GUARDIANS
OF THE GALAXY
ROCKET RACCOON & GROOT

STEAL THE GALAXY!

AN ORIGINAL NOVEL OF THE MARVEL
UNIVERSE

MARVEL

GUARDIANS OF THE GALAXY

ROCKET RACCOON & GROOT

STEAL THE GALAXY!

AN ORIGINAL NOVEL OF THE MARVEL
UNIVERSE

DAN ABNETT

GUARDIANS OF THE GALAXY: ROCKET RACCOON & GROOT — STEAL THE GALAXY! PROSE NOVEL. Published by MARVEL WORLDWIDE, INC., a subsidiary of MARVEL ENTERTAINMENT, LLC. OFFICE OF PUBLICATION: 135 West 50th Street, New York, NY 10020. Copyright © 2014 Marvel Characters, Inc. All rights reserved.
ISBN# 978-0-7851-8977-0

Printed in the U.S.A.

ALAN FINE, EVP - Office of the President, Marvel Worldwide, Inc. and EVP & CMO Marvel Characters B.V.; DAN BUCKLEY, Publisher & President - Print, Animation & Digital Divisions; JOE QUESADA, Chief Creative Officer; TOM BREVOORT, SVP of Publishing; DAVID BOGART, SVP of Operations & Procurement, Publishing; C.B. CEBULSKI, SVP of Creator & Content Development; DAVID GABRIEL, SVP Print, Sales & Marketing; JIM O'KEEFE, VP of Operations & Logistics; DAN CARR, Executive Director of Publishing Technology; SUSAN CRESPI, Editorial Operations Manager; ALEX MORALES, Publishing Operations Manager; STAN LEE, Chairman Emeritus. For information regarding advertising in Marvel Comics or on Marvel.com, please contact Niza Disla, Director of Marvel Partnerships, at ndisla@marvel.com. For Marvel subscription inquiries, please call 800-217-9158. **Manufactured between 5/5/2014 and 6/16/2014 by SHERIDAN BOOKS, INC., CHELSEA, MI, USA.**

First printing 2014
10 9 8 7 6 5 4 3 2 1

COVER ART BY MIKE PERKINS AND ANDY TROY
TITLE PAGE ART BY SKOTTIE YOUNG
BACK COVER ART BY TIMOTHY GREEN II AND ANDY TROY

Stuart Moore, Editor
Design by Nelson Ribeiro

Senior Editor, Special Projects: Jeff Youngquist
Assistant Editor: Sarah Brunstad
Associate Managing Editor: Alex Starbuck
SVP Print, Sales & Marketing: David Gabriel
Editor In Chief: Axel Alonso
Chief Creative Officer: Joe Quesada
Publisher: Dan Buckley
Executive Producer: Alan Fine

Acknowledgments

My heartfelt cosmic thanks to Stuart Moore, Jeff Youngquist, Axel Alonso, Dan Buckley, Sarah Brunstad, and James Gunn for their support in this project.

Humble fan-boy appreciation must go to Bill Mantlo, Keith Giffen, Roy Thomas, Jack Kirby, Dick Ayers, Mike Mignola, Arnold Drake, Gene Colan, and Stan Lee for the (Marvel) Universe-building and the inspiration. Growing up would not have been nearly as exciting without you. And you're just the start of the list.

Disconcertingly humanlike fist-bumps to Ronald Byrd for continuity-fu, and to Nik Vincent for first reading.

This book, however, is for Jim Starlin. Marvel wasn't properly cosmic until it met you.

STEAL THE GALAXY!

AN ORIGINAL NOVEL OF THE MARVEL
UNIVERSE

DAN ABNETT

LAST
ORDERS

A talking raccoon and a mobile tree walk into a bar—

Wait. My linguistic circuits inform me that in the vernacular of more than one hundred and fifty-six *thousand* civilized cultures, that opening sentence definitely sounds like the start of a joke.

The sort of joke that might also include the words "Why the long face?" or "I'm afraid *not*" or "Ouch, it was an iron bar."

Please understand, gentle reader, what I am about to tell you is most certainly not a joke. It is a story about the fate of worlds. The Destiny of the Universe, no less. It is a story during which this Galaxy, and possibly many other galaxies—not to mention several terations of the *entire* space-time Multiverse—will be in *serious* jeopardy on more than one occasion. This is a serious tale. Billions of innocent lives depend upon its successful conclusion. One false step in our narrative, and stars will snuff out, spiral galaxies will unwind, supergiants will detonate in clouds of luminous atomic heartbreak, and the ancient and mighty civilizations of the cosmos will fall, screaming, as the dreadful blackness of eternity rips out the throat of All Creation.

So let us not, loyal and friendly reader, get off on the wrong foot by thinking that I am about to tell you a joke.

I am not. Are we clear? I will suspend my literal speech protocols {*literal speech protocols suspended*} because that's possibly what's causing the problem. I will try to be more...informal and more *human* (because I am presuming that you are human, loyal reader. You look human, at any rate. Except for those eyebrows. Really? *Really*? Did you trim them yourself?). I am a synthetic. A synthetic humanoid. I am an instrument of measurement. A recorder of data. I was manufactured in the matter forges of Rigel. I was made to observe. So cut me some slack, okay? I don't do organic nuance.

Where were we?

Oh yes, right. A talking raccoon and a mobile tree walk into a bar.

The bar is in Dive-town, a minor suburb of the continent-spanning supercity/starport cosmopolis of Lumina on the planet Xarth Three. Occupying a long-season, "sling-loop" orbit around the binary stars Fades Primary and Fades Secondary in the Xranek Group, Xarth Three is a class M world with a population of 9.9 billion and a gross industrial export principally comprising—

{*halt expositional protocol*}

—just checking with you, loyal reader, but that's going to become tiresome, isn't it? If I keep reverting to data-delivery mode every time I hit a proper noun? I am an encyclopedia. But I want to tell this story without *sounding* like one. Here's an idea...if I'm going too fast or not explaining things, tell me, and I'll back up and fill in details. I'm very good at filling in details. If details are what you want, you've come to the right place.

{*resume narrative mode*}

The bar is in Dive-town. The suns are setting like hot coals spitting as they sink into murky water. In the streets outside, neon lamps are pulsing. Necrodroidal trash-gangs are howling at the rising moons, eager to begin a night of vicious turf wars and lucrative organ scavenging.

The bar is called Leery's. No one who frequents the bar can actually remember who Leery was, or why the bar bears his (or her, or its) name. Not even Nrrsh, the Skrull who runs the place.

Nrrsh has been wounded (presumably in the course of numerous Kree-Skrull wars) so many times that a great deal of his biomass has been systematically replaced by cybernetics and prosthetics. It's fair to say that he is not so much a Skrull with cybernetic parts, but rather a collection of cybernetic parts with one remaining Skrull arm vaguely involved. This does not in any way prevent him from being fiercely Skrullian and singing the traditional anthem "Tarnax! Tarnax! Always shifting!" lustily every Skrull-Day, or when he has had one too many Timothies.

{*data note—we'll come back to the subject of the Timothy later*}

Leery's is typical of most Dive-town hostelries: split-level, multi-bars, a dancefloor, an orchestra pit, a ranged sequence of fighting arenas, and a quasi-siderial gateway to the Multiverse that no one ever uses because they are too busy getting hammered, betting on the arena fights, dancing, or having a flarking good time of it.

As our talking raccoon and mobile tree enter it, Leery's is business as usual. The dancing girls are dancing (I *say* dancing girls—I mean a shoal of eighty coalescent pseudo-moebea swirling in stylish, syncopated formation. With ostrich feathers). The band is playing (I *say* band—I mean a close-harmony squadron of Kymellian interpolatory trumpatoonists who are using brass acoustic-tubes to produce disconcerting and frankly uncomfortable horse-fart noises at ultralow frequencies. With a samba beat). The joint is jumping (I *say* jumping—and it is. The deep and immense rock-fuse piles upon which Dive-town was built, bored down into the planet's mantle in ages past by the first constructors of Xarth, are actually being affected by the ultralow infra-sound frequencies of the Kymellian band's horse-farting and are beginning to twitch. Just a little bit. Oooh, just a little bit).

"My kinda place," announces Rocket Raccoon with relish.

"I am Groot," his towering companion agrees, nodding.

A talking raccoon and a mobile tree. As heroes go, they're not much to record home about. That was certainly my reaction when I met them. I am presuming that it is yours, too, loyal reader, as you observe them for the first time stepping into my expertly woven narrative. A raccoon and a tree. One talks, one walks.

Surely, I hear you say, loyal reader, *they* are not the heroes of this tale? Surely, you add anxiously, the fate of the Multiverse does not depend upon *them*?

Well, yes. Yes, it *does*. Loyal reader, if this idea alarms you, then maybe the fate of the Multiverse isn't something you should think about *too* hard.

If it matters at all, and I hope it does, my first impressions of them were similarly underwhelming. It took a while for me to fully appreciate that Rocket Raccoon and Groot of Planet X were proper, Multiverse-saving heroes. Quite a while, actually. I'll shout out when, in the course of this narrative, it happens.

Anyway...

"My kinda place," says Rocket Raccoon with relish. He is very much less than a human meter tall. His coat is glossy and in wonderful condition. His spectacular tail is bouffant. He walks upright in a way that makes the human in you want to exclaim, "Lookit the little man! Lookit! Walking on his back paws! *Oooooaww!*"

Do not do that. *Ever.* If you do that, he will shoot you to death as many times as necessary. Rocket Raccoon has, I'm sorry to say, experienced a twisted and unpleasant background (an "origin," as I suspect you might regard it, loyal reader), but that twisted and unpleasant background has made him the glossy-snouted, cheeky-as-a-button space warrior he is today. I may reveal some details of his "origin" as this tale advances. I can't promise. I was warned with actual guns not to reveal certain particulars. Look, if you know him as I do, you'll know his heart is in the right place (in the upper-left-hand quadrant of his thorax), and he has a very specific moral code ("Flark everything and everyone!" © 2014 Rocket Raccoon. All rights reserved), and he likes unfeasibly large guns.

One of which is strapped across his back as he enters Leery's. Look at him! Look at him, walking upright! Like a trained dog! Gawwww! Good boy! Good boy!

Sorry.

And then there's the hands. Look, this is the thing. I can't get past it. Rocket's hands...they're so disconcertingly *human*. It's uncanny (not in the mutant sense, obviously. Mutants are uncanny in an entirely different way). It's amazing, astonishing, astounding, incredible, adjective-less...okay, it's just *distressing*. Rocket Raccoon's hands are disconcertingly human in the *most* distressing way.

Let's think about something else for a moment, because the *hands* thing is creeping me out a bit.

Something else, something else...okay, Rocket is wearing a uniform. It's dark blue, militaristic, with red flashing and frogging. It's the uniform of the Guardians of the Galaxy, a cosmos-defending supergroup that really doesn't get the respect it deserves. Or the publicity. Or anything. Mention the name, and most people will go, "Huh? Guardians of the where now?"

Rocket is enjoying a sabbatical. The Guardians, you see, are on a bit of a hiatus between their efforts to save an ungrateful cosmos (and guard a sniffily "I don't need to be guarded" Galaxy). Star-Lord's off doing this. Gamora's off doing that. Drax is off... destroying. That's just a guess.

So Rocket and Groot, they've gone back to what they do best: make a little action, develop a little cash. They have the keys and papers for a subcompact jump freighter and a fresh cargo of zunks. Forty-eight tons of zunks, in fact. They've come to Leery's because they've got a lead that a zunk trader might be in the house tonight—a zunk trader looking to move between forty-seven and forty-nine tons of zunks. So this is business time for Rocket...just him and his trusted pal Groot.

Speaking of which...Groot is a tree. Imagine an ancient, giant oak tree with a face, arms, and feet. Imagine it walking toward you. Groot has to duck as he comes in through Leery's doorway—and even though he does, twigs scrape off and clatter to the floor.

Rocket looks at the almost entirely *not* Skrullian barman.

"Two Timothies!" he declares.

"I am Groot," says Groot.

Rocket sighs.

"Okay, make that one Timothy, and one bitterbark and soda."

Nrrsh scurries to his task. Rocket glances up at his leafy friend.

"Lightweight," he says. Then he sniffs the air with his glossy button nose. He smells snake oil and leather. He smells reptiles. He smells lizard belly.

"Flark it," he says. "Badoon."

It is not long after this that the fight begins.

· CHAPTER TWO ·

A SPOT OF BOTHER

THE drinks arrive. Groot sips his, his littlest twig finger extended politely. Rocket regards his Timothy with healthy caution and respect, the sort of respect that a veteran tamer of Denebian face-eaters shows for the predators he has spent his career taming. They may let him get into the cage with them every day, they may be used to him, they may even allow him to scratch them behind the ears or feed them treats, but they are still Denebian face-eaters, and their name is not in any way euphemistic.

The Timothy is, loyal reader, a truly splendid beverage. It sits upon its napkin on the bar, glowing with a kind of inner light that promises merriment, conviviality, and ultimately a merciful memory blackout. The exact recipe for the Timothy is, of course, a secret closely guarded by the Most Honorable Galactic Fraternal Guild of Bartenders and Mixologists, but it is rumored to contain Arkuan spirit, Kree brandy, shaved zark-seeds, a shot of vooosh-juice, a jigger of sentient remorse squeezed out of the collective memory of a dying species using a quantum press, lemon zest, and a small antimatter charge just strong enough to sustain the hyperspatial cascade at a molecular level. When first concocted, it was given a completely terrifying name that accurately reflected the experience of drinking one. This honesty was found to be off-putting in the retail environment, however, so the drink was renamed "The Timothy"—a Monicker that was felt to be much more reassuring and mild.

Rocket Raccoon looks at his Timothy for a moment, his eyes narrowing. One does not rush into a Timothy. One does not casually knock back a Timothy. A Timothy requires a certain degree of mental preparation before it is confronted. A certain degree of mental preparation, a deep breath, and a long run-up. Like a ravine. Or a flying tackle. Or a Kree-Skrull War.

It is worth noting that the Timothy is the only beverage in the known Universe to have repeatedly made it on to the Shi'ar Imperial Guard's watch list of prohibited and outlawed weapons.

"I am Groot," says Groot, noting his companion's pensive nature.

"As a matter of fact, I *have* got something on my mind, ol' buddy," replies Rocket. "I'm worried about our cargo of zunks. If we don't find a d'ast buyer soon, we could be left with forty-eight tons of overripe zunks. We could be seriously out of pocket. I thought zunks were a smart investment. They always used to be. But since they opened those mega-farm plantations in Gamma Eridani, the market's been awash. That's what's on my mind. Or at least it was my chief worry until we came *in* here."

He sniffs the air again.

"I can definitely smell Badoon," he says.

As if on cue, the Badoon appear.

There are ten of them. They are especially large specimens of their race. Judging from the "talon-and-forked-tongue" silver insignia on their War Brotherhood wargear, and their satin-sheen black battle pants, they are warriors of the elite War Brotherhood "Devastation" Cadre—a division not known for taking a lighthearted approach to love and life, even by Badoon standards.

And it is clear that these large and aggressive reptilian warriors are looking for something. Unblinking amber eyes dart to and fro, scanning the environment for traces. Forked tongues flicker between steel-enhanced war fangs. The Badoon leader keeps a firm grip on the jeweled handle of his ceremonial War Brotherhood plasma exterminatron.

Rocket turns back to his Timothy.

"Don't make eye contact, ol' buddy," he murmurs to Groot. "We don't want to get involved in any trouble. The last thing we need is a fight with Badoon."

"I am Groot," agrees Groot.

"Exactly, pal. A spot of bother is not where we want to be right now. Ignore any provocation."

"I am Groot."

"Yeah. Even if it is hugely tempting to ease our troubles by laying some righteous smackdown on good-for-nothing, pointy-eared lizard bullies."

"Excuse me," says the Badoon leader from behind them. Rocket stiffens. He thinks soothing, calming thoughts. Slowly, he and Groot swivel their bar stools to face the Badoon.

"War Brotherhood Commander Droook," says the Badoon leader by way of introduction. "Sorry to bother you. Have you by any chance seen a Rigellian Recorder?"

"A Rigellian Recorder?" Rocket replies. "I don't believe so."

"We have a scan image," says the leader. His forked tongue dances and flickers. "Warrior Lorg, show the scan image on your War Brotherhood tactical display."

One of the lizard warriors steps up and holds out a data tablet on which glows the image of what is almost definitely a Rigellian Recorder unit.

"Face doesn't ring any bells," says Rocket.

"The Recorder is a fugitive," says the Badoon leader. "He has absconded with sensitive data. We believe he has come to this establishment in search of a starpilot or freetrader prepared to offer him passage off-world. Are you a starpilot or freetrader?"

"Hey, I can offer you a sweet deal on forty-eight tons of zunks," says Rocket, "but beyond that..."

The Badoon leader hesitates and considers Rocket closely. Badoon are not easy to like. They are aggressive, cruel, and self- important. They have, in the course of their long and bloody history, conquered and oppressed great swathes of the Milky Way Galaxy. Their cultural development is such that very early on, certain traits such as social grace, good humor, patience, and sympathy became— like their tails—firstly evolutionarily redundant, then vestigial, and then gone entirely.

But even that doesn't properly explain the mutual dislike between Rocket and the Badoon. It's a primordial thing, the animosity that exists, and has always existed, between small mammals and large snakes. It's instinctive, hereditary, a cobra-mongoose dynamic. They just make each other uncomfortable.

So it is with great self-control that the Badoon leader says, "Sorry to have troubled you," and with equally great self-control that Rocket replies, "No problem whatsoever," and turns back to his Timothy.

"Phew," says Rocket to Groot as the Badoon move away. "That was close."

It is at this point that one of the Badoon warriors' War Brotherhood tactical scanners detects Rigellian technology in the crawlspace under the bandstand.

"War Brotherhood Commander! Sir! I have found something!" the warrior cries. The Badoon close in, drawing their War Brotherhood laser disruptors and War Brotherhood combat swords. The Badoon believe that there are no words or phrases in the Galaxy that can't be improved by the addition of the prefixes "War" or "Brotherhood," or preferably both.

The Badoon's unlucky quarry, which is now revealed to indeed be a Rigellian Recorder unit—a robotic humanoid device designed and mass-manufactured by the Rigellians for data-gathering and galactic surveying—emerges from the crawlspace under the bandstand and tries to flee.

There is alarm and consternation. The Badoon rush the Recorder. The Recorder emits an electronic squeal of dismay. It was built for neither combat nor speed. Many patrons of Leery's scatter; others jeer at the Badoon. Bouncers close in. Behind the bar, Nrrsh yells, "Oy!" and points with his one Skrull arm to a sign on the wall that reads, "Please do not draw or discharge firearms or energy-disruption devices on these premises as a Skrullian punch dagger in the kidneys often offends."

Rocket just keeps staring at his still-untouched Timothy.

"I am Groot," says Groot.

"Yes, I know it's kicking off," Rocket sighs.

"I am Groot."

"Yes, I know the right thing to do would be to help that poor robot guy and stick up for him against the Badoon, because if we don't, who will? We just...have to ignore it. We want to stay out of trouble, don't we?"

"I am Groot."

"Yeah, I *am* well aware that the only thing necessary for the triumph of evil is for good men to do nothing."

Behind them, the fracas is escalating. The Recorder has run headlong into a waitress and sent three trays of glasses crashing to the floor. The Badoon leader has drawn his War Brotherhood plasma exterminatron. Customers are screaming and shouting. The Recorder is trying to get back onto his feet, apologizing to the waitress. The Badoon leader has a clear shot. One squeeze of the War Brotherhood trigger will send a supercharged bolt of War Brotherhood laser-jacketed plasma spitting across the bar. It will fuse and burn out the base of the Recorder's spine, preserving the data in his memory banks but preventing him from running ever again.

The Badoon leader fires.

An odd thing happens. Its dramatic significance will only become apparent much later, loyal reader—along with its causal relationship to the rest of space-time, and destiny, and fate.

Suffice to say for now that there is a sudden flash of de-mat energy swathed in a halo of cracking light, and what appears to be a Galadoran Spaceknight in unusual matte-black battle armor appears in the middle of Leery's bar. He appears, in fact, directly in the firing line between the Badoon leader and the flailing Recorder at the split-second the War Brotherhood plasma exterminatron discharges.

The Spaceknight takes the full force of the deadly blast. The Spaceknight's advanced null-shields absorb the worst of it and deflect the rest. But even so the impact sends the warrior flying across the bar, demolishing the lower rails of the bandstand.

The deflected plasma bolt, robbed of most of its lethal charge, whines sidelong across the bar area, missing the Recorder and striking, instead, a glass standing on a napkin, destroying it entirely.

"That does it," snarls Rocket Raccoon, leaping up and drawing his unfeasibly large blaster cannon. "Flarking Badoon spilled my drink! Lock and flarkin' load!"

CHAPTER THREE

THROWDOWN

ROCKET RACCOON's current unfeasibly large gun of choice is a Nitro Weapons System Model 66 B.P.B. ("being-portable blaster"). It has a number of attractive, user-friendly features—including ergonomic hand-grips (useful for those with disconcertingly human-like hands), a reflexive auto-targeting system, an inertially buffered stabilization system, and a patented recoil minimizer.

However, its most immediately appealing feature is the "KZZWARK" sound it makes when it blasts out a pulse of blue-white death ray.

KZZWARK! says Rocket Raccoon's unfeasibly large gun. Rocket is standing on the seat of his barstool as he shoots; despite the recoil minimizer, the rifle's back-slap causes him and the seat to spin around three times.

The pulse of blue-white energy streaks across Leery's and hits the Badoon leader in the face. The Badoon leader is, as befits a high-status cadre commander, equipped with an automatic bodyshield, a personal force field that snaps on when it pre-senses incoming energized or ballistic munitions. The bodyshield saves his life, if not his dignity. It stops the shot's explosive force, but it cannot deal with the overwhelming kinetic hammerblow delivered by such an unfeasibly large weapon.

Knocked off his feet, Droook, War Brotherhood Commander of the elite War Brotherhood Devastation Cadre, leaves the main saloon area, clears the fantail stage, and ends up facedown in the salad bar.

His men do not react to this well. Uttering a War Brotherhood battle-howl, they rush the area of the bar where, until a few seconds earlier, Rocket and Groot had been furiously trying to mind their own business. The first to reach them is a burly Badoon warrior with a War Brotherhood combat sword and steel-reinforced War Brotherhood battle teeth.

He swings his sword at Rocket. Rocket exclaims, "Yip!" and dives out of the way. The sword, a superb piece of Moordian steel with a quantum-sharp edge, slices Rocket's barstool in half.

Then Groot punches the Badoon warrior.

The warrior reels across the room and collides with a party of Kree businessmen who were simply hoping for a nice night out where no one would end up accusing anyone of anything. The combat sword, knocked from the Badoon warrior's nerveless hand, spins twice in the air and ends up embedded and quivering, tip-down, in Leery's well-carpeted floor.

A certain amount of what might be described as "pandemonium" has now broken out. The bar was pretty crowded, and there's a lot of general screaming and running around in progress—what with the discharge of two major power weapons, bisected barstools, and trees punching things.

Rocket Raccoon is a tactical genius. The primary reason you

might know this about him is that he freely tells everyone he meets that he is.

However, his track record speaks for itself. He has guarded, not to mention saved, the Galaxy on several occasions. He reads a fight like very few practitioners of warfare. And he's a flarking good shot.

Rocket uses both the pandemonium and his stature. He is effectively screened by the patrons fleeing around him. The Badoon can't draw a bead on him. Wild shots ring out. A chandelier explodes. The dancing girls shriek and stampede toward the dressing room in a cloud of ostrich-feather fibers.

Rocket rolls into the cover of an ornamental pot-plant, and fires his Nitro 66 again.

Oh, that satisfying KZZWARK!

The shot hits one of the Badoon attackers. Unlike his War Brotherhood Commander, this Badoon was not high-status enough to warrant an automatic bodyshield. The Badoon warrior takes a brief moment to reflect on the inherent unfairness of the perks afforded to the officer classes, and how it's always the common fighting Badoon who end up paying in the long run. Then he glances down wistfully at the haze of vapor previously occupied by his torso, and he topples over.

{Death will stalk this tale, loyal and gentle reader. I make no excuses for it. The Universe is a cruel place; life and death go, if not hand in hand, then at least chained together, like Tony Curtis and Sidney Poitier in The Defiant Ones. Yes, it is entirely my pleasure to tailor the thematic references of this story to your Human Culture. The Badoon are warriors. Rocket and Groot are warriors. The fate of the Universe is a life-or-death matter, and sometimes it is decided by the speed of a *trigger finger, or the unfeasible largeness of a gun and its owner's willingness to use it. It is worth relating that one of the other attractive, user-friendly features of the Nitro Weapons System Model 66 B.P.B. (being-portable blaster) is the toggle that allows the owner to select a nonlethal "stun" setting. Rocket had owned the Nitro 66 for eight months before Groot pointed this feature out to him. When he did so, Rocket laughed for nine minutes, then asked, "Why would you need that?"}*

First blood—*proper* blood—to Rocket Raccoon. A line has been crossed. Rocket refers to this line as the "Oh What the Flark Event Horizon."

There is no going back now.

"Groot, ol' buddy, ol' tree!" he yells. "We've crossed the Oh What the Flark Event Horizon! The gloves are off!"

Groot is puzzled, because he was not wearing any gloves in the first place. With a simple nod to his tiny mammalian friend, he turns and delivers an uppercut that sends another of the Badoon out of Leery's through a hole in the roof not previously there.

Groot is an example of the rare genus *flora colossus*, indigenous to a planet known as X. He is a surprisingly complex individual and only ever punches things out of necessity—and because he is extremely good at it.

Groot reels, struck by a blow of immense force. Nrrsh, the bar owner, has attacked him from behind. Nrrsh is wielding the ugly cyber-cudgel that he reserves for particularly boisterous and uncooperative patrons at closing time.

"No one starts a flarking firefight in my bar!" he snarls.

"I am Groot!" Groot tells him.

Nrrsh hits him again. The energized cudgel shatters bark and draws sap.

This annoys Groot. Groot slugs Nrrsh, and the Skrull performs an entirely involuntary flick-flack over the bar and brings down six shelves of bottles.

Nrrsh has, however, employed a number of highly skilled bouncers to police his establishment. They are huge fighting Cyberneti-cons from the Raxus war zones. As they close on Groot, they switch to ogre-mode, bulking up and armoring themselves with overlapping sheets of dense alloy and subcutaneous force fields.

The first ogre-mode punches Groot. The second lays another solid fist home. Groot staggers, hurt, then lashes back, slamming one ogre-mode over the bar and another back into the wall. The third and fourth close in, fists balled.

"I am Groot," Groot decides.

Meanwhile, Rocket has become the focus of the Badoon's wrath. They are firing multiple War Brotherhood laser guns at him. The bombardment has blown holes in the floor, the wall, the side of the bar, and the bandstand, and has come very close to scorching the tip of Rocket's silky and wonderfully voluminous tail.

He dives, rolling and firing his gun. Part of the ceiling explodes and falls in. The Badoon scatter for cover. One Badoon finds entirely inadequate shelter behind a dessert trolley and spends far too much time trying to mimic the shape of a three-tiered gateau.

Rocket scurries for cover. Ducking under a table, he hears a voice say, "I do appreciate the help."

He looks around and finds himself face-to-face with the Rigel-lian Recorder, who has chosen the same table to hide beneath.

"I am a Recorder," the Recorder says. "I am Recorder 172, built by the Colonizers of Rigel to travel the spaceways until the end of all time, and survey and record the known Universe. I fear I am in a great deal of trouble."

"Why the flark do these d'ast Badoon want you so bad?" Rocket asks.

"I do not know, sir," the Recorder replies. He is an aesthetically pleasing, sleek humanoid android finished in green and gold. His face is the sad side of impassive.

"I have been damaged in some way," he says. "My recollection is impaired. I am not entirely sure what is happening, except that I wish it wasn't."

"Well, Recorder ol' buddy," Rocket says, "we've already crossed the Oh What the Flark Event Horizon."

"Query? Meaning?"

"Meaning I was trying to stay out of trouble tonight—but seeing as that didn't happen, I may as well make my trouble count for something."

"Query? Meaning?"

"You want protection from these Badoons, Rigel-boy, you got it."

"I am gratified. I do not mean to be a burden."

Rocket bares his teeth. Badoon laser shots are skimming the top of the table they are cowering beneath. He slams a fresh power-mag into his unfeasibly large gun.

Then he glances at the Recorder.

"I don't suppose," he inquires sadly, "that you happen to know any zunk traders looking for a little action?"

"I'm sorry, but I don't."

Rocket shrugs.

"Had to ask. Okay, keep low and follow me."

With that, Rocket Raccoon leaps out from under the table, unfeasibly large gun blazing, and performs the most savage and effective twenty seconds of sustained anti-Badoon warfare I have ever witnessed.

And that, gentle and loyal reader, is how we met.

I am a Recorder.

I am Recorder 127 of the Rigellian Intergalactic Survey.

CHAPTER FOUR

EXIT STRATEGY

THEY start to run. I should say, *we* start to run. The nature of this narrative has shifted in the telling. You, loyal reader, are now aware that I am one of the three individuals at the epicenter of this mayhem.

"That way!" Rocket Raccoon bellows.

"I am Groot!" his brave comrade responds.

Rocket Raccoon hesitates. He has now seen the armored ogremodes that Groot has drawn his attention to—and the fact that Nrrsh is getting back onto his artificial feet and racking a cut-down ion shotgun. It does not take a tactical genius to see that "that way" is not a promising exit route.

I have certainly noticed this.

"That way is blocked by at least seven dangerous combatants," I point out. "That way does not seem a way that should be considered, especially if one is evaluating options based on concerns such as health, safety, success, our continued vital function, the avoidance of dismemberment—"

"From you, not so much of the talking," Rocket Raccoon advises me. I suspend speech functions immediately.

Rocket Raccoon turns.

"This way!" he orders.

Sadly, "this way" is also not overburdened with positive advantages. Several of the Badoon have been felled, but a support squad has arrived. War Brotherhood weapons are drawn and firing. The air is filled with a blizzard of laser rounds and exterminatron bolts. From his forward command point behind the salad bar, War Brotherhood Commander Droook is yelling orders and expletives in equal measure.

"Okay, okay!" Rocket Raccoon concedes. "Not *this* way, either!"

He slams off two more shots to keep the Badoon troopers ducking, then aims his unfeasibly large gun at the floor. The blast, almost point blank, blows a large hole clean through the deck of the bar level. The edges of the hole crackle and glow with molten metal, dissipating superheat.

There is a void below.

"Groot!" Rocket yells. "We're going the other way instead! Cover my tail, pal!"

Groot is still slugging it out with the enraged ogre-modes. Each punch and impact makes the air ripple, as if from a sonic boom. Groot puts an ogre-mode through a window, then sends another sprawling onto its side—its alloy armor dented, and its subcutaneous force shields fritzing and misfiring. But there are too many of them. Twigs snap off. Bark cracks. Sap leaks. Groot looks like a prizefighter on the ropes in a final, grueling round.

"Groot!" Rocket yelps. He hoists his unfeasibly large gun up above his ears with both of his disconcertingly human-like hands and hurls it across the bar. Groot catches it. He wields it as a club at first, knocking aside the immediate threat of the nearest ogre-mode, then starts firing from the hip. The Nitro Weapons System Model 66 B.P.B. does not seem so unfeasibly large in his massive grip. It seems like a toy: a submunition gun or a carbine. He does not aim with any special care. He hoses, quick-fire. Ogre-modes fly backward like struck bowling pins. Nrrsh utters something quite un-Skrullian and seeks urgent cover.

"Let's go! Let's go!" Rocket shouts. He has drawn his backup weapons, a matched brace of long-barreled Spartoi laser pistols. He brandishes them, arms straight, a deadly pistol in each of his disconcertingly human-like hands. Your Human Culture thematic reference point here, loyal reader, would most likely be the two-handed gunplay of Chow Yun-Fat. Or a buccaneer.

Yes, most definitely a buccaneer. The only thing that would make Rocket Raccoon look more like a buccaneer right now would be a macaw or some rigging.

He fires at the advancing Badoon: right, left, right, left—one pistol muzzle rising with the recoil as its partner blasts. Three War Brotherhood warriors caught by the shots collapse sideways into one another and sag, sliding halfway to the floor and forming a tragic Badoon teepee.

Rocket Raccoon is about to look even more like a buccaneer.

"Groot! I said we're high-tailing it now!" he shouts over the thunder of gunfire. "Stop having fun and get with the program! It's time to make like a tree!"

"And leaf?" I inquire, suspending mute for a second. I cannot help observing and enjoying the old heroic-banter trope.

"No," Rocket snaps, correcting me. "And *fall!*"

With that, he leaps into the hole he has shot in the floor.

I hesitate. The presumption is that I should follow this reckless course, but now that the moment is actually upon me, I find myself reluctant.

At that point, however, I am picked up by a tree and tucked under its arm. Then the tree makes the decision about jumping for me, and I am obliged to go along with it.

THUMP!

I am...dazed for a second. I realign and reboot, stabilizing my sensory systems. Gyro positioning tells me we have descended approximately eight meters. Groot puts me down. I find myself standing on ground made from a dusty, mica-based sand material. It is, I notice, stained in patches.

There is a roaring noise. An excited, lusty ululation.

It is coming from the crowd. The crowd is, it seems, surprised but pleased to see us. It seems collectively keen to see what happens next.

"The general layout schematics of Leery's," I observe, "indicate it is possible that the pit-fight arenas are situated directly beneath the main bar level."

Rocket Raccoon turns very slowly and glares up at me. I feel that this is his way of informing me that I might have mentioned this fact earlier. Before we jumped, for example.

The pit is a broad, circular arena. The baying crowd—now unanimously punching the air with many fists, and exchanging rapid wagers and counter-wagers—is contained behind the high stone wall that surrounds the ring. On the sand around us, various large gladiators and pit-fighters—clad in brutal spiked plate-armor, clutching hatchets, cleavers, pikes and tridents—assess us with professional curiosity. So do the vast fighting beasts specially imported from Sakaar. They snort and whinny; saliva drools from their immense, fanged maws.

The stains on the sand, processing tells me, are blood...at the very least.

Groot glances up wistfully at the hole in the roof. It suddenly seems much more like a worthwhile escape route than it did from the other side. It is, however, absolutely out of reach.

"Oh well," mutters Rocket Raccoon with a world-weary affect. He twirls his pistols defiantly in his upraised, disconcertingly human-like hands and growls, "Place your bets."

CHAPTER FIVE

LET THE GAMES BEGIN

A SIREN sounds, urging the start of combat, but it is superfluous. The gladiators are already rushing us. The squealing Zen-Whoberian ring girls barely have time to scatter and get themselves and their round cards behind the pit barriers.

Rocket aims his pistols at the nearest charging gladiator, a raging Saurid giant in a houndskull helm. He fires.

Nothing happens.

Rocket gurgles, "What the flark?" and ducks hard. He darts between the legs of his oncoming foe, allowing the armored bulk of the gladiator to pass right over him and smack face-first into Groot's waiting fist. Suddenly, the houndskull helm is not so much a wolf as a bulldog.

The gladiator drops on his front.

"My blasters don't work!" Rocket yelps, trying them again to be sure. Groot is also attempting to discharge the Nitro 66, without success.

"The pit levels are fitted with jamming fields that prevent the firing of energy weapons," I point out.

"Why?" Rocket begs, rolling hard to avoid the downswing of a battleaxe the size of a patio table.

"Because that would be unsportsmanlike," I reply.

"Un-what?"

"Unfair. The sport here is close-combat pit-fighting," I explain. "The use of ranged and energy weapons would disadvantage the gladiators."

"Disadvantage the gladiators?!" Rocket shrieks back at me. He is being chased around in circles by an immense cyborg creature with a sword the size of an ironing board. Rocket has a point. The disadvantage is all ours. Of the three of us, only Groot is physically capable of contending at this level. He is punching anything that gets close. Rocket is surviving by speed alone—running, jumping, darting, ducking, and leaping. He is too small and fast to hit. For now.

I am, myself, only surviving because Groot is being kind enough to keep picking me up out of the path of danger and putting me down again somewhere temporarily less risky. It is as though he is fighting while simultaneously using me as a chess piece. This is an activity that, I fear, cannot be successfully maintained for long.

The crowd is on its feet, howling.

Rocket ducks under the cyborg's sword, executes a leap that uses another gladiator's shield as a springboard, and somersaults into the air. He lands on the shoulders of a Shi'ar brute with a huge gene-amped musculature. This pit-fighter has immense steel shoulderguards and an intimidating, low-slung, chrome sallet helm. Rocket has holstered his pistols. He grabs the rim of the gladiator's helm with his disconcertingly human-like hands and yanks it down around the brute's ears. The Shi'ar barks in outrage, dropping his cleaver and hand axe, and staggers around blindly trying to loosen his sallet helm and pull it back up. It will take him some time and effort to realign his eye-slits.

Rocket bounds off him, lands on the sand, and scoops up the discarded hand axe. It was a small thing to the Shi'ar, just a secondary hacking tool. To Rocket, it is a mighty battleaxe, and he has to prop the haft over his shoulder to get a good grip.

Another pit fighter rushes him. Rocket swings the axe, deflecting the prongs of the fighter's trident. The fighter stumbles. Rocket swings again and puts a dent in the fighter's belly plate, winding him. The fighter drops to his knees, and Rocket brings the flat of the axe blade down across the back of the fighter's head, rendering him unconscious.

"Who else wants some?" Rocket snarls, darting away and glancing around. He dashes up the spine of a Taurian gladiator coming for me, and brains him with the axe, leaping off his shoulders as the thug starts to sprawl.

I have the distinct impression that, despite everything, Rocket Raccoon is almost enjoying himself.

The gladiators are one thing. The pit beasts are quite another. They are monsters, loyal reader, born from fevered nightmares. Each one is at least the size of a modest building. Their origin world was the notorious planet Sakaar, a place that no longer exists except in memories or databases (or for those with access to temporal technology), but its monstrous creatures were so feral and impressive that many specimens still exist in arena bestiaries the Universe over.

One of the things sharing the pit with us is some kind of centipede the length of two or three subway cars. Hellish, spiked limbs ripple around the sides of its churning, segmented body. Its razor-sharp mouth-parts clack and chop.

Another resembles a vast, pustular toad with the head of a deep-sea fish. It has an underbite and eight rows of needlelike teeth, any one of which would have served Rocket Raccoon as an adequate lance. Its glistening flesh is almost translucent, so that its bones and some pulsing organs are actually visible. Its eyes are great, dead orbs like milky ponds.

Another is a giant, ursine quadruped with a spiked collar. It is partially armored across the back, flanks, and cranium with plates of rusty iron. It is trailing heavy chains that seem, distressingly, to have been snapped. Its mouth, jutting from beneath the rim of its iron head-guard, is so large that a small family car could easily be parked inside it. Its teeth are like sharpened tombstones.

The ursine surges forward, roaring. It tramples several unlucky gladiators and tosses others high into the air. Groot sees the ursine coming and moves me out of its path, but this places him in the way of the centipede thing. It sweeps toward him like a runaway train on a curved section of track, legs rippling. It reeks of ammonia.

Groot is still carrying the Nitro 66. It is the only weapon he has at hand. Because it won't fire, he jams it into the thing's jaws in an attempt to thwart the snapping mouth-parts.

The shearing mandibles bite down on the gun. Though the arena's jamming fields prevent the discharge of energy weapon systems, they have no power to affect the explosive containment failure of a power-mag that has been bitten in half.

The unfeasibly large gun explodes as the entire energy load of its munition pack releases in one go.

The blast, a white-hot ball of light, throws Groot onto his back and disintegrates the head of the metameric monster. Yellow ichor and fragments of chitinous plating fly in all directions. Galvanized by neural aftershock, the immense, segmented body of the suddenly headless arthropod convulses violently. The entire freight-train length of it whips and thrashes in the most devastating fashion, churning up the sand and hurling hapless pit-fighters, broken and mangled, into the air. Then it all but up-ends, and its lashing body and flailing legs topple into the wall of the ring and into the crowd.

A section of wall collapses under its grinding weight. Venomous leg-claws and squirming, spiked body segments do grievous harm to a large section of the audience in the cheaper seats.

The crowd is no longer roaring. It is rather more screaming and flooding for the exits. Suddenly the pit fight doesn't seem so much like a good night out anymore. This is a definition of the term "bloodsport" for which the crowd had not signed up.

The centipede thing takes a long time to accept that it is dead. Its thrashing, snapping body brings down more of the wall and smashes four tiers of seating—and the crowd members in them—over into the arena. Pit-handlers and marshals try to contain the mayhem, but the task is far beyond their abilities.

The translucent toad-beast smells blood and hurls itself through the collapsed section of wall. Perhaps it merely identifies a way to escape its prison, or perhaps it realizes that members of the audience will make less challenging snacks than its usual diet of armored gladiators who fight back.

Besides, the crowd has been jeering at it for far too long.

Rocket Raccoon surveys the carnage. Given that the "Oh What the

Flark Event Horizon" was comprehensively crossed earlier in the evening, he has no idea what kind of event horizon this is.

However, I realize that he is deep in the machinations of tactical genius. I am disappointed with his initial findings.

"We've got to get out of here," he says.

"I am Groot," Groot agrees. There is clearly more to Rocket's plan than I have appreciated.

Rocket is scooping spare power-mags out of the pouches of his bandolier. He starts to scamper away from us. I see he is plucking the containment plugs out of the power-mags.

The consequences of the centipede thing biting the Nitro 66 have given him an idea.

"Grab the Recorder-dude!" he yells over his shoulder. Groot obligingly picks me up and starts striding across the sand after his tiny friend.

At first, it looks as though Rocket is heading for the immense portcullis gate that leads out of the pit into the animal pens. But no, this is not the case.

He is heading for the ursine quadruped.

The ursine, only moments earlier, had thundered past us chewing on some gladiators and pitmarshals who had the misfortune to wind up in its parking-garage mouth.

Rocket leaps and manages to grab hold of one of the broken chains it is trailing. He races up the links, climbing up the beast's flank and onto its plated back. This is a deed akin to climbing the reins of a runaway horse. But Rocket is nimble and agile, and his disconcertingly human-like hands evidently afford great prehensile grip.

He is on its back. He is between its shoulder blades, hanging on to the huge, rusty spikes of its collar. All we can see of him is his bushy tail, flapping around at the back of the ursine's head. From our vantage point, loyal reader, it appears the ursine is wearing what you would call a "Davy Crockett hat."

"Steer, flark you!" he yells at the ursine he is riding. The ursine does not respond to the various tugs and heaves Rocket is applying to the spiked collar, so Rocket snakes his admirable, silky brush of a tail around and uses the tip to tickle the beast's right ear.

That does it. Irritated, the ursine steers to the left, directly toward the cage gate of the animal pens.

Rocket yells, "Yeeeeee-haaaw!"

He rises in the saddle and hurls the power-mags.

Power-mags are containment reservoirs that hold considerable amounts of energy, as the now-headless centipede thing will no doubt attest. They are designed to remain inert and highly stable— not exploding or releasing all their energy in one go, for example— to survive the rough-and-tumble of space war.

That is, unless the containment plugs are deliberately removed, something a sane person would only do the moment before sliding a power-mag into a weapon's receiver slot.

The destabilized power-mags sail through the air. As was the case with the one bitten in half by the centipede, they are not in any way influenced by the arena level's jamming fields.

They strike the bars of the portcullis and detonate.

The portcullis explodes. The archway surrounding it shivers upward in a cloud of flame, then rains down in an avalanche of stone blocks. This in turn causes another large section of the ring wall and the seating tiers it supports (along with quite a number of fight-night aficionados) to collapse. Utter mayhem ensues.

{*halt expositional protocol*}

—the superlative limits of the term *mayhem* will evidently need to be upgraded and redefined during the course of this narrative. I estimate I should have done this at least three times already, and we have only just started, really.

{*resume narrative mode*}

Rocket leaps from the ursine's back. It keeps going at full gallop and crashes through the ruined gateway, tearing down everything that the power-mag blast hasn't.

Still carrying me under his arm, Groot follows Rocket through the ruins of the gate. They pick their way over smoldering blocks and twisted shreds of metal. Up ahead, we can hear the noisy devastation being caused by the still-galloping ursine.

"Gotta be a way to an exit somewhere," Rocket advises. "A loading dock, something."

A few pit-workers run past, ignoring us. The air is full of smoke. Debris rains down from the ceiling. A figure looms out of the murk. It is the Shi'ar gladiator with the chrome sallet.

Rocket reaches for his pistols, but the Shi'ar just looks at us and shakes his head.

"No fight from me," he growls. "This is not what I signed on for. I'm just looking for the exit."

"Any suggestions?" Rocket asks him, raising his hands to show he is no longer going for his sidearms.

"Me, I'm heading for the subbasement," says the Shi'ar. "They say there are ways out down there. Into the Dive-town undercity, the rock-pile levels. Maybe from there to the trash wastes. Who knows?"

"Good luck with that," says Rocket Raccoon.

"Good luck yourself," the Shi'ar replies darkly. "All hell's coming down. The cops are inbound. Nova Corps. I even heard someone say the Luminals had mobilized."

"Xarth's Mightiest, huh?" says Rocket.

"I don't plan on sticking around to find out," the Shi'ar says. "I'm just going to slip out the back door. You got other plans?"

"Always," Rocket replies.

The Shi'ar turns to go. He pauses.

"Who are you people?" he asks.

"Rocket and Groot," says Rocket.

"Never heard of you," says the Shi'ar.

"Same old, same old," sighs Rocket.

The Shi'ar vanishes into the smoke, shaking his head.

"I am Groot," says Groot.

"The undercity?" asks Rocket. "No, not that way. Even with the heat coming. We need to accelerate our exit strategy. Let's get up to the landing pylons."

We start to move again, clambering through the wreckage. Rocket locates a broken security shutter that leads into a dank stairwell. Sounds of explosions, screams, and redefined mayhem echo down the concrete shaft.

Just inside the doorway, a man is propped up against the wall. He's a Xarthian, wearing the robes of a merchant. Something, probably a galloping ursine, has recently trodden on him. He has crawled into the stairwell to find refuge. Rocket pauses to see whether there's anything he can do for the poor fellow. It becomes rapidly apparent that an ursine footprint is not the sort of injury you can easily bandage.

"Just...j-just came looking for a q-quiet night..." the man murmurs through his pain. "H-have a drink...maybe d-do a little b-business..."

"What line of work are you in?" Rocket asks, trying to distract the man from his mortal injuries.

"Z-zunks," the man says. "I'm a zunk trader. I w-was just hoping for a little b-business...not *this*. Just a little d-deal. Something sweet. M-maybe looking to move between forty-seven and forty-nine t-tons of zunks. N-not a lot to expect, eh?"

"No," says Rocket. "I tell you what —"

But the man is dead.

Rocket looks up at Groot.

"You know what that is, pal?" he asks.

"I am Groot."

"Precisely. *Irony*."

IT takes a further fifteen minutes to climb the stairwell to the landing pylons. We do so cautiously. Smoke and the sounds of chaos still thread the air, and many alarms are blaring. From outside, we hear the distinctive klaxons of Nova Corps pursuit vehicles and emergency fliers. We pass a few other people, but they pay us no attention. They are merely interested in getting the flark out of Leery's. Possibly the flark out of Xarth itself.

Rocket tries to pop the landing-deck shutter, but security has locked it down. He pulls out a small sonic jimmy set and uses a couple of the delicate steel probes to pick the lock. The picks seem like surgical instruments in his disconcertingly human-like hands.

The shutter opens. Cold night air rushes in. The landing deck is one of several large platforms supported by the pylon that extends above the rooftops of Leery's. Parking for patrons only. Stepping out, we see the vast sweep of the city at night, a dirty haze of neon and the lit windows of skytowers. Thick smoke billows from the building beneath us. The busy air traffic of the high-rise city is being held back by the hovering pursuit vehicles of the Nova Corps: Xandar's finest, peace officers, the Galaxy's boys in blue. The night sky is filled with pulsing, flashing lights—blue, red, and bright yellow. There is a constant whine of lift engines.

"Come on," says Rocket. "Time to grab our wings and go."

He leads the way over to a little subcompact jump freighter, parked on its landing skids at the edge of the platform. It is not the most reliable or well-maintained spacecraft I have ever seen. I do not believe it is entirely necessary for it to have flame-effect nose art scrolling back from the exhaust vents, or a bumper sticker that reads, "Honk if you want to go faster-than-light."

"Excuse me," says War Brotherhood Commander Droook from behind us. "I think you have something that belongs to me."

We turn slowly.

"Hi there," says Rocket. Droook has several of his men with him. They are dirty and bloodstained, their War Brotherhood battle pants have brand-new War Brotherhood tears in them, and none of them look like they've seen the funny side of anything recently.

"I said I think you have something that belongs to me," hisses Droook.

"I belong to no one except the Rigellian Colonial Collective—" I start to say, but Rocket cuts me off. He looks Droook in the eye.

"Something that belongs to you, huh?" he asks. "I guess I do."

The landing platform is not covered by jamming fields like the arena level. Rocket's brace of pistols is out, and he is firing them faster than it is possible to believe. I think this is, in terms of Human Culture thematic reference, known colloquially as "gun-fu."

The Badoon scatter for cover—those that do not simply drop dead on the spot, that is. Droook is protected by his automatic bodyshield and stands his ground, screaming in rage as he fires back.

Groot opens the side hatch of the jump freighter, energy bolts smacking off the bodywork around him, and drags me aboard. Rocket follows, firing and running backward.

"Go! Go! Flarking go!" he yells.

The interior of the jump freighter is cramped, dark, and rather shabby. Groot drops me onto an acceleration couch littered with old take-out cartons and half-read holo-mags, and hauls himself into one of the cockpit seats. He hits *launch mode/engine start* before he's even strapped in.

Rocket leaps aboard. With a strangled whine of complaining, cold-started engines, the freighter lifts off. The side hatch is still open. Shots smack into the hull outside and the freighter yaws to the left, unsteady. Rocket backs across the sloping deck and almost falls out of the open door.

"Higher! Higher!" he yells, clinging on. "Straighten up and fly right!"

The freighter levels and begins to climb. It swings away from the platform edge, nose down, its landing gear still deployed. Badoon gunfire chases it.

"I am Groot!" Groot yells.

Clinging to the frame of the open hatch, Rocket peers out. He can see Droook and the Badoon hastening to their own craft, a sleek and very well-armed War Brotherhood Assault Ship.

"Flark!" he murmurs. He slams the hatch and dashes into the cockpit, sliding in beside his pal.

"Take us up and out!" he orders. "Full burn!"

"I am Groot!"

"Yeah, yeah, I can hear it!" Rocket replies. So can I. The comlinks are suddenly blasting out loud challenges.

"This is the Nova Corps! Jump freighter, cut your engines and land! Repeat, cut your engines and land! You do not have permission for orbital exit!"

We hear klaxons. Flashing hazard lights fill the sky, underlighting the clouds.

But we are not stopping. We are still climbing. Groot is dragging the sublight throttle levers all the way back.

The War Brotherhood Assault Ship screams into the air after us. It also ignores the frantic demands of the Nova Corps, and several of the Corps' pursuit craft are forced to veer wildly to avoid collision with the accelerating Badoon ship. It opens its forward battery covers and extends its gun turrets, which pop like ugly blisters from its sleek hull.

In the cockpit of our little jump freighter, hazard alerts start to scream. *Multiple target lock. Multiple target lock. Multiple target lock.*

Rocket glances at his pal.

"Only one thing for it," he says. "We need extra lift—and a little distraction."

"I am Groot!"

"You said it!"

Rocket leans over and hauls on a large lever. It is the lever that opens the freighter's rear cargo hatches.

The freighter zooms forward, suddenly lighter by almost exactly forty-eight tons.

"Not such a lousy investment, after all," says Rocket Raccoon.

It is, perhaps, the first and only time in the history of the Universe that a Badoon War Brotherhood Assault Ship is taken out by forty-eight tons of almost overripe zunks. The payload—tumbling, scattering, and bursting—hits the ship like a mass birdstrike, clogging intakes, jamming gunports, and pulping through thermal exchangers.

The War Brotherhood Assault Ship falters, wobbles, flutters, and then peels away in a vast and spectacular crash dive, trailing flames, mangled engine parts, and ingested debris. It arcs away and down across the outskirts of Dive-town in a trajectory that no amount of fighting with the helm controls, hitting the braking jets, or screaming futile, outraged orders can arrest. A brief, bright starburst of light and a shock wave mark the spot where it impacts—almost, but not quite, missing a municipal sewage treatment plant.

The Nova Corps ships maintain high-speed pursuit of the jump freighter, and their orders to desist become quite shrill and indignant, but Rocket and Groot are not stopping. Not even for The Law.

"Hit it!" Rocket yells.

"I am Groot!"

"Yeah, I *know* we're still inside the atmosphere! Hit it!"

Groot mashes a huge, gnarly hand down on the big red switch that lights the freighter's FTL drive. A significant and instantaneously generated storm explodes through the upper atmosphere as the ship goes to plus-light speed inside the atmospheric envelope. The traumatized weather pattern will continue to bring unseasonal rain, high winds, lightning, and snow to the streets of Dive-town for another week.

Aboard the jump freighter, we are suddenly encased in the blessed silence and ethereal starlight of FTL travel. There is a gentle, frosty glow outside the window ports, a silvery sheen. Inside, our faces are lit by the multicolored displays of the instrument panels. Xarth, and the Xarthian system, is already a memory far behind us. There is a little throbbing hum from the jump drives. There is an aftersmell of ripe zunk.

Rocket looks over at me from his pilot seat.

"I think it's about time we found out more about you," he says.

"I think that would be a good idea," I agree. "I, for one, am anxious to know."

Rocket Raccoon lets out a deep sigh and sinks back into his seat.

"I need a Timothy," he declares.

Meanwhile, forty-three minutes earlier on Alpha Centauri...

CHAPTER SIX

MEANWHILE

(FORTY-THREE MINUTES EARLIER ON ALPHA CENTAURI...)

EACH window of the Executive Boardroom of Timely Inc. Corporate Headquarters was a kilometer square that looked out on to a stunning vista of the dynastic ritual palaces carved by expert icesmiths into the Gon-Ket Glacier. The view was a stunning, peerless blue-white.

The view was also unusual because Timely Inc. Corporate Headquarters was situated on the principal continental landmass of Alpha Centauri, and the Gon-Ket Glacier was at the southern pole of the Kree homeworld, Hala.

"Could we change the vista settings?" asked Senior Vice Executive President (Special Projects) Odus Hanxchamp from the head of the Executive Boardroom table. "We've a couple more items on today's agenda, and the view is making me chilly."

Around the immense Executive Boardroom table, the one hundred-plus executive officers, department heads, vice presidents, and senior vice department officers nodded and made a show of shivering and turning up the collars of their immaculate pinstripe suits to indicate they felt the same. They did not feel the same, but everyone liked to be seen to be in agreement with Senior Vice Executive President (Special Projects) Odus Hanxchamp.

"Would you, Mrs. Mantlestreek?" Hanxchamp asked.

"Of course, sir," replied Mrs. Mantlestreek, Hanxchamp's prim, elderly personal assistant. She rearranged her horn-rimmed spectacles to better see the controls of her actuator wand, then waved it in the direction of the windows. The Gon-Ket Glacier glimmered for a second more, then vanished in a swirl of pixels. For another second, they were treated to the drab and uninspired landscape of Alpha Centauri outside. Then they were bathed in a warm, golden glow as the windows revealed a breathtaking view of the dusty Temporal Mausoleums of Calofxus in the deserts of the fifth moon of Spartax—moldering edifices twice as old as time, washed by the baleful red light of an ancient sun.

"Much better," said Hanxchamp. "Right, moving on...item one sixty-two, 'product development update, beverage containers.' Gruntgrill, where are we on this?"

"R&D has done a lot of work on this, sir," said the Kaliklaki-born Senior Vice Development Executive Arnok Gruntgrill, leaning forward and using his actuator wand to punch up a hologram suspension over the table. "As you know, Timely Inc. leads the way in innovationized development to make all of its products optimated for maximum market-agreementabilization. It's our core philosophy. We want to resolutionate the lives of all our purchase benefactors and redactify the problemistic areas of their day-to-day existence experience with synergetic solutionoids."

"Hear hear," said several vice executives.

"As you can see from this graph," said Gruntgrill, "market research has confirmed a key difficultized issue regarding beverage containers."

"Summarize, Gruntgrill," Hanxchamp said testily. "We've been here three hours already."

"Of course, sir," laughed Gruntgrill. It was a nervous, synthetic laugh. A boss-soothing laugh. His antennae quivered anxiously, and he adjusted the knot of his tie. He fought back the urge to vocalize the characteristic "tik" noise distinct to the Kaliklaki. He knew that it annoyed people, so he had spent a lot of money on speech therapy to lose the habit. But it welled up every time he felt stressed.

"Exhaustive market research has revealed that beverages are, in general, thermally awkward," he said.

"Thermally awkward?"

"Yes, sir."

"Meaning?"

"They tend to be hot."

"Are we sure about this?" asked Hanxchamp.

Gruntgrill smiled confidently.

"Nineteen years of audience studies across twelve quadrants, canvassing eighty-two trillion consumers, sir," he said proudly. "We're pretty d'ast sure."

Hanxchamp nodded.

"Okay, I'm seeing it now," Hanxchamp said. "Beverages are hot. So the beverage containers *also* get hot?"

"Exactly, sir."

"And thus become thermally awkward?"

"Spot on, sir."

"Leading to?"

"Uncomfortable hand experiences," said Gruntgrill solemnly.

"Also instances of scalding, cuff damage, and—in some cases—actual spillage."

Around the table, many execs tutted and shook their heads. Someone in the Beverage Containment Division was for the chop, and they were all very glad it wasn't them.

"Okay, Gruntgrill," said Hanxchamp, "you paint a very ugly picture. I presume you've got good news? Solutionize me. Go!"

Gruntgrill allowed himself a quietly triumphant smile.

"R&D has been working on this little baby for a decade, sir," he said proudly, "and we think it's a doozy. See for yourself."

He wanded up a fresh hologram. It was a design schematic.

"What the flark is that?" asked Hanxchamp.

"Marketing is still blue-skying a name, sir," said Gruntgrill, beaming. "For now, we're calling it the Manual Easification Curve."

"Talk me through it, Gruntgrill."

"As you can see, sir, the Curve is built *directly* into the side of the beverage container. Digits, fingers, or pseudopods can slip around the Curve easily, thus allowing the beverage container to be raised, lowered, or otherwise manipulated with zero loss of comfortable hand experience, and no scalding issues."

There was a long pause.

"It's a work of flarking genius," said Hanxchamp. "Sheer flarking *genius*."

Gruntgrill blushed a deeper shade of green.

"Kudos to the guys in R&D, Gruntgrill. Take that to them from me personally."

"I will, sir."

Hanxchamp thought for a moment.

"Hang on...hit me with the downside. What's this going to cost, implementation-wise?"

"That's the beauty part, sir," said Gruntgrill. "Market research was less than six trillion. R&D came in under eight. We calculate another sixteen trill to upgrade beverage-containment manufacturing, and only one hundred and eighty trill on top of that for the market-awareness campaign. Frankly, it's so extremiatedly well under budget, it's scary."

Hanxchamp sat back in his chair.

"I love it," he said. "I want to marry it and have offspring with it. It's a true synergetic solutionoid. It's exactly the thing that makes Timely Inc. a Galaxy leader."

He looked around the Executive Boardroom table. Everyone present realized it was time to *ooohh* and *aaahh*.

"Come on, people," Hanxchamp said. "Idea-shower me. Comments? Brain-ideas? What do we think?"

"Work of genius like you said, sir," said Blint Wivvers, the M'Ndavian head of Legal.

"It's the simplicity I love," said Sledly Rarnak, the Skrull in charge of Corporate Pamphlets. "I look at it and I think, why has no one thought of this before?"

"I'm literally speechless," said Pama Harnon. She was a sultry blue-skinned Kree and the Chief Finance Officer of Special Projects. "I mean, the budget underage gives me literal goosebumps, but it's the *idea*. We identified an oblique user needage, and we flarked that sucker."

"I'm just thinking out loud here, boss," said Homus Staplebunt, Vice Senior Junior Executive in charge of Responsibilities, "but what if...what if..."

"You're not a Watcher, Staplebunt," said Hanxchamp. "Spit it out."

"Well, what if our target purchase benefactor wanted to manipulate the beverage container from the *other* side?"

"What are you saying?" asked Hanxchamp, leaning forward again.

"Uhm, okay," said Staplebunt, "check my thinking here, people, but from that display it's clear the Manual Easification Curve is situalized on the *right-hand* side of the beverage container?"

"This is just a mock-up," said Gruntgrill.

"Right, right," said Staplebunt, warming to his theme. "But think. What if you wanted a *left-hand*-side hand experience? I mean, how would that work? The Curve would be on the wrong side."

"Flark," said Hanxchamp, noticing the truth of it with a sigh.

"Way ahead of you, kid," said Gruntgrill, glancing at Staplebunt. He waved his actuator wand and the displayed image began to rotate slowly. "This was the hard nut to crack, actually, but we've anticipated this feedback. You see? You turn the beverage container *around*."

"Flark, that's brilliant!" exclaimed Rarnak.

"Turn it around?" asked Staplebunt. The Zundamite sagged slightly and tilted his oversized head on one side, gazing at the hologram display. "I guess you could. Wouldn't it...I'm just thinking with my voice here...wouldn't it be better to have a curve on *both* sides?"

"Well, that would -tik!- double the costs," said Gruntgrill in a thin, fretful voice.

"No way are we doing that," said Hanxchamp. "One curve. And maybe we include an illustrated instruction manual with each beverage container explaining how 'container turning' works."

Everyone around the table nodded.

"Okay, good," said Hanxchamp. "That's covered. Mrs. Mantlestreek, did you get all that down?"

The elderly P.A. reviewed her minutes.

"I think so, sir," she said. "Let me check...*invented the handle*... yes, I got it."

"Excellent," said Hanxchamp. "Right, let's move on. Last item. Ah yes, Project 616. Right, people, this is Senior Special Projects clearance only, so that lets most of you off the hook. Good meeting, thank you all."

The vast majority of the hundred-plus executives around the table mumbled their appreciation, shuffled away their papers, and headed for the exits. Some, who had only been attending the meeting telepresently, vanished in wafts of light. Several others teleported away.

"We have the room, sir," said Mrs. Mantlestreek.

Apart from her and Hanxchamp, there were only six execs left at the meeting: Rarnak; Pama Harnon; Gruntgrill; Wivvers; Xorb Xorbux, a fierce Z'Nox in charge of Corporate Security (Special Projects); and Allandra Meramati, a dignified Shi'ar noblewoman who headed up the Executive Executization Department.

"Clandestine fields on, please," said Hanxchamp. Mrs. Mantlestreek obliged. Her wanded command surrounded the Executive Boardroom with a subtle cone of silence generated by the miniature black hole in the basement of Timely Inc.'s headquarters. Nothing and no one outside the room could see them, listen in, or be privy to any exchange that now took place.

Hanxchamp got out of his seat and regarded the view of the Temporal Mausoleums of Calofxus.

"Six-one-six," he said. "The biggie. The big one-a-roonie. 616.
Nothing else matters. This is the mother lode, people. This is the one
that secures Timely's economic power. It will secure it for a million
years. Total market stability. Total Timely dominance. We stand at
the threshold of a new era. The great empires and cultures will fail
and fade. Only the megacorporations will exist. They will dominate.
This is the megacorp future, my friends. Corporations more powerful, stable, and resilient than any individual flarking species. And
Timely will lead the way with the greatest market share of all."

He turned and looked back at them.

"It's going to be a beautiful, beautiful thing," he said sadly. A
cloud crossed his face. "But flark me. It's taking longer than a Kree-
Skrull war. No offense."

"None taken," said Rarnak.

"I literally hear that," said Pama Harnon.

"Datacore," said Hanxchamp. "Where are we at?"

"Percentile stands at eighty-seven," replied Meramati smoothly.
"The datamap is eighty-seven percent complete, which is to say we
have eighty-seven percent of all existential truth."

"Less of the 'truth' stuff, lady," snapped Hanxchamp. "You sound
too much like one of those happy-clappy, killy-silly freaks from the
Universal Church of Truth."

"My apologies, sir," Meramati replied, her elegant feathered
crest ruffling slightly.

"Is eighty-seven enough?" asked Hanxchamp.

Gruntgrill shook his head.

"One hundred percent seems unlikely to be achievable," he said,
"but we think we can go live at ninety-six percent-plus."

"Why is this taking so long?" asked Hanxchamp. "I thought the Rigellian Solution was supposed to speed things up?"

"It was, and it has," said Meramati. "Project 616 was originally scheduled to take three millennia to accomplish. By opting for the Rigellian Solution, we have brought it down to just six years. That's a serious result, I think."

Hanxchamp nodded.

"But we're still not there?" he asked.

"The basic problem remains," replied Xorb Xorbux. "One Recorder unit is unaccounted for. It contains the percentile data balance we need."

"It's missing?"

"It's on the run, sir."

Hanxchamp frowned.

"So find another one to do the job."

"Not so simple, sir," said Xorb Xorbux. "The missing Recorder viewed the entire datacore while it was being reprogrammed. It knows everything. It knows more than it realizes. It is too valuable to be allowed to remain at large. It is essentially a greater and more complete version of our datacore. We need it back to obtain the data unique to it and complete Project 616. We also can't allow it to fall into anyone else's hands."

"We can't destroy it?" Hanxchamp sighed.

"It's too valuable," replied Meramati.

"Solutionize this for me, please!" demanded Hanxchamp.

Xorb Xorbux coughed gently.

"We need to go off book for this, sir," he said, his voice dropping to a growl. "In my opinion. Time is short, and there's too much at risk. I request permission to bring in a private security provider. He's unorthodox, but reliable. Talented. He'll get the job done and retrieve the missing Recorder. But this has to remain budget-concealed. We need to bury it in the back-budget, or the shareholders will go flarkazoidal."

"Literally, not a problem," Pama Harnon stated.

"Okay, approved. Who are we talking about?" asked Hanxchamp.

Xorb Xorbux rose and wanded open the side door to an annex. A tall figure walked out and stood before them. They all recognized the sleek and complex armor of a Galadoran Spaceknight at once.

But this being was markedly different from the chrome-and-shiny Spaceknights of legend. His armor was matte black and scarred from many battles. On his belt, he wore a heavy blaster, a cyclic broadsword, and a nullifier. He was menacing, almost evil. They felt a chill that no amount of virtual desert radiance could dispel.

"This is Roamer," said Xorb Xorbux. "Once of Galador."

"No longer of Galador?" asked Hanxchamp.

"I fought for the light most of my life," said the Spaceknight, his voice dull and heavy through the speaker of his cowled helm. "For Galador. For what is right. I fought the Wraiths, and all evils."

"And?"

"I suffered. I lost things that mattered to me. I lost my faith."

"In what way?" asked Hanxchamp

"I will not speak of it," replied the dark Spaceknight.

"Hey, buddy," said Hanxchamp, gesturing around himself with both tentacles. "Clandestine field? State of the art? No one can hear you?"

"*You* can hear me," said the Spaceknight.

"Roamer has excellent credentials," said Xorb Xorbux. "His work is immaculate. His past is his own affair. We need not pry. Consider him a *h'jel, a ronin,* a *gonaktofaj,* a masterless warrior. He wanders the spaceways, selling his extraordinary military craft to the highest bidder. I propose we retain him to find and recover the missing Recorder."

"And how will he literally do that?" inquired Pama Harnon.

"I have my ways," replied Roamer gruffly.

"And they will be supplemented," said Xorb Xorbux. "Show them."

Roamer turned slowly to reveal a small device bolted to the back of his matte-black armor. The casing of the device bore the Timely Inc. logo.

"Hey!" said Gruntgrill. "How did you get hold of that? That's an Interpolation Inserter! That's still in testing! It hasn't even been tried!"

"Needs must," replied Xorb Xorbux humorlessly.

"What does that thing do?" asked Wivvers.

"It's essentially a teleport device," replied Gruntgrill, "but it operates off tachyon-state temporal energies. It contains a multi-phase destiny generator, totally experimental, that, once triggered, calibrates the causal nature of reality, recognizes the pathways of the Universe in terms of satisfying dramatic progressions, and deposits the user at..."

"At what?" asked Hanxchamp.

"Well, sir," said Gruntgrill, "in theory, exactly the right place in time and space to effect the greatest dramatic consequence. It assesses universal life as a story, and places the user in precisely the right moment to influence that story. That's the idea, anyway. The Entertainment Division was developing it, but they found it ended movies and vid-plays before they even began, so it was shelved. It's never been adequately field-tested. It could potentially disrupt and collapse the causal tension of reality. It's-tik!-*dangerous*."

"I'm not afraid," said Roamer, turning back to face them.

"This doohickey will take the dude to wherever the Recorder is because it makes dramatic sense?" asked Hanxchamp.

"Possibly, sir," replied Gruntgrill. "In theory, it harnesses narrative energies, reads the Universe as an ongoing continuity, and interpolates the user directly to the most dramatically satisfying moment. In practice -tik!- it could shred the entire Universe on a cause-and-effect level."

Hanxchamp thought about this.

"Do it," he said.

The Spaceknight nodded slightly.

"Approve his fees, whatever they are," Hanxchamp told Harnon. "Let's get on with this. Bring that Recorder back to us."

The Spaceknight nodded again. He activated the device. There was a halo of crackling light. The Executive Boardroom momentarily smelled of plot twist and shock reveal, with an aftertaste of page-turn splash.

And the Spaceknight vanished.

"Good, good. Great work, people," said Hanxchamp, sitting down again. He turned his chair and looked at the view. He smiled.

"Is it me, or is it suddenly getting hot in here?" he asked.

CHAPTER SEVEN

RESUME NARRATIVE MODE

I LIKE space. Deep-field space. I have spent much of my life in it, voyaging between destinations on behalf of the Rigellian Colonizers who made me and programmed me. Of course, loyal reader, I have also spent much of my life *in situ*, observing and recording the data of my destinations, but it has been the time *between* those experiences that has given me the greatest satisfaction.

The time spent traveling. The time spent in the dark, starlit void of great, tumbling galaxies. I have voyaged, alone, sometimes for decades, always silently, hearing nothing but the whine of neutrinos as they stream past my moving form. During those periods of transit, I have had little to do—apart from recording starmaps and navigational markers, and observing the changing color of young stars and old stars alike, obviously—but think. For *myself.* These have been periods of meditative reflection and self-discovery.

And now I am in space again. I'm aboard the little jump freighter belonging to Rocket Raccoon and Groot, and we are traveling at high FTL passage away from the complex and downright troublesome situations of Xarth Three. My problems, perhaps temporarily, slide away behind me at faster than light speed.

It is quiet, apart from the sub-deck throb of the engines. Outside the hull ports, the view is a frosty one of chilled stars and distant light. There is a calm and a solitude. There is a respite.

I take the moment to search my memory records and experiential data-logs for some clue as to why any of this is happening. I have, I can see, many blanks. Many lacunae. I am loaded to approximately eighty-three percent of data capacity, and I have no difficulty recovering most of it. I can, for example, explain in detail the underworld hierarchies of the planet Krul. I can tell you what the manufacturer Triplanet Metals Inc. has constructed throughout its history (a list, incidentally, that would include the very jump freighter that now conveys us). I can tell you why the oath "Trigon's Bones" is common in one Galaxy and not another. I can describe, in extensive detail, the sunrise on Chandilar and the weather forms that accompany it at different times of the year. I can relate the specific observable nature of sunset on Adrinax. I can recite and compare the legal systems of eighteen hundred cultures, including the inevitably complex Code of Law practiced and prosecuted by the Nova Corps of Xandar. I can tell you how to feed and care for a Kymellian hopping shrew. I can remind you of the best psionic defense against Kt'kn. I can tell you how to say "Cheers!" in Kodabak.

I have, on balance, a very great amount of data in my brain case. It is the equivalent of many encyclopedias. It covers all subjects, and it is both specific and general. You are, I believe, especially proud of your "Wikipedia." You consult it for homework shortcuts and easy stump-speech research. You rely upon it. It is, for a primitive pre-stellar species, remarkably thorough.

Imagine, if you can...and you *can't*...but imagine having access to the Wikipedias of ninety-six thousand cultures—including data that they don't even know about themselves, but that I have patiently observed. Imagine having that in your head, instantly accessible (no network problems, no...what is it you call it again? Ah, no "broadband issues"). Imagine that *being* your head. Imagine knowing so much detail about so very, very much.

Are you doing that? Are you?

Okay, good try.

Now imagine that in the middle of that there are *blanks*. Things you don't know. Things you know that you know, but that you can't understand. Imagine knowing everything about almost everything, except the reasons that you know them.

Imagine gaps.

I am scared of the gaps. I am scared of the *not* knowing. I am scared of the confusion, of the lapses, of the breaks in my mechanically thorough memory that mean I don't know connective things that I should know.

I know that I know things I cannot access or account for. I know I know things that I cannot remember. It feels, my dear gentle reader, my new friend, like a terrible weight. A burden.

I do not know why people are hunting me. I do not know why the Badoon were chasing me. I do not know where the Spaceknight came from. I do not know, apart from my obvious intrinsic worth as a source of data, why I should be valuable to anyone.

And I do not know why a genetically engineered Halfworld Raccoonoid and an arboreal life-form from the closeted Planet X should be acting so kindly toward me. They saved me from doom.

I suspect, though I have nothing to back this up, that the motive may be less than altruistic.

I think they see money in me.

"We have to get to the bottom of you," says Rocket. The ship is on auto-nav and flying itself, so he has popped what he calls a "cold one" and retired to the bench booth behind the cockpit space where I am sitting. He leans back, regarding me with curious, beady eyes. His disconcertingly human-like hand grips the frosty beer bottle.

"The Badoon wanted you real bad," he says. "Why was that?"

"I don't know," I reply.

"Aw, come on, Recorder 127 of the Rigellian Intergalactic Survey," he replies with a grin. "You must. I mean, you're an impressive piece of kit. Ultra-tech. A walking, talking multipedia. But the Badoon sicced an entire War Brotherhood War Cadre on your heels— knowing they were on an advanced civilized world, knowing that they would tangle with the Nova Corps and the Luminals and worse."

"I assure you," I tell the Raccoon, "I do not know. I know I do not know, with some certainty. There is a marked and alarming gap in my understanding where a piece of knowledge should exist. It is blank."

"Hmmmm," says the Raccoon.

Groot, having run a situation test on the auto-nav, joins us. He has popped a cold one of his own and produced a pack of playing cards. He starts to deal them out onto the table.

"Not the time for Skrull Hold 'Em," Rocket observes, but Groot continues dealing. His dendrite fingers are astonishingly dextrous. And in no way disconcertingly human-like.

I immediately understand that this is how they unwind during long FTL trips. They sit back in the bench booth, play cards around the little table, and sink a few beers. I say beers. Neither of them are actually drinking beers.

"I am Groot," Groot says as he finishes dealing.

"Yes," I say, "the gaps *are* most troubling."

Groot nods his huge wooden face. Rocket leans forward.

"Wait a sec," he says, wiping his muzzle on the back of his disconcertingly human-like wrist. "Wait a sec here. I just realized the flark out of something here. You...*you* understand what he's saying."

"Of course," I reply.

"You have all along," Rocket muses.

"Of course," I reply.

He frowns. Frowning does not suit Raccoonoids.

"But...and here's the meat of what I'm saying," he says, "most people assume that my old buddy Groot just says the same thing, all the time."

"I am Groot," Groot nods.

"Exactly that," says Rocket.

"Well, of course they do," I reply. "Acoustically speaking, that is all he ever says. That is the sound he makes. But beneath the repeated sound, there is a wealth of breath nuance. The breeze whispers through the branches of a tree, and it seems to make the same sound, but there is much variety in it if you listen closely."

"Well..." Rocket ponders.

"*You* understand him," I venture.

He nods. "But no one else ever claims to, except..."

"Except?"

"Last time someone did, it was Maximus the Mad," he replies.

"Troubling indeed," I agree.

"I am Groot," says Groot.

"Really, don't worry about it," Rocket and I say at the same time. We look at each other.

"You're smart, Recorder," he says. "Or crazy. Either of which, I'm down with. Okay, Recorder, ol' buddy, let's sort this pickle out. What *do* you know?"

"You'd be amazed," I reply.

"So amaze me."

"Where would you like me to start? Issue a data command to me."

"Uh-huh...okey-doke...where are we?"

"Aboard a Triplanet Metals Inc. jump freighter, compact class— the 'Fast-Leap' model, second generation, with custom modified shift-drive."

He nods. He sinks some beer.

"Go on...?"

"It is nineteen weeks past its last service. There is a knocking in the generator flux that you think should be looked at. Groot has made some peripheral adjustments, which is why there is a trace of bark residue around the engine-inspection panels over there. The shine on the screw heads shows that they have been taken off and replaced recently."

"He's good," Rocket says to Groot.

"I am Groot," Groot replies.

"We are traveling comfortably at sub-thirty over FTL," I continue. "The ambient cabin temp is 19 Celsius, Earth gauge. There are thirty-eight spent disposable beverage containers rolling around under the deck grilles."

"I ditch them. I keep getting scalded," Rocket says.

"You have informally named this ship the *White Stripe*, because it plays upon your characteristics—i.e., your bushy tail—but is also a cheeky reference to the appearance of stars at high light speed."

"How did you know that?" he demands.

"The name is written in biro on the left-hand side of the main navigation console in the cockpit."

"Okay, okay, what else..?"

"There is a frankly alarming copy of *Playbeing* scrolled up under the locker opposite us."

"That's not mine!" Rocket cries.

"Your disconcertingly human-like fingerprints are all over it," I say.

"Man, I just read it for the articles."

"I am Groot," Groot laughs.

"Indeed. These playing cards," I continue, "are a novelty set that features pictures of popular woodland forms. It was manufactured on Arborus. The Queen of Hearts, a particularly attractive-looking birch, is your favorite, though the nine of spades, the billowy ash, also has some appeal."

"I am Groot!" Groot exclaims.

"Don't dish it if you can't take it, bud," Rocket laughs.

"You are drinking a bottle of Zero-Beero; it is your preferred drink, excepting a Timothy, which no one in his right mind would attempt to mix on a warp-transiting spaceship. Groot is drinking a jug of garglesap. It is his drink of choice when he is kicking back."

"I am Groot."

"Exactly. The afterburn and the mouth-feel. I get it."

"You...you read us that fast?" Rocket asks.

"It is my program. I am a Recorder."

"So...so you *not* knowing something...that's a big deal?"

"It is."

Rocket sighs. He looks at Groot.

"Okay, buddy, get up in the cockpit and set us a course for Kno-where."

"I am Groot."

"Yeah, I know what I'm doing. I'll even smile while it's happening and put up with that flarking Soviet Labrador. Our new buddy has a head fulla stuff, and I think it includes stuff he doesn't know he has a headfulla. The freelance tech-gurus at Knowhere are the only people in the entire flarking Galaxy that I think might be able to rip his memory out."

Groot gets up and heads for the cockpit.

Rocket looks at me.

"We're jumping to Knowhere," he tells me. "I have contacts there. Contacts that will sort out this mess. Contacts that will get to the bottom of this conundrum."

"But you have reservations also?" I ask.

He nods.

"Yup, I do. We're on the lam, and the cosmic cops are after us. We hafta get to the freestate station Knowhere before they find us."

Groot makes a course correction. The jump freighter *White Stripe* snarls as it comes around, its light engines straining.

Twenty-seven seconds later, the cops pull into view.

Nova Corps. Lamps flashing. High-speed pursuit.

Trouble in anyone's book, either side of the law.

"Flarkity flark flark flark," says Rocket Raccoon.

CHAPTER EIGHT

CUT TO THE CHASE

IN the tight, G-adjusted cockpit of his X-Class Pursuit Ship, Nova Centurion Grekan Yaer frowned and made a subtle adjustment to the joystick. Obediently, the supple, ultra-high-tech, high-speed chase ship yawed and accelerated.

Centurion Yaer was an impressively big individual, a male Korbinite with a heavy muscular frame and orange skin. He had been recruited by the Worldmind to serve the Nova Corps of Xandar eighty Earth years earlier because of his determination, high moral standards, and devotion to equality and justice.

Since that day, he had obediently served the Law Code of Xandar—which was, in effect, the single most consistent criminal law system in the Galaxy.

He synched his comlink.

"This is Centurion Yaer. Subject vessel is coding red on my ident systems. Engage full pursuit."

"Corpsman Starkross, aye!"

"Corpsman Valis, affirmed!"

"I hear that, Corpsmen," Yaer replied. "Looks like this isn't going to be a training flight, after all. Follow me in."

The three Nova Corps chase ships banked in formation, Yaer's in the lead, and rocketed after the lone jump freighter. As they accelerated to eighty-eight gravimetric, the three X-Class Pursuit ships opened their spiked starshields. This enabled them to achieve greater FTL speeds by widening the wake of their gravimetric engines; it also made them resemble the distinctive starburst insignia on the brow of every Centurion's helmet, a universal symbol of law and order.

All three ships began to pulse their hazard lamps and broadcast subspace sirens.

Yaer frowned again. It was hard to see his frown entirely because he was wearing the golden, cheeked helm of a Nova Corpsman. Sleek and gleaming, it covered everything but his mouth and chin. His powerful body was sleeved in a dark blue armor suit, the uniform of the Corps, gauntleted in strips of radiant gold metal. On his chest, the three circles of his rank glowed with incandescent power.

"Worldmind?" he said. "This is Yaer, operative 19944-56712. I am in pursuit of a suspect vessel. You have my coordinates. Sending you the details now."

In front of him, the solemn face of the Xandarian Worldmind appeared in ghostly holographic form.

"Reading you, Yaer," it said in an ageless voice. "Processing. Suspect vessel is identified as a Triplanet Metals Inc. jump freighter, compact class, the 'Fast-Leap' model, second generation, with custom-modified shift-drive. It is not capable of outrunning you. It was last seen departing without permission from Xarth Three. Outstanding warrants there issued now follow: absconding to FTL without permission, suspicion of smuggling, suspicion of violent acts, suspicion of extortion, suspicion of theft, possession of illegal firearms, murder, murder with intent, murder with unfeasibly large guns, breach of the peace, breach of the peace in a public arena, atmospheric disruption, unauthorized use of an FTL drive, refusal to comply, refusal to obey a direct order of the Nova Corps, malicious damage to a Corps officer or Corps vehicle, imbibing a Timothy—"

"I getcha, Worldmind," Yaer replied. "They're bad guys. Show me in pursuit at this time."

"Centurion Yaer," said the Worldmind. "Am I to understand that you are taking the novice Corpsmen Starkross and Valis into this action with you?"

"They gotta learn sometime, Worldmind."

The Worldmind said nothing for a moment.

Then, "Centurion Yaer, desist. The Corpsmen are young, barely graduated, and not suitable for a mission of this jeopardy. I urge you to curtail engagement."

"Yeah, well, we're here now," said Yaer, flicking the hologram away. "This, Worldmind, is real life."

He opened his comlink channels on broad.

"Suspect vessel, suspect vessel, this is the Nova Corps. You are a vessel of interest following an incident on Xarth Three. Cut your drives and drop to sublight. We're coming alongside. Prepare for boarding and inspection."

He waited.

He repeated the order.

No response.

"Suspect vessel, suspect vessel, I'll take that as a 'no.' Choice was yours. We are coming to get you, and we will take no flark from you. You are advised."

Yaer switched to helm-to-helm.

"People, we're taking this son-of-a-flark down. You know the drill. You were trained for this. Catch and keep. Expect exceptional bad-assery."

"I hear that, Centurion," replied Starkross over the link. She was a young Xandarian, steady but untried. She was eager for this chance to prove her worth and advance in the Corps.

"Affirmed, C-Centurion!" replied Valis. He was a young Kymellian, nervous and unpredictable. Yaer knew he had to watch him. Valis might fly off at any second.

Hell, he knew he had to watch them both. They were his responsibility.

On top of that, he had to catch and keep a ship full of very, very bad types. It might get messy. It might get stone-cold. It was going to be a busy night with lots of professional risks.

Then again, it was *always* night out here.

"Suspect vessel, suspect vessel, this is your last warning—"

He had barely started the comlink challenge when the jump vessel in his holo-cross-hairs began to accelerate. Then it executed an amazing turn-and-dive.

"The flark?" Yaer muttered, banking hard after it. G-force slammed him. "Who the d'ast is flying that thing? Flark, they're good..."

"Say again, Centurion?" Starkross commed.

"I said *stay with them*!" Yaer barked.

He kicked in higher, feeling the acceleration straps automatically tie him back into his seat. The stars were like stripes. Yaer loved speed. The gravimetric powers of the Nova Force with which he had been joined had taught him a love of speed.

But this was almost too much.

"Stay close!" he warned his cadets. They were still tight, remaining in pursuit formation, though Valis was having difficulty keeping with the pack.

"They're not heeding me," Yaer told his pupils. "Gonna fire a warning shot across their bow."

"Understood."

"Read that."

Hand stiff on the bucking stick, Yaer took aim through the cockpit display and fired—one, two, *three* shots from his chase ship's gravimetric battery.

He fired them wide, but no one in the Universe would risk getting hit by blasts of that strength. That kind of warning always brought suspects to a sudden, frightened halt.

Not these idiots, apparently.

They were going for it—full burn.

Yaer cursed.

"I don't want to kill them, but they're giving me no choice..."

The jump freighter zagged again, executing a perfect port-side turn.

"How's he doing that?" Yaer wondered.

"He's diving—" Valis replied.

"Asteroid field! Asteroid field!" Starkross yelled in alarm.

Yaer's pupils widened very slightly, but he reacted with impeccable speed and dexterity. He'd been so intent on the suspect vehicle, he'd taken his eyes off the navigation projection and thus any notification of shipping hazards ahead.

It was an asteroid field, a big one, filled with lazy, tumbling rocks—some the size of boulders, some the size of small moons. It was a dense field, too. A flier would have to be crazy to take a ship of any size into a rock-swarm that close-packed.

And a flier would have to be certifiably flarkazoidal to do it at FTL speeds.

But the suspect ship was going for it. It was going to try to lose them in the asteroid field.

"Sublight! Sublight!" Yaer yelled into the link. All three chase ships cut their FTL drives hard, their gravimetric engines protesting, and decelerated to what felt, by comparison, like a standstill—though they were still moving at many thousands of distance units per time period.

Yaer kept his eyes on the forward screen, expecting at any second to see the flash-and-flare of the suspect vehicle's inevitable impact. Typical end for a typical overzealous joywarper. Yaer had been in the Corps long enough to see his fair share of speed-freaks trying to outrun a high-speed pursuit, and ending up losing control and leaving the road, so to speak.

But this lunatic was good.

"D'ast, this lunatic is good," Yaer murmured.

"He's cut his FTL!" Starkross yelled over the link.

He d'ast well had. At the very last microsecond, the fleeing jump freighter—executing an almost suicidal, corkscrew nosedive into the edge of the field—had killed its jump-drive so abruptly it would probably never work again. But the ship dropped instantly to very low sublight speeds and slipped almost elegantly between two rocks the size of mountains.

"Starkross! Valis! Hold your positions! I'm going in after him!" Yaer barked.

"We're coming with you, sir!" Starkross linked back eagerly.

"That's an absolute negatory, Corpsman. Stay the flark here and hold position. This is way too risky for you kids. Understood?"

"Corpsman Starkross...aye."

She sounded disappointed. Yaer smiled. He admired her pluck.

"Corpsman Valis, affirmed!"

Valis sounded relieved. Yaer kept his smile. He admired the kid's healthy attitude toward risk taking.

"Get on the link," he ordered, yanking on the stick. "Contact the nearest Corps Heavy and tell it to route our way at max. If I nail this lunatic, I want to be able to cart him all the way to Xandar!"

"Affirmative, sir," linked Valis.

"Good luck," linked Starkross.

"Luck, Corpsman, has nothing to do with it," Yaer replied. "But thanks."

He had begun his approach, nursing his sublight speed. He had a partial lock on the suspect's tail. Glory, but those asteroids were looming fast. Some of them were spinning irregularly. This was going to be tight.

Foolishly, though it made him feel better, he breathed in.

He closed his ship's starshield, reducing its lateral profile, then turned on his side as he passed between the first two rocks. It *was* tight. He could have reached up out of his cockpit and taken a surface sample.

Almost immediately, he was climbing hard to avoid a rock tumbling right at him, then jinking left and right to dodge between smaller rocks that were spinning toward him from different directions.

Where was the suspect? *Where was the d'ast suspect?*

His protection screen was really busy. It was tracking and marking more than nine thousand asteroid masses at once, and that was just the immediate part of the field he was cutting through. He had to roll hard, then duck under a rock, then bank at high G to miss another. The asteroids around him—the small ones, especially— were beginning to move even more unpredictably. The powerful backwash of his gravimetric drive was causing a ripple; rocks were starting to spin, pushed by the wake. Some collided with each other, splintering and sending out showers of deadly debris.

Two large rocks bashed into each other so hard there was a bright flash as matter annihilated.

"Too close," Yaer murmured.

"Sir? Sir? Are you okay?" Starkross linked. She sounded scared. "Sir, we saw a flash from out here. Are you—"

"I'm fine as flark. Hold position. Any word from the Heavy?"

"—skkzzk—inbound now and skkzzk—within twenty skkzzk—"

Great. Yaer knew that he was far enough into the dense field for the high heavy-metal composition of the space rocks to start blocking his link. The mineral-ore interference was also messing with his tracking and projection systems. He couldn't read anything except inert, hyper-density rock. How the flark was he going to detect the jump freighter? It was like hunting for a single ember in a blizzard.

Yaer was calm. His heart rate was super-mortally low. Years of training had cut in, and his mind was clear.

He didn't have to detect the suspect vessel. He could see where it had *been.*

Just as with his own gravimetric drive, the backwash of the jump freighter's sublight engines was causing a cascade tumble pattern in the rock field.

Yaer killed his projection screen and went eyes-only. His enhanced mind and vision read the intense, ever-moving complexity of the asteroid field ahead of him and watched for tell-tale signs of—

There!

A tumble of rocks, spinning erratically against the field's overall tidal ebb. A backwash.

He steered hard. The cunning flarker had tried to double back. Rocks rushed at him as he course-corrected, pushing his velocity as high as he dared. Rocks flew past: over him, under him, to the left, to the right, some so close they almost scraped his golden hull finish. With super-normal speed, his hand was operating the joystick— jerking, twisting, pulling, yawing. Only a Nova Centurion possessed this level of mental speed and hand-eye coordination.

Well, only a Nova Centurion and a flarkazoidal nutzooki in a jump freighter, obviously.

He was in the suspect's backwash now, and the asteroids were perturbed to such a degree they were no longer predictable. A big spinning rock came right the flark at him, and he barrel-rolled frantically to duck it. Immediately, there was another one behind it, right in his face.

No way to miss it. No way...

Yaer gritted his teeth and thumbed the fire stud on his joystick, atomizing the rock with a thunder-punch from his gravimetric cannons.

The rock flew apart. Yaer's chase ship powered through the heart of the dissipating debris. Small chunks, some the size of fists, exploded off his forward shields. Some got through and smacked the hull, leaving dents. Even the dust-size particles were potentially lethal at this speed. Yaer knew his chase ship's beautiful golden hull was going to look like it had been sandblasted.

A series of red lights flicked on across his control board. Damage sensors. It was all minor stuff—though one of his vector-thrusters had been misaligned, and that was going to reduce maneuverability.

Never mind. He had, in more than the obvious way, dodged the big one.

He plowed on, gunning the jets, slaloming through the unstable swirl of the field.

"Where are you, you son of a—"

Just for a second, he glimpsed the hot yellow glow of sublight afterburners between the rocks ahead of him. He hard-rolled to chase it.

The move was hasty. He had turned too tight. An asteroid the size of Xandar's Hall of Justice clipped his starboard side and ripped off one finial of his closed starshield. The chase ship bucked hard, and Yaer fought to retain control. The stick shook. The engines wailed. Vibrations juddered through the mainframe.

He stabilized just in time to avoid smashing nose-first into a space rock ninety times as big as his ship.

He saw the glow again. He locked on.

"You're mine, flarker," he breathed. It was the first time he'd exhaled in a long while.

The suspect vehicle saw him and began to accelerate. Dumb move. Yaer could see that, in its haste to escape, it had already taken several dents and scrapes of its own. Accelerating was the last thing it should be doing.

The suspect was desperate. *Really* desperate.

Dodging the pelt and rush of the swirling asteroid shoal, Yaer got closer. He was almost in range to activate the chase ship's gravimetric tractor-beam and snare the flarker. Just a little closer. *Just a little closer...*

The jump freighter tried to dart away. It had to bank hard to avoid collision, then came out the other side of the roll and clipped a small rock. There was a flash, a spray of sparks, and chunks of torn hull plating scattered back at Yaer.

The jump freighter pulled out and stabilized, but it was hurt. It seemed to be bleeding propellant from a ruptured tank. The liquid propellant trail spattered off Yaer's shields like rain on a windshield.

He had him. He had the crazy son of a d'ast.

He gunned again.

The jump freighter spurted forward, as if scared by the approach. It dodged another rock, went between another two and then—insanely—through the hole in the middle of a donut-shaped asteroid. The hole was scarcely big enough. Sparks trailed back fiercely as the jump shuttle's hull scraped the rock in several places.

Yaer went after it. He punched through the hole, leaving two more starshield finials behind.

A targeter sounded: a sudden, bright chime in the small cockpit space.

Tractor-beam range achieved.

Yaer punched the beam activator and felt the sudden pull on his momentum as he snared the fleeing ship. He had the suspect, had him *tight*, like a chain was connecting them, taut and unbreakable.

But the suspect was not killing his engines. He was actually dragging Yaer along, unwilling to admit defeat and pull over.

"D'ast you!" Yaer yelled. "Know when to quit!"

They were tied together. They were d'ast well *tied together*. Yaer could kill the tractor and cut free, but he was damned if he was going to let the suspect go.

His gloved hands flew along a row of control touch plates. He killed his engines—he had no need of thrust now, as the jump freighter was doing all the work for both of them—and channeled all gravimetric power to the beam. In effect, he was now a ball and chain bolted to the jump freighter. And he was increasing his mass gravimetrically, making his chase ship heavier and heavier.

The jump freighter began to slow rapidly, its afterburners lighting to white hot as it strained its engines to break free.

"That's it, you idiot," Yaer said, "burn your d'ast drives out."

Then the lunatic flying the jump freighter did something *more* lunatic, even by his own previously demonstrated high standards of lunacy.

He braked and hard-turned to starboard. He almost—*almost*—collided with a big rock in the process, but somehow missed it.

Yaer let out a cry of alarm. He had killed his engines—his chase ship was, in effect, an inert mass being towed by the freighter. All the physical laws of the Universe were against him. The jump freighter's hard turn jerked his ship around like a dead weight on the end of a rope. Converted momentum was forcing him to fly out to port hard, sideways, dragged and yanked simultaneously.

Collision alarms screamed. A rock came at him hard from his port side. He could see it out of his left-side canopy ports. His ship was being swung sidelong into an asteroid.

No chance! No chance! No chance at all!

"Eject! Eject!" Yaer screamed.

But it was too late. Far too—

Yaer's golden chase ship struck the asteroid side-on and disintegrated, releasing a brilliant, scalding explosion of light, debris and energy.

Total annihilation.

CHAPTER NINE

THE REST IS SILENCE

BLACKNESS.

Then more blackness.

Then a little bit more.

Then a slowly unfolding light.

Yaer woke up. He was spinning slowly in zero G, in absolute silence, tatters of his chase ship glinting as they tumbled around him like leaves.

His head was swimming.

Think. *Think*.

He had managed to eject. That's it. Okay. At the very last minute, he had managed to eject. Now, like a drowned body in an ocean swell, he was tumbling through the silence of the void.

But Grekan Yaer was a Nova Centurion. Though the Nova Corps of Xandar used chase ships and star cruisers for convenience, each member of the Corps was effectively a ship in his or her own right. Yaer's blue-and-gold armored uniform and his access to the extraordinary Nova Force made him a humanoid rocket.

Yaer reached out and accessed the Nova Force, activating his super-mortal power. He swept his fists forward like a diver coming off a high board. His chest circles glowed brightly. He sped forward, leaving a twinkling wake of gravimetric power behind him.

Asteroids rushed past him. Yaer was like a missile—not as fast as his poor, lost chase ship, but far more agile. Via his helmet's visor, he plotted and tracked thousands of asteroids, whipping his course between them, watching for the backwash wake of the suspect vehicle.

It was dead ahead of him.

It had dropped speed sharply, assuming no more pursuit. It was in reach. It was banking and diving to exit the underside of the asteroid field and jump away.

The Worldmind spoke in Yaer's head.

"Centurion Yaer. Telemetry has recorded the destruction of your vessel. Are you intact?"

"Yes," Yaer replied.

"Are you still in pursuit?"

"Yes," Yaer replied.

"Centurion Yaer, I am reading your vital signatures. Your heart rate is raised. Your adrenalin is accelerating. You are sweating. You are channeling a great deal of the Nova Force. Are you all right?"

"Oh, I'm *marvelous*," Yaer said.

The jump freighter was right ahead of him. It was limping along—swooping and twisting between the rocks, trying to find a way out. He doubted he even showed up on its sensors, if it had any left.

He closed in, reaching out. He directed the Nova Force through his gold-spurred gauntlets. The beam, firing from his fists, struck the jump freighter and snuffed out its drive.

It tumbled, drive dead.

He swooped in and grabbed it by the hull plating. He hauled it after him, using the invincible power granted to the Nova Corps.

"You're mine now, flarkhat," he murmured.

He cleared the field, dragging the battered jump freighter after him.

Open space. He breathed out. Open, clear, deep space surrounded him. He loved that: the freedom—the freedom to soar, alone, free of a ship as he was now.

The asteroid field—a trillion spinning, sunlit rocks— fell away behind him in the galactic glow.

Two Nova Corps chase ships stood in position ahead, waiting for him with starshields open and hazards blinking.

"Centurion? Sir?" Valis linked.

"I got him, Valis," Yaer replied.

"We...we thought you were dead, sir," Starkross linked. Yaer could hear tears. That kid. So ballsy, but so emotional.

"I'm fine, Starkross. Seriously. In fact, I feel great. Lost my ship, bagged a bad guy. That's a *good* day in the Corps."

"Yes, sir."

"Starkross? Valis? You did real good. I'm proud of you both."

"Corpsman Starkross, aye."

"Corpsman Valis, affirmed."

Tugging the dead weight freighter behind him, Yaer allowed himself a smile. The kids were good. Really fine. One day, they would both make superb Centurions.

One day they might remember the crusty old Korbinite who had showed them the ropes, and maybe raise a glass of synthol to his memory.

Because Grekan Yaer would be long dead by then. Especially if he continued to pull crazy-flark stunts like this.

The Nova Corps heavy cruiser behind the two waiting chase ships was so vast it was almost invisible. It loomed like an eclipse out of the starfield, a subtle magnitude of brown shadow.

"Hello Heavy, hello Heavy," Yaer linked.

The cruiser's lights came on, illuminating it like a city block at night. Searchlights reached out to pinpoint him and the ship he was dragging.

"Hello, Yaer," the link replied in a cheerful, warm female voice. "You been a crazy boy again?"

"That you, Centurion Clawdi?" Yaer teased.

"You know it, Grekan. Always here for you and your... exploits. What do you have for me?"

Clawdi was a gorgeous little Tsyrani and a superlative Centurion. She'd been classmates with Yaer at the Academy; they'd always had a thing, though they had never acted on it.

Yaer sighed.

"I've got an absconding jump freighter, Lolet. Charges on file. Read them down—they're quite a package. And open your hangar-bay doors so I can bring it in."

"Wow, you weren't kidding, crazy boy. Okay. Opening the bay doors now."

The belly gates of the vast heavy cruiser opened, and light flooded out. It was like coming home.

Yaer steered in and set the jump freighter down on the deck. The chase ships followed him. The hangar-bay shutters closed behind them.

Yaer stood on the grilled decking of the hangar bay and stepped back from the battered, smoldering jump freighter. It was bashed up to hell. That'll teach you, Yaer thought.

Atmosphere and gravity began to come up. The lighting increased. Yaer let the Nova Force ebb out of him, keeping a little in his gauntlets in case of trouble.

Leaping out of their open canopies, Starkross and Valis ran to his side. Starkross pulled off her golden helm. Yaer could see the kid had been crying, but she was trying to show she hadn't. She was a pretty thing. A heartbreaker.

"That was amazing, Centurion," she said. "I mean...we thought... we thought..."

"I know what you thought, Corpsman," Yaer said and briefly touched her cheek. "Thank you."

Valis, helm still in place, aimed his equine muzzle up at the much taller Yaer.

"That was unorthodox, sir," he said.

"It was."

"I should really write a report."

"You should."

"I won't," said Valis. "I mean—"

"No, you should. Just try not to make me sound too crazy."

Valis offered his hand. Yaer shook it.

"It's an honor to be in your tutelage, sir," he said.

"Oh, don't be telling him that. His head will swell, then he'll be crazy as flark all over again."

Centurion Lolet Clawdi was advancing across the hangar deck to join them. She was smiling. Her golden helm was under her arm. She shot a wink at Yaer that no one could have missed. Sixty Nova

Denarians followed her, bearing grav-batons and riot shields. Millennians with team-served heavy gravimetric cannons set up their tripods and power boxes, and took aim at the jump freighter around the perimeter.

"So who are we dealing with here, Grekan?" Clawdi asked Yaer.

"No idea, Lolet. Fugitives from Xarth Three. You saw the rap sheet. Mucho dangerous perps, at the least. Very bad news. We should be prepared and armed for whatever emerges from that wreck."

"Oh, I am," she grinned.

She waved a team of Denarians forward. They were carrying cutting torches and raid-rams.

"Open the sucker up, boys," Clawdi ordered. "Everyone else? One hint of a gun, we blow the flark out of them."

The entry team of Denarians prepared to storm the jump freighter.

They hesitated.

The landing ramp was suddenly extending, and the main hatch behind it started to open.

"Steady, boys," Clawdi warned, stiffening and raising her fists. Nova Force glowed within her gauntlets.

The hatch opened. Stale air fumed out.

A figure appeared.

It was small. Short. Shorter even than the Xanthan Nova Cadet Kurrgid whom Clawdi, Yaer, and everyone else in their class had teased at the Academy.

It skipped down the ramp—bright of eye, sleek of pelt, and bushy of tail. At the foot of the ramp, it stopped and smiled winningly at the circle of riot cops and tripod-mounted weapon crews.

The riot team stiffened, drawing their armor-shields together with a concerted clack and raising their batons to charge. Safeties clicked off. Gun charges rose with a whine to fire status.

A pause. A terrible tension. A standoff.

"Evening, officers," said Rocket Raccoon. "What seems to be the problem?"

CHAPTER TEN

XANDAR

I AM in what I believe is known as an interview room. On either side of me, at the very rugged maxteel table, are Rocket Raccoon and Groot. Our chairs are composed of very rugged maxteel, as well.

The chamber is entirely inhospitable and spare. The walls are plated in matte-finish maxteel, and the ceiling is an acoustic mesh. To one side, there is a blank window that I am sure is a one-way mirror for observation.

We are on Xandar, in the heart of the Hall of Justice. This is where the Nova Corps heavy cruiser has brought us after seven hours of jump-travel.

I am not nervous, gentle reader, for the very fact that I have no nervous system. But I am, still, apprehensive about this situation.

It is, quite clearly, not a good situation for anyone to be in.

"Let me do the talking," advises Rocket Raccoon in a tone that suggests that this would be A Good Idea.

The hatch opens. Two people walk in. They are both Nova Centurions in full armor. The hatch closes.

They take their seats opposite us.

They put flat-screen tablets down on the table in front of them, sit back, and remove their helmets, which they also place on the table. One of the Centurions is a muscular Korbinite male. He glares at us, eyes narrowed.

The other is a short, curvaceous Tsyrani female.

"Record on," she says. "Let the record show Centurion Lolet Clawdi interviewing."

"Centurion Grekan Yaer interviewing," the male says.

"Would you identify yourselves?" Clawdi asks us.

"Rocket Raccoon, like I told you already," Rocket says, eyes down. He is fiddling with a part of the table's lip that is slightly deformed, as if some previous interviewee has struck it. Or bitten it. In either case, it is not possible for me to tell whether said act is voluntary or involuntary.

"I am a Recorder," I say in turn. "I am Recorder 127 of the Rigellian Intergalactic Survey."

"I am Groot," says Groot.

"Okay, planets of origin?" asks the male Centurion.

"Halfworld," says Rocket.

"Rigel, essentially," I reply.

"I am Groot," says Groot.

I sense, at this point, that there is going to be a problem.

"Planet of origin?" the Korbinite Centurion asks Groot harshly.

"I am Groot."

"We can play this game all day, buddy," the Korbinite Centurion replies.

"Planet X," says Rocket anxiously. "Put Planet X. That's where he's from."

The Korbinite Centurion sighs.

"Explain your activities on Xarth Three," says the female Centurion.

"Just doing business," replies Rocket.

"What sort of business?" asks the Korbinite.

"You know...a little of this, a little of that," replies Rocket Raccoon.

"No, I don't," the male Centurion counters gruffly.

"Well, you know...zunk trading, basically."

"Zunk trading?" asks the female.

"Right. But it's a tough game. A *really* tough game. A hard market. We didn't know what we were getting into."

"Is that why you ran?" asks the male Centurion.

"Well, *obviously*," says Rocket Raccoon.

The Korbinite Centurion looks at me.

"Is this correct?" he asks

"Utterly," I reply. "It is utterly congruent with the details you have presented."

"What about you?" the male Centurion asks Groot. "What's your take on this?"

"I am Groot," Groot replies.

"You, flark-face, are really beginning to rile me up," growls the male Centurion. "If you're not going to cooperate, at least say, 'I refuse to comment,' okay? Okay?"

"Easy, Grekan," the female Centurion hisses sidelong.

"Cooperate, all right?" the male Centurion warns Groot.

"I am Groot," replies Groot sincerely.

The male Centurion thumps the edge of the table angrily. I begin to see a possible origin for some of the dents and deformations in the maxteel surface.

"You trying to wind me up, buddy?" the male Centurion asks.

"I am Groot," Groot responds, aghast.

"Flark!" the male Centurion exclaims.

"Easy!" the female Centurion hisses.

"This joker has to realize what he's facing here," the male Centurion says to the female. "The charge list alone could put him in the Kyln for more year-growth rings than he'd care to consider. Add to that failure to cooperate with a formal interview..."

"What would happen then?" Rocket asks, brushing his whiskers with a disconcertingly human-like hand as if he doesn't really care two hoots about the answer. "What are you saying, big guy? You have ways of making us talk?"

"Less lip from you," the male Centurion tells Rocket. "Sure, we have ways. Your pal says that again, and I'm going to fetch a chain saw and a wood chipper."

"Grekan!" the female Centurion warns.

"One last chance," the male Centurion tells Groot. "What were you doing on Xarth Three, and how come you had to leave in such a d'ast hurry?"

There is a pause. Groot hesitates, leans forward, and looks past me at Rocket plaintively.

"Just tell the truth, buddy," Rocket says.

Groot sits back. He looks down.

"I am Groot," he whispers, reluctantly.

"You flark-taking little voidzoid!" the male Centurion cries.

{*halt expositional protocol*}

—I think, loyal and kindly reader, that this was the point at which I decided to act. It was less out of concern for our terribly compromised situation, and more because I empathized with Groot. I felt his discomfort and helplessness. I also remembered that he and Rocket had, between them, saved me in my hour of need. In several of my hours of need, in fact. I wanted to return the favor.

{*resume narrative mode*}

"Verbal Abuse of a Detainee," I say.

"Huh?" the male Centurion says, flicking his angry gaze toward me.

"Verbal Abuse of a Detainee," I repeat. "Nova Corps Code of Conduct, item 171777454. 'Detainees shall not be subjected to verbal or physical abuse during interview or custody. Nova Corps officers found guilty of such acts will be subject to penalties including loss of privileges, reprimand, severe reprimand, suspension, demotion, and—in extreme cases—expulsion from the Corps.'"

"Oh," says the male Centurion, sitting back and getting a measure of me. He is still confident, the alpha male in the room. "So look who turned out to be smart."

"And, uhm, *correct*," the female Centurion whispers.

"Leave this to me, Lolet," the male snaps back. "You saw the rap card. You know what these guys have done."

"Even so..." says the female.

"We do not know what we are alleged to have done," I say. "Xandar Criminal Code, paragraph 1112 (a), subsection iii: 'All detainees should be notified of their rights and informed of charges prior to interview.' It is very clear."

The male Centurion glares.

"You little fl—"

"Verbal Abuse of a Detainee," I say. "Nova Corps Code of Conduct, item 171777454."

"I should beat the goop out of you—"

"Physical Threat to the Body or Person of a Detainee," I reply. "Code of Conduct 876888."

"Yeah? Yeah? This is a sound-blanked room, metal-head!" snarls the male Centurion, rising to his feet. I feel the fizzling power of the Nova Force welling up in his gauntlets. "Who's gonna know you didn't just fall down while resisting?"

"This interview is being recorded," I reply. "You told me that yourself."

"I—"

"And she would know," I add, looking at the female Centurion. "I observe that she is uncomfortable with this line of interrogation. She does not approve of your methods. Her opinion of you has been modified."

The male Centurion pauses. He looks at the female.

"Lolet..."

"Simmer down, Grekan. Please. We know these guys are bad types. We know they tried to kill you."

"Excuse *me*," says Rocket Raccoon.

The female puts her hand out and touches the male's arm, urging him to retake his seat. He does so.

"Grekan nearly died bringing you in. You flarked his ship," she says. "It's on the list of charges."

"Which we still have not been allowed to see," I point out. "Xandar Criminal Code, paragraph 1112 (a), subsection iii: 'All detainees should be notified of their rights and informed of charges prior to interview.'"

The Centurions look at each other. Then the female rotates her tablet and slides it across the table. Rocket Raccoon reaches out to take it, but I pick it up first.

I review.

"This is quite extensive," I say after a while, still reviewing.

"You bet your tin ass it is," says the male. "What? Are you going to exercise your right to a lawyer? You want a lawyer?"

"Well, on balance, that's not such a bad idea," says Rocket.

"There is no need," I say.

"Because?" asks the female Centurion.

"There is nothing a lawyer would know that I do not," I reply. "Proceed."

"Oh, I'll *proceed*, all right," says the male. "First off, resisting arrest—"

"That is not 'first off,'" I say.

"What?"

"The Xandarian Criminal Code operates on an enshrined context of procedure and protocol. It respects, above all, due process. No matter the charges, any case that breaks due process is liable to be thrown out by the Xandarian High Chamber."

"What the flark are you talking about?" the male Centurion asks.

"A suspect must be informed of his rights and the charges he faces before interview," I say. "Xandar Criminal Code, paragraph 1112 (a), subsection iii and after. This has not been done. We have only seen the charges now, after the formal commencement of interview."

"So?"

"A breach of due process. The case would be thrown out."

"That's nonsense!"

"Perhaps," I say. "Given the magnitude and variety of the charges listed here, a tribunal might overlook the procedural lapse because of the significance of the case. A heat-of-the-moment thing."

"Exactly," says the male Centurion.

"There is more, however. Formal identification of a suspect vessel must be made prior to charging. Xandar Criminal Code, paragraph 82 (a), subsection iv."

"You were tracked and pegged leaving Xarth!" the male rages.

"Incorrect," I tell him. "Many ships left Xarth Three that night. Many may have been the same type and class as ours. You identified ours via the Corps' 'red-flag' system, which is generally accurate but requires specific confirmation. Such confirmation was not obtained. It says so right here on the list. You suspected we were the ship leaving Xarth, and you have not yet confirmed it. Breach of due process. Case thrown out."

"We can easily match serial codes—" the female begins.

"Yes, but you have not done so," I reply. "Continuing. Suspects must be identified formally before charging may take place. Xandar Criminal Code, paragraph 6768 (a), subsection i."

"We can put you in a lineup, if you like," says the male.

"To what end? Who would formally identify us? There are roughly eighty-eight trillion sentient beings in this part of the Galaxy alone. What formal identification could be made to specify *us*?"

"A Rigellian Recorder, a walking...tree, and...and whatever that hairball is!" the male Centurion shouts. "How much doubt could there be?"

"Enough," I answer. "I am one of many, many Recorder units. Raccoonoids and specimens of *flora colossus* are commonplace."

"Commonplace?"

"Commonplace enough in this infinite Universe for there to be a considerable element of doubt without precise formal identification. Doubt equals breach of process. Case thrown out."

{As I have previously indicated, loyal and gentle reader, it is entirely my pleasure to tailor the thematic references of this story to your Human Culture. To that end, I feel I should say that, at this point in the proceedings, I am beginning to feel like Henry Fonda in 12 Angry Men *or Atticus Finch in* To Kill a Mockingbird. *Or the rather dashing Matthew McConaughey in entirely every movie based on a John Grisham novel.}*

"We can get prints," the male Centurion tells me. "We can get prints, hair residue, DNA, bark samples—whatever you like. We can make a formal ID like that." He snaps his fingers.

"Yes, you can," I agree. "But you have not. Rush the samples from Xarth Three. Teleport them, if you like. Fast-process them through your labs. It is too late. You should have done it before beginning formal interview. Xandar Criminal Code, section 45, paragraph 23. Breach of due process, Centurion Grekan Yaer. Case thrown out."

"I've met slick attorneys like you before," Yaer glowers.

"Two things: One, I am not an attorney. I am Recorder 127 of the Rigellian Intergalactic Survey. I merely know what I know, and I apply that data if necessary. Second, no you *haven't*."

"But you resisted—"

"Unproven. Breach of due process. Case thrown out."

"But we have charges that—"

"Unsupported by fact. Breach of due process. Case thrown out."

"D'ast it! You tried to kill me and—"

"Not shown in evidence. You risked your own person during a high-speed pursuit while we were simply attempting to navigate a dangerous asteroid field. No charge upheld. Breach of due process. Case thrown out."

"I—"

"Also," I add, "none of us has been offered sustenance or even a beverage since custody began—"

"I could really use a beverage," sighs Rocket Raccoon. "But, you know, one of those cups with a little handle, because I hate to spill."

"—none of us has been offered a beverage since custody began," I continue. "Nova Corps Code of Conduct, item 1770134. 'Detainees shall be furnished with sustenance and/or a beverage at regular intervals prior to interview, without their demand, as upheld by the Universal Codex of Sentient Welfare, section 2, paragraph 12345671111.' Breach of due process. Case thrown out. You should have provided us with beverages, Centurion Yaer. You should have provided us with beverages."

Yaer falls silent. He looks glum.

"I'm checking this via the Worldmind," Centurion Clawdi says. "Flark. *Flark*. Everything the robot said...it's on the statutes. Every line and citation. He's got us cold."

They look at us, stunned.

"We will be leaving now," I say.

"I am Groot," says Groot.

"I'd love that beverage, though," says Rocket.

"Do not push them," I advise. "Know when we're done."

"But we get our ship back, right?" Rocket asks Yaer. "And it had better be all fixed up and hand-valeted."

"Do not push us," says Yaer quietly.

"We will get your ship back from impound," I tell Rocket. "We will effect repairs ourselves. We incurred our own damage. Surely you have insurance?"

Rocket mumbles something.

I look at the Centurions. They both seem a little...deflated.

"Good day to you both," I tell them.

I wish I had a folder of case files or a dossier to straighten with a tap on the maxteel table before I turn to go. I wish I had a brief-case.

I wish I looked like Matthew McConaughey.

Meanwhile, ten days earlier in the Negative Zone...

CHAPTER ELEVEN

MEANWHILE
(TEN DAYS EARLIER IN THE NEGATIVE ZONE...)

SHE hated the Negative Universe. It was counter to every fiber of her matter. It was utterly *alien*.

Also, it stank worse than a Brood's armpit.

Steam hissed from the gas vents dotting the blasted landscape around her. The ragged planetoid on which she stood was rotating far too fast around a pair of Negative suns. They drizzled ugly light. Day and night, and day and night went by every few minutes.

She should have turned down the job. She knew that now, no matter the paycheck. Coming to the Negative Zone made her sick. She was a being of the Positive Universe, and that was where she belonged.

Still, she was between jobs. She needed the cash. Times were surprisingly hard when you weren't guarding the Galaxy. They were also hard when you were, but that was different. Lean times made you a mercenary. You went where the work was, even if it was the Negative Zone.

The stink of the place was in her nose. She prowled forward. Her blades were heavy in her hands, heavy and ready. How many had she diced so far?

She'd lost count.

From behind boulders, camouflaged by the shifting shadows of the repeating sunset/sunrise, the next two attacked.

Both were gibbering, multiarmed warriors, waving far too many blades and cleavers. She ducked, kicked one back with a long, lean leg, and then sliced her right-hand blade through the other. Three limbs flew away in a shower of ichor. So did the top of the thing's head.

The other one rallied and came at her, chopping and slashing.

She dropped to her knees, raised her left-hand blade, and let the creature impale itself. It shuddered, its weight upon her, and went limp. Ichor streamed down over her sword hilt, her hands, and her thighs.

She rose, shaking the thing off her sword in revulsion. She switched her blades in the air beside her to fling off the blue body fluid.

"Enough," she cried.

"Enough indeed," replied Annihilus.

It flew forward into view on its grav-platform, a hunched and wizened insectoid mannikin half-cased in purple organic armor. Below its jaw, its Cosmic Control Rod glowed a harsh yellow, throbbing with immense, cosmos-altering power. She made no move against Annihilus. She knew, full well, that the insectoid on the grav-platform was one of the most powerful beings in *any* universe.

It slowed to a halt and hovered in front of her. Behind it, a host of warriors emerged, rattling forward like a swarm of locusts.

"You have performed well," it hissed in a voice like crackling paper.

"I don't like tests," she replied. She had had enough of those growing up.

"Eighty-two of my foremost warriors dead," said Annihilus, ruler of the Negative Zone. "An impressive audition. You are truly the Deadlies Woman in the Universe."

"*A* Universe," she sneered. "Not this one. Get to the point."

Annihilus laughed. It was the sound of a dog retching.

"Project 616."

"Means nothing to me," she replied.

"Heh," it replied.

"So how do I fit in?" she asked.

"There is a target," Annihilus crackled. Its chitinous skin creaked as it moved. "I want it obtained and brought to me."

"Finder's fee as mentioned?"

"No," it said. "*Double* it. Whatever it takes."

"I like your talk."

"Good."

"I don't like you."

"Few do," Annihilus replied. "I have built my reputation on it."

"Why can't you do your own dirty work?" she asked. "You've got the manpower. Why hire an agent?"

"None of my people could function well, or operate undetected, in the Positive Universe," Annihilus replied. "We would be showing our hand too early. You, however, creature of the Positive, can move without notice there. Do this for me, and you will be rewarded. You will be rewarded beyond your dreams."

"The target?" she asked.

One of Annihilus's warriors stepped forward nervously and handed her a data-block.

She speed-read it.

"This? This is what you want?" she asked.

"This is what I want," Annihilus replied. "Can you perform?"

She nodded.

"Yes. No problem. Arrange my transvacuation to the Positive Universe, and I'll begin at once."

"Agreed. It will be done," Annihilus replied. "One last thing—"

Three warriors rushed her. She decapitated one, bisected the second, and impaled the third.

"You can stop doing that," she said. "Tests are over. I've taken the job."

"That wasn't a test," said Annihilus. "That was a taste of the horror you will face if you fail to deliver."

Behind Annihilus, the insect army pulsed and chittered, quivering their wing-cases. Tough as she was, she knew she'd never take them all. And Annihilus was as powerful as a god.

"I *always* deliver," she said.

"Good."

"And I always expect prompt payment."

"Of course."

"I'm going now," she said. She turned. She paused.

She looked back at Annihilus.

"Just by the way, don't ever threaten me. *Ever*," said Gamora.

CHAPTER TWELVE

OUR AL CAPONE MOMENT

SEE? Once again, see how I make Human Culture references to ease your comprehension of the story, gentle and generous reader?

Oh, I realize I am also foreshadowing. I hate that. I will cease and desist from this moment.

{*But just to explain, Al Capone was a notorious criminal of your 20th Earth century. Despite his horrendous acts of felony, he was only jailed because of a comparatively minor charge of tax evasion. I have recorded this fact thanks to repeated viewing of an exciting Kevin Costner movie, which also features Sean Connery* not *doing an accent. And that, gentle readers, is the Chicago way.*}

We are in the impound dock of the Nova Corps HQ on Xandar, reviewing the frankly parlous state of our ship, the aforenamed *White Stripe.*

Rocket Raccoon keeps slapping me on the shoulder. So does Groot. The latter hurts rather more.

"That was amazing, Recorder, ol' pal, ol' bud," Rocket says to me. He seems genuinely grateful.

"I am Groot," says Groot.

"I know, I know...how incredible was that?" Rocket agrees. He looks at me. "You just took them to school, Recorder. You took their ol' Xandarian rule book and fed it back to them, chapter and verse. All the ways I'd imagined getting out of the clutches of the Nova Corps, and it never occurred to me to beat them at their own game. It was a thing of beauty to watch. An absolute thing of beauty."

"It wasn't difficult," I reply.

"It wasn't?"

"I just know these things. It is my purpose. I realized all I had to do was simply apply the knowledge in my head."

"Well, pal, you aced it," says Rocket.

"I am Groot," Groot agrees, as he slaps me once again on the shoulder.

After I pick myself up, we inspect the ship.

The *White Stripe* has seen better days.

"FTL drive?" asks Rocket.

"I am Groot."

"What about the sublight?"

"I am Groot."

"Flark's sake...environmental?"

"I am Groot."

"Shields?"

"I am Groot."

Rocket looks at me.

"It's going to be a while," he says. "Lot of repairs to run. We're going to need parts and spares, and probably a good mechsmith, too."

The impound dock is not a friendly place. A dank concrete box open to the sky, it is bathed in cold inspection lights; the tops of the walls are festooned with defense cannons and tractor-beam relays. There are two other ships parked on the concourse beside the *White Stripe*: a shot-up Xeronian warp shuttle with impound stickers and evidence markers all over it, and a K-class Nova Corps prowl cruiser that is in for repairs. Nova Corps tech teams wander about, working and talking, but they pay us little heed.

"We should effect repairs," I urge, "and then go to this place you mentioned. This *Knowhere*."

"I am Groot," opines Groot.

"I hear that," replies Rocket. He sighs. "We have some cool tech skills, but this might be a tad beyond us."

"I apply knowledge," I say. "I am not a mechanic of any sort, but I apply knowledge. Fetch me the user's manual."

It is brought to me. It is a tablet device, and I have to wipe off the smears of old beverage stains and crumbs of "salsa" corn chips.

Within half an hour, under my guidance, we have the sublight working again.

"Now, the FTL," I say, turning to page one thousand and eight. "It says, 'Insert a ratchet driver into access port viii, and remove the cover plate to expose the outer warp-ignition circuit. Then—' Uhm."

"Then what?" asks Rocket, his welding goggles pushed up on his brow and his overalls stained with oil spots.

"Nothing," I reply. "Just a part about needing an accredited warp engineer to do this, in case of cross-mixing the antimatter core and thus triggering a chain reaction that could blow a planet in two."

"Ah, that," says Rocket with a dismissive wave of his disconcertingly human-like hand. "It always says things like that. Go on."

"I am Groot," says Groot.

We both look up. Groot is correct. Nova Centurion Grekan Yaer is indeed walking across the bay toward us. He looks alarmingly pleased with himself.

"Not him again," says Rocket. "What does he want?"

"Gentlemen," says Yaer, coming to a halt and staring at us. "A little issue."

"Yeah?" says Rocket.

"You talked and walked your way out of everything. I'm impressed. Believe me, I am. But there's always one thing that trips you up, isn't there? The little thing?"

"Go on," says Rocket warily, hoping that the little thing is not him.

"I checked. This ship has no valid insurance. Not anywhere, on any system."

Rocket shrugs.

"I got behind on the payments. So what? You're going to bust us for insurance, after all we went through?"

Yaer thinks about this.

"Yes," he says, amused. "Yes, I am. It's a thousand-unit fine or two days in lockup. You see what I did there? I formally explained the charge and penalty, as per code, and now I'm going to read you your rights. Would you like a beverage before interview?"

"A mocha would be nice," says Rocket.

"Do not speak," I say, rising to face the Centurion. "I see what you are doing, Grekan Yaer. You are going by the book, so we can be arrested and processed with no technical problems. Once arrested, we can be re-examined for all the other charges on the rap sheet. You have reopened the investigation on a technicality in order to reapply the more serious charges."

"Yeah. Smart, right?"

"Very smart."

"Any clever rule of law or code citation you want to throw back at me to stop me?" Yaer asks.

I think. There are none.

"No," I say.

"Good," says Yaer. "So how's this going to go? The easy way, or my way? Go on, flarks, make my day. Resist arrest."

"Do not resist arrest," I tell my new friends. "We will find another course out of this."

Yaer shakes his head sadly.

"Ah, you spoiled it. Okay...Recorder 127, Rocket Raccoon, and 'I am Groot,' I am arresting you on suspicion of Using a Jump Vehicle Without Valid Insurance. You do not need to say anything, but any comment you make may be recorded and used in court. Follow me."

He pauses.

"Oh," he adds. "Is that a broken taillight I see? Fifty-unit spot-fine."

"You can't be serious about this," says Rocket.

I am sure that Yaer is, but we never have time to find out. Something very curious happens.

I get a presentiment of it for a second, like dramatic foreshadowing. I get a whiff of twisting plot and a hint of reversal of fortune.

There is a crackle of light. It appears between us and Yaer, on the impound-bay pad. Reality bulges, buckles, and bubbles—like a frame of old cine film caught in the projector and melting as it heats from the light.

Reality pops open like a blister, and suddenly the matte-black Spaceknight is standing there.

"Who the flark are you?" Yaer asks angrily. He steps forward, his gauntlets rising.

The Spaceknight suddenly has his nullifier drawn in his hand. The squat-nosed, boxy weapon fires once, emitting a shriek of power. The vicious beam puts Yaer through the dock wall.

Nova techs run for cover. Alarms wail.

The Spaceknight turns to us. Evil red light simmers like furnace coals behind the eye-slot of his visor.

"You know what?" says Rocket Raccoon. "I think I preferred the other guy."

A SUDDEN SURPRISE TWIST

SO THEN—

{*Oooops! I am sorry, genial and forgiving reader—I realize I have done it again. Foreshadowing, that is. I am like, I suppose, the jerk in the movie house who talks all the way through the flick and gives away the ending. Calling this chapter "A Sudden Surprise Twist" sort of spoils that twist and its surprise quality, doesn't it? I realize that now and apologize for any detriment caused to your robust enjoyment of this narrative. Maybe I should start again. I think I will. This is Chapter Thirteen, a number considered unlucky by twenty-seven hundred cultures, so maybe it would be altogether better to make a fresh start with Chapter Fourteen and forget about this whole affair. Okay? Right. Let's do that.*}

Resume—

{*Just a thing, though. Forgive me. Am I getting the Contemporary Terran terminology right? I worry. I want to make this accessible to you, kind and increasingly patient reader. For example, "movie house?" Is that what you call them? What about "Cellulose Image Projection Theater" or "Grand Cinematic Hall" or "Moving Picture Building?" I*} *must make a note to revisit Earth again soon and catch up. Please, do tell me where my vernacular is outdated or obsolete.}*

Resume—

{Cineplex! Cineplex! THAT was the word I was searching for! Anyway...}

· CHAPTER FOURTEEN ·

IN WHICH THERE ARE NO SUDDEN SURPRISE TWISTS WHATSOEVER

(DISSEMBLING MODE ACTIVATED)

RESUME—

The matte-black Spaceknight steps slowly toward us. The malevolent and ruddy light of stars burning out at the end of their lives throbs behind the slit of his helmet visor.

"Hello," I say, tentatively, over the wailing of sirens.

"Forget 'hello,' lock and flarkin' load!" Rocket yells. He has fetched an unfeasibly large weapon from his secret stash aboard the *White Stripe*.

"I do not think it would be advisable to shoot at this fellow," I suggest, but I am outvoted by Rocket's trigger finger and simultaneously drowned out by the roar of the Plasmatica Arms Inc. 50 Energy Bombard.

The Spaceknight is knocked back a few paces by the horrendous blast, but his null-fields absorb the lethality of it.

"Bad move," he growls.

"As I think I pointed out," I add.

He aims an armored finger at me.

"I want him. The Recorder," he says.

"Well, you can't have him, pal!" snaps Rocket Raccoon.

"Give me one good reason," says the Spaceknight.

Groot does so. He uppercuts the Spaceknight in the face so hard the Spaceknight achieves low orbit.

"Cool," whistles Rocket Raccoon.

It is, I suppose, in a purely "Man, did you see *that*?" kind of way. But it has not resolved our issues. In the cloudy skies of Xandar above us, the Spaceknight arrests his upward trajectory, turns, and starts to powerdive back toward us. We hear the high-pitched whine of his armor's propulsion system.

"I think we should—" I begin.

"*Take cover!*" Rocket yells.

The first blasts rip down out of the sky: dazzling orange beams of quanta-laser fire, utterly deadly, emitted by the heavy blaster weapon the diving Spaceknight has drawn.

The blasts strike the ground around us—blowing craters in the bay's concrete floor, scattering grit and debris in flaming cones of detonation. Each time we try to run, a beam strikes the ground in front of us.

I feel he is herding us, containing us.

The six automatic defense cannons atop the bay walls wake up, sensing an aerial assault. They start firing, their twin pneumatic barrels pumping bolts of gravimetric energy that look like streams of tracer rounds. The ground-to-air defenses lock in, and the six individual pulsing streams sweep together to triangulate the diving

Spaceknight. He is fast, and he banks to evade the chasing firepower, but his null-fields start taking hits.

Without slowing, he adjusts his aim and fires six perfect shots with his blaster. Each one annihilates a defense cannon. Around the wall top, the batteries explode, showering debris and flames down into the bay—and causing some of the inspection-light arrays to come crashing down, too.

The Spaceknight is a formidable shot. I am convinced he was containing us with his earlier blasts. If he'd wanted to kill us with a direct shot, he would have been able to do so effortlessly.

Another thought strikes me. I am the one he wants. I am the individual he wishes to capture intact. He has shown restraint toward Rocket and Groot thus far, but he has no particular reason to continue to do so if he decides they are hostile or simply in the way.

Indeed, Rocket is being both of those things. He has opened up with his Energy Bombard, streaking deadly red beams of light into the sky in an enthusiastic but wildfire fashion.

He might as well be wearing a neon sign that reads, "Shoot me."

The Spaceknight does.

It is just a nanosecond of my life, but thanks to the fluid-resolution pico-processing systems with which the Rigellian Colonizers equipped me, I observe and record every detail with absolute clarity.

The Spaceknight shoots Rocket Raccoon. The orange quanta-laser beam sears down to obliterate him. The predictive subroutines of my pico-processors flinch as they anticipate recording the sight of a small Raccoonoid disintegrating in an explosion of light, heat, and tufts of fur.

This does not, however, happen.

About one Raccoonoid arm's length from Rocket, the beam stops short in a huge flare of dissipating energy as something blocks it.

Rocket opens one eye.

"Am I dead?" he asks. "Is this the afterlife? Because if it is, it looks oddly identical to regular life, and that comes as a disappointment."

The Spaceknight swoops into the bay, lands on his feet, and starts running toward us. He aims the blaster at Rocket and takes another shot.

Like the first, it is mystifyingly stopped short.

"*Not* going to happen," says Centurion Grekan Yaer and knocks the Spaceknight flying with a gravimetric blast from his right gauntlet.

I realize Yaer was protecting us with a gravimetric field. The applications of the Nova Force are many and various.

The Spaceknight comes flying back at Yaer, but the Centurion is ready for him this time. Yaer's first punch smashes the Spaceknight's head sideways, and a deft gravimetric pulse rips the blaster out of his hand and crumples it. The Spaceknight hits back with a chin jab that staggers Yaer and splits his lip. Yaer blocks the next blow with his forearm, then delivers a straight punch that connects with the Spaceknight's visor. The Spaceknight lashes back. Yaer ducks, then comes up hard to put a super-mortally enhanced fist into the Spaceknight's midriff. The Spaceknight returns with a devastating spin kick that sends Yaer stumbling.

Then they start trading blows *seriously.*

We, meanwhile, take advantage of the super-mortal combat to seek cover.

"*Why* am I alive?" Rocket asks.

"I am Groot," says Groot.

"Groot is quite correct," I affirm. "The Nova Centurion screened us from harm with a gravimetric force field."

"Okay, again," says Rocket, "why am I alive? Why the d'ast would that flarkhat Nova-dude bother protecting us? Just a second ago he was gleefully trying to send us to the Kyln for life times twenty hard labor without possibility of parole!"

"It is his ethical duty," I reply. "Not only is it a Nova officer's sworn obligation to protect any and all individuals from the aggression of others, it is enshrined in their Code of Conduct, item 1246613, that they are morally responsible for the welfare of any individual or individuals in their custody or detention. Yaer arrested us, and thus he must do everything at his disposal to protect us under the terms of that arrest."

"Our problems just became his problems?" Rocket asks, with what seems to me to be a little too much relish.

"Just so," I reply. I am about to go on to add that the same edict applies to the Nova Corps as a whole—we are detained by the Nova Corps, not just an individual officer, and have thus become the responsibility of each and every officer—when events themselves demonstrate this fact.

Eight Nova Corps officers, including Centurion Clawdi, arrive at rocket speed to assist Yaer. The alarms are still blaring, and it would seem that the entire (and vast) Xandarian Hall of Justice complex is on high alert. The impound bay itself, one of many on the western fringe of the space-terminal facility, is being locked down to contain the incident. Heavy blast doors are sealing the bay's exits (not that we could reach any of them, anyway, due to the extremity of the combat). Very soon, more officers will be overhead, along with riot teams and heavy-duty squads. Meanwhile, we are trapped in the impound bay with all the combatants.

It is mayhem. {*Note previous definition, and raise it.*}

We have found insufficient shelter behind a maintenance trolley parked close to one wall. There really isn't enough room for all of Groot.

"We've got to get to our ship and make a fast goodbye!" Rocket declares.

We start to move, edging along the wall to avoid the shock wave blasts of energy and occasional tumbling Nova Corpsman. The matte-black Spaceknight is taking them all on. If anything, he has upped his game. I do not know how he intends to get out of this with the whole of Xandar closing in on him, though I assume he is confident that whatever strange process conjured him here will also conjure him back out if the need arises.

The Nova officers attack him from all sides, trying to restrain him. He knocks a Denarian unconscious with a ferocious punch, then draws his nullifier and blasts a female Corpsman back into the bay wall, making a female-Corpsman-shaped dent in the concrete. Two more come at him; he smashes one aside with his fist and sends the other backward, rolling and flailing, with a null-blast.

Yaer goes for him again, blood leaking from his lip. His uniform is scuffed in places.

"Stand down!" he yells. "Stand down and surrender now! That's an *order*!"

Yaer dives at him. The Spaceknight meets the attack with a backhanded slap so brutal that the very air winces. Yaer flies backward across the bay and smashes into the *White Stripe*.

This does not improve the *White Stripe*'s air worthiness in any way.

"My ship!" Rocket squeaks in dismay.

Yaer rolls clear of the damaged jump freighter, shakes his head to clear it, and then rises. He picks up the *White Stripe*, which is trailing debris from multiple busted hull plates, and briefly hefts it above his head with both hands before hurling it at the Spaceknight.

"*Hey!*" Rocket shrieks in a voice so high-pitched with indignation only canines could hear it.

The jump freighter lands on the Spaceknight. Its career as a functional space vessel ends as it becomes a pile of crumpled and twisted metal on top of a rogue Galadoran warrior.

The Nova Corps officers close in, those that were airborne landing on their feet. Their gauntlets seethe with power, ready to fire. Centurion Clawdi sets down in front of us.

"Stay down," she tells us sternly. "You are under our protection."

She turns her back to us, covering us.

"You done?" Yaer asks the pile of wreckage.

The Spaceknight is *not* done. The screaming blade of his cyclic broadsword rips up through the wreck of the *White Stripe* as he cuts himself out from under it.

He climbs out of the wreckage, hunched and glowering, blade in one hand, nullifier in the other.

"Take him!" Yaer yells.

They try. Even the lowliest Corpsman is a significantly empowered being, and the two Centurions present are full-on super-mortal. I doubt the Spaceknight is in any real degree stronger than either of them, nor is his matte black space-armor significantly more durable than their gravimetrically shielded bodies. But he has *something*. It is, I think, battle-smarts. It is sheer combat experience. The Nova Corps are highly trained and do not shrink from a fight, but they are peace officers. The Spaceknight is a stone-cold warrior. He faces them down with tenacity, and a sheer weight of confidence in his own skills. When he strikes, it is ruthless, devastating, and unorthodox—yet finely nuanced. He has learned tricks, many of them dirty and brutal, during his long years as a warmaker. He unleashes them now.

As they come at him, he knocks them back with fists, kicks, headbutts, and the frequent use of his nullifier. The screaming cyclic broadsword almost removes Clawdi's head, but she dodges and is able to wrench it from the Spaceknight's grip with a desperate application of ultra-high-magnitude gravimetrics. She effectively makes it so heavy he can no longer hold it.

The combat continues.

"Now's our chance!" Rocket says.

"I am Groot!"

Groot is quite correct. The impounded Xeronian warp shuttle looks like our best bet. Ducking a Nova Millenian who somersaults over us, we rush for the shuttle.

"I reckon I can hotwire that," Rocket says as we run.

I reckon he's right. He does not get the chance. Centurion Yaer gets his revenge for the punch that smashed him into the poor *White Stripe*, and manages to hit the Spaceknight with a powerful gravimetric blast from his gauntlets. The Spaceknight is thrown across the bay, and his bulk demolishes the engine nacelles of the Xeronian ship.

History repeats itself, in reverse.

The Spaceknight gets up, seizes the warp shuttle, and throws it at his enemies. Scattering a wake of broken scrap, cables, and drive rings, the ruined shuttle makes a brief, final flight across the bay—not under its own power.

Clawdi, Yaer, a Denarian, and one of the Corpsmen react fast—as might be expected of beings possessed of the mercurially rapid Nova Force. They blast the shuttle in midair before it lands and crushes them. The combined, tight-focus gauntlet blasts rip the vehicle apart. It disintegrates in a vast blizzard of debris. Many thousands of separate pieces—twisted metal, buckled plating, wires, shards of window ports—rain down on the bay floor or ping and ricochet off the walls. The Nova officers shield themselves from the whirling metallic rain.

The Spaceknight is already coming for them again. The vicious hand-to-hand battle resumes.

"Okay, right," sighs Rocket. "Not the warp shuttle, then."

We turn and rush in the opposite direction, toward the K-class Nova Corps prowl cruiser.

It is a sleek thing, finished in burnished gold with a red starburst on its prow. It is designed to carry a team of four to six, with room aft for prisoner transportation. The ramp is down.

We clamber aboard. The interior is equally sleek and finished with the classic design elements of the Nova Corps—seen in their uniforms, their iconography, their architecture, and their starships. Just looking at the rake of the windshield and the sweep of the grav-seats, you can tell it's more than *just* fast.

Rocket clambers into the pilot seat. I take my place beside him in the copilot's chair. Groot crowds in behind us.

{*halt expositional protocol*}

—I just want to point out that despite the ongoing jeopardy, this is terribly thrilling. I have never sat up front in a high-speed jump ship before, and certainly not while trying to make my escape from certain...if not death, then definite *unpleasantness.*

{*resume narrative mode*}

Rocket looks frantically at the sleek touchscreen controls.

"I'm not sure I can hotwire *this*," he moans. "I mean, it's all touch-sensitive. It probably needs palm-print ID recognition. Flark it, it's a Nova pursuit ship. They wouldn't design them so any old perp could steal one!"

"I am Groot!" Groot warns.

"Okay, I *will* just push something!" Rocket snaps back.

He lunges with a disconcertingly human-like hand and jabs at the main console in front of him. It lights up with a scintillating blue holo-display. Then a big red X appears across the display.

"Forbidden," says an automatic voice.

Rocket jabs another control surface. The big red X pulses.

"Forbidden. Function denied."

Rocket jabs yet again, exasperated. The big red X pulses once more, as if annoyed.

"Forbidden. This vehicle is programmed for exclusive use by the Nova Corps. This vehicle cannot match your palm print, disconcertingly human-like though it is, to any ID registered in the Nova Corps database of authorized users. You do not have permission to use this vehicle."

Another jab. Another X pulse.

"Desist," says the automatic voice. It is quite calm, though firm. "You are not an authorized user. You are not Nova Corps. Desist and remain with this vehicle while this vehicle summons Nova Corps assistance."

"Flark it!" Rocket exclaims, jabbing something else.

"Desist. This vehicle cannot establish your identity. This vehicle deems it likely that you are fugitives and/or criminals attempting to steal this vehicle. Further attempts to jab at touchscreen control surfaces will result in the automatic locking of all hatches and the release of anaesthetic gas. Desist and remain with this vehicle while this vehicle summons Nova Corps assistance."

Rocket goes to jab again. Groot grabs his arm and stops him before he can.

"Okay, okay," Rocket says, shaking off Groot's grip. He leans forward and looks at the big red X

"Please?" he says. "We're in a spot of bother, and we could really do with a ride out of here. *Please*?"

I believe he even flutters his eyelashes.

"Forbidden. Your identity is not recognized. You are not Nova Corps."

Rocket begins to serially use almost all of the vernacular curse words popular on this side of the Western Spiral Arm.

I hold up my hand to hush him.

"Vehicle," I say gently. "We are not Nova Corps. We are not authorized."

"Then why do you persist in trying to operate this vehicle?" the automatic voice asks.

"We are in jeopardy," I reply. "We have been arrested and taken into custody by Nova Centurion Grekan Yaer."

"That identity is verified. So you admit you are criminals. You *are* trying to steal this vehicle."

"We admit nothing!" harrumphs Rocket, folding his arms.

"We are suspects in custody," I clarify. "Extreme jeopardy, harm to our persons, and general threat exists in the bay outside. Please use your external sensor equipment to confirm this."

A pause. "Situation confirmed."

"Nova Corps Code of Conduct, item 1246613," I say, "enshrines that the 'Nova Corps is morally responsible for the welfare of any individual or individuals in its custody or detention.' Yaer arrested us, thus he and all agencies of the Nova Corps of Xandar must do everything at their disposal to protect us under the terms of that arrest."

There is another pause.

"So this vehicle, as a functionary unit of the Nova Corps, is obliged to remove you to a distance that might be considered appropriately safe for the duration?"

"Precisely," I say.

"What distance might be considered appropriately safe?"

"Orbital," says Rocket. "Definitely orbital."

"Given the scale and the ferocity of the situation," I suggest, "orbital might be appropriate."

"Or even, you know, another star system entirely," says Rocket.

"One thing at a time," I tell him. I look back at the display. "Vehicle? You now understand the gravity of this incident and the laws that apply to it. What does your programming tell you?"

The big red X pulses again, twice. Then it vanishes.

"This vehicle suggests you fasten your harnesses," it replies.

We do not have time. The hatches slam and the prowl cruiser

launches, as is so often the case with elements of the Nova Corps, like a rocket at hypervelocity. We shoot skyward out of the bay like a golden bullet. Rocket and I are crushed back into our seats. Groot disappears backward down the cabin behind us with a strangled "I am Groot!" and ends up crumpled upside down against the bars of the suspect transport cage in the rear.

Far below us, the magnificent vista of Xandar and the Hall of Justice recedes, bright in the sunlight. Sunbeams lens-flare through the window ports. In the impound bay, the Spaceknight slugs Yaer away from him, looks up to see us depart, and activates his propulsion system to give chase. He soars after us, struggling to match the prowl cruiser's velocity. Yaer, Clawdi, and more than two hundred other Nova officers take to the air in pursuit. Chase ships and arrest fliers of the Corps join them. High above, heavy cruisers and mass-driver vessels move in to blockade the orbital route.

"The identified jeopardy is following this vehicle," the automatic voice tells us. "This vehicle will attempt to achieve appropriate safe distance."

The prowl cruiser accelerates. Hard.

We experience extreme G-force push, a pressure so intense that our cheeks begin to flap. Well, mine don't, gentle reader, because they are made of synthetic polyalloy. But Rocket looks like a dog with a migraine grimacing in a wind tunnel.

Behind us, the Spaceknight knows his efforts are wasted. He cannot keep up with us. Moreover, the heavy cruisers in close orbit have target-locked him with their main batteries—main batteries more than capable of incinerating even a relentless and determined Galadoran warrior.

He activates whatever exotic device first brought him to us and vanishes in a blister of torn reality.

The prowl cruiser immediately begins to decelerate. However, we are already almost eighty million distance units out from Xandar.

Rocket slumps forward, the G-force lifted. From far behind us, Groot groans.

"Why are you slowing down?" Rocket asks the console. "Hey, hey! Keep going!"

"The jeopardy has gone," the automatic voice replies. "This vehicle will now return you to Xandar and into the custody of Grekan Yaer."

"No, no, *no!*" Rocket yelps. He thumps the console in frustration.

The big red X reappears and pulses.

"Forbidden. Your authority is not recognized. Don't make this vehicle use the gas."

"Sorry, sorry," gabbles Rocket. "My bad. I'm sorry! It's just, we were doing so well. You, us, on our way to who knows what adventures. Come on, it was kinda fun, wasn't it?"

"The jeopardy has gone," the automatic voice repeats. "This vehicle will now return you to Xandar and into the custody of Grekan Yaer."

"But the adventures? The fun?" Rocket asks in a quiet, disappointed voice. "We were going to have such adventures...uh... vehicle."

"The jeopardy has gone," the automatic voice insists. "This vehicle will now return you to Xandar and into the custody of Grekan Yaer."

Rocket turns and looks at me with a sigh.

"Oh well," he says.

Of course, one does not always have to go *looking* for adventures, gentle and generous-hearted reader. Sometimes adventures come to find you. And they are not always *good* adventures.

A force seizes the prowl cruiser. Alarms blare, but the vehicle cannot fight the tractor-beam holding it.

"What the flark?" Rocket has time to say.

We get a brief glimpse of an immense battlecruiser de-cloaking in front of us, and then a trans-mat beam dematerializes us and the prowl cruiser along with us...

...and rematerializes us in the stark belly-hold of the gigantic battlecruiser. It is a cyclopean space, like the interior of a temple designed by a minimalist.

"Do not be alarmed, criminals," the automatic voice says calmly. "Jeopardy has been identified, and this vehicle will protect you with all the means at its disposal."

"That doesn't really reassure me," says Rocket. "Look at the flarking size of this place!"

Outside, hatches open, and fire teams of warriors rush onto the hold floor to surround us. Their green-and-white uniform armor design is unmistakable.

"Kree?" exclaims Rocket. "It's the d'ast-damned flarking *Kree*?"

A statuesque figure walks out behind the troopers. She wears a powered exoskeleton over which she is draped in distinctive, hooded uniform robes. The robes are emerald green; the exoskeleton armor is black. In her left hand, she carries a ceremonial power-hammer.

"You in the ship!" she booms in a voice that would intimidate a Skrull armada. "Hear me! I am Sharnor the Accuser! I hold the high rank of Accuser as a governor and jurist, to arbitrate law and control across the Kree Stellar Empire! I bear these responsibilities according to the lasting, eternal edicts of the Supreme Intelligence! Get out of the ship and kneel before me! *Now*!"

"Flark," says Rocket.

"This vehicle is not quite sure what it can do about this particular jeopardy," says the automatic voice.

"I am Groot," says Groot.

I did not know, either. We suddenly found ourselves prisoners of one of the most powerful and militaristic cultures in known space. And we did not even know why. This was a reversal of fortune. This was utterly unforseeable.

This was a sudden, surprise twist, gentle reader.

You didn't see that coming, did you?

CHAPTER FIFTEEN

IN WHICH WE STAND ACCUSED

(*DISSEMBLING MODE DEACTIVATED*)

CAUTIOUSLY, we emerge from the prowl cruiser. Ranks of first-echelon Kree warriors face us, proud and formidable in their sculpturally crested helms and green-and-white uniforms. The uni-beam weapons they aim at us are even prouder and more formidable.

Steam billows across the mesh deck, rolling away from us like ground mist as the internal atmosphere of the prowl cruiser exhales and blows the vapor back. There is no sound except the quiet clicking of the prowl cruiser's cooling engines, the muffled crackle of the Kree soldiers' helm intercoms, and the distant, half-audible announcements from other parts of the immense battlecruiser. Because of Kree physiology, the air in the hold has a slightly raised nitrogen content.

The towering figure of the Accuser regards us coldly. Unlike most of the warriors around her, she is blue-skinned, indicating that she is of the "purebred" racial minority. Evolutionarily, the blue-skinned elite—considered the most racially ancient and original form of the species—are more gracile and less robust than the pink-skinned majority. There is, however, nothing that might remotely be described as "gracile" about Sharnor the Accuser. I suspect her undoubtedly impressive physique is the result of extensive genetic engineering and possibly cybernetic enhancement.

She studies us for a moment longer. Then she turns to the Kree officer at her side.

"Captain Yon-Dor, instruct the helm to reactivate the aura of negativity and make best speed for Hala."

"Yes, Accuser."

"We are deep in Xandarian territory, and out of jurisdiction. The Worldmind of Xandar will have detected us the moment we decloaked. If we remain here, it will wish to challenge us. It may even consider our presence here an act of aggression."

"Yes, Accuser."

"Also, establish an Omni-wave link to Hala. Inform Stellar Command that we have acquired the Rigellian artifact."

The Captain salutes and turns to gabble instructions into his helmet com.

The Accuser returns her icy gaze to us.

"Not much to look at," she murmurs. "I hope all this effort was worth it. But if this ensures the future survival of our race and our continued dominance in the Galaxy—"

"*That's* a lot to ask of us," says Rocket.

She glares at him.

"Anyway, this is nice," Rocket continues, turning in a slow circle and looking up to admire the truly colossal space of the hold around us. "Love what you've done with the place. And wow, Hala, huh?"

He looks back at the Accuser.

"A free trip to Hala, birthworld of the Kree. Nice. I haven't been to Hala in the longest time. Tell me, they used to mix a mean Timothy in the Pleasure Palaces of Lar-Lux, you know, down south on the coast there? They still—"

"Do not talk," snaps the Accuser. "Do not speak unless it is in answer to a direct question. Do you understand?"

Rocket hesitates.

"Do you understand?"

"Oh," says Rocket. "Was that one of the direct questions?"

"Yes."

She waits.

"Answer!"

"Sorry," says Rocket. "I was confused. You see, 'yes' isn't a direct question. Neither is 'answer!' actually, so I really shouldn't be speaking now. What was the question again?"

"Do you understand?!"

"I reckon I do," says Rocket.

"Bring them!" the Accuser tells her soldiers. We are duly brought. As we leave the hold, surrounded by a phalanx of unsmiling Kree warriors with unsmiling heavy weapons, we hear an automatic voice call out faintly behind us.

It says, "This vehicle will just stay here and wait, then? See you criminal guys later, this vehicle guesses..."

We are brought down a long way. We are marched along the lofty and gleaming hallways and corridors of the massive battleship. The decks are throbbing gently, and I realize we are under way and traveling at high warp.

We are brought through monumental drive chambers, crossing these stupendous spaces on long, slender walkways that bridge one side of each chamber to the other at high level. Below us, prodigious drive units—each one the size of a city block—pulse with inner light as they generate Nega-energy to power the ship. The Kree engineers maintaining the drive units far below look no bigger than dust mites. I do not have a chance to observe and record the view for long, because we are being brought rather briskly. Besides, the soaring walkways have no guardrails whatsoever, and the drop is making me a bit giddy.

Finally, we are brought down a long corridor where the walls, high ceiling, and deck are so polished they seem like mirrors. The haughty Sharnor the Accuser leads the way. Her men stamp along on either side of us, rigid and uniform as automata. At the far end is a massive blast door. It is guarded by a towering Sentry, one of the Kree Stellar Empire's indomitable humanoid war robots. It is significantly taller than Groot and broader than a bulldozer. It is so broad, in fact, that it looks stocky despite its imposing height. Its complex armored bodywork gleams purple with pale blue highlights.

Sharnor the Accuser halts in front of it.

"Sentry #212," she says.

It answers with a deep, electronic grumble.

"Observe these three prisoners. Store their identities in your database."

It issues another electronic rumble.

"My orders, Sentry #212," says the Accuser. "These prisoners are not permitted to leave the ship without my express authority. If they attempt to escape, you will pursue them. You may obliterate that one—"

She points to Rocket.

"—and that one."

She indicates Groot.

"That one," she says, pointing to me, "must be recovered without damage and brought to me intact. Are my orders clear?"

A deep electronic rumble indicates the affirmative.

"Open the chamber door," she says. "Soldiers? Bring them."

The hatch whirrs open like the door of a bank vault. The Sentry stands aside to let us pass.

As we are brought for the final time, I notice the signage above the hatch. It reads, in High-Halan, *Chamber of Examination*.

WE enter a large, circular compartment. There is a raised, round podium in the center of the floor, bathed from above in cold blue light. Facing it, around the edge of the chamber, is a semicircle of large, raised thrones.

The hatch closes behind us. A brisk gesture from Captain Yon-Dor indicates that we are expected to mount the short flight of steps and stand on the podium. Sharnor the Accuser takes a seat on the central throne and rests her chin on her fist, studying us. The warrior escort withdraws to the back of the room.

We stand there awkwardly for a few moments, caught in the harsh blue glare.

"Tell me of Project 616," says the Accuser.

We shuffle a little.

"Speak!"

"Was...was that a direct question again?" Rocket asks.

Glowering, Sharnor activates a touch control on the arm of her throne. The blue light around us shivers and intensifies. We all feel a jolt of neural discomfort—even me. As organics, Rocket and Groot suffer it more greatly.

"Ow!" gasps Rocket.

The intensity dims, and the discomfort recedes.

"Every time you evade, withhold, dissemble, attempt to play verbal games, or simply refuse to answer," says Sharnor, "I will deliver a burst from the Psyche-Agonizertron."

She demonstrates its effect again. The blue light intensifies. The discomfort this time is greater.

"Yeeoouch!" cries Rocket.

"Every time," continues Sharnor as the pain ebbs, "I will increase the Psyche-Agonizertron's setting. Do you understand?"

"Yes," says Rocket immediately.

"Good. Tell me of Project 616."

"I don't know what that is," says Rocket plaintively.

Pain again, worse than before.

"I really don't!" squeaks Rocket.

"What about you?" Sharnor asks Groot.

"I am Groot."

The pain is even worse this time. It is almost unbearable.

"I am losing patience," says Sharnor as we pick ourselves up, trembling. "I will ask again. Tell me of Project 616."

This time, she is directing the question at me.

I would, at this juncture, swallow nervously if I possessed an Adam's apple. I can see what is going to happen, and there is nothing I can do about it.

"I'm afraid I have no idea what that is," I reply.

CHAPTER SIXTEEN

MEANWHILE

(TWENTY MINUTES EARLIER ON ALPHA CENTAURI...)

FEW people ever entered the outer office of Senior Vice Executive President (Special Projects) Odus Hanxchamp without a prior appointment, and even if they *had* a prior appointment, entry was generally through the door.

Not on this occasion.

Behind her desk, Mrs. Mantlestreek, Hanxchamp's glacial P.A., looked up through her horn-rimmed spectacles and watched with some distaste as reality unfolded like reverse origami and the matte-black Spaceknight dropped through. He landed on one knee, hands flat on the floor, his head bowed. Smoke and vapor fumed off his armor, which was scratched and dented. He had singed the carpet beneath him.

Slowly, he raised his head until the venomous glow of his visor met her withering gaze. She did not blink.

"Hanxchamp," he said.

Patiently, Mrs. Mantlestreek made a show of scrolling through the daybook.

"I don't believe you have an appointment, Mr. Roamer," she replied. "Senior Vice Executive President (Special Projects) Odus Hanxchamp is in a meeting just now."

He rose to his feet.

"Hanxchamp," he growled.

She arched one eyebrow.

"Sir, he is in a meeting."

The door behind the Spaceknight flew open, and two Timely Inc. Corporate Security guards entered the outer office in the more traditional manner. Their Timely Inc. Subduematic phase pistols were drawn and aimed in highly professional two-handed stances. Xorb Xorbux, the Z'Noxian head of Corporate Security (Special Projects), rushed in a few seconds later.

"Flark!" he cried in dismay. He looked at the security guards. "Put those away, boys," he instructed. "Everything's optimate. I'm sure I can redactify this problemistic situation right away."

The guards withdrew. Xorbux approached the smoldering Spaceknight.

"Roamer," he said. "What the flark's going on? You can't just burst in here—"

"Hanxchamp," the Spaceknight replied. "Now."

Xorbux looked at Mrs. Mantlestreek anxiously. Though perfectly unruffled, she was already dialing.

She exchanged a few quiet words, put the handset down and looked at Roamer.

"You can go in," she said.

The door to the inner office slid open, and Roamer entered with Xorbux on his heels.

Senior Vice Executive President (Special Projects) Odus Hanx-champ's inner office was opulent and stylish. Situated on the eight thousand and first floor of the Timely Inc. Headquarters building, it enjoyed precipitous views across downtown Alpha Centauri—though today the window showed instead rainbow streams of an-nihilated planetary material circling the event horizon of the Procyon black hole in majestic candy-cane spirals.

"Hey, Spaceknight pal!" said Hanxchamp, not getting up. "A little unscheduled, but what the heck? We were just having a Senior Spe-cial Projects meeting here, so I guess you fit right in."

There were others in the room: Senior Vice Development Execu-tive Arnok Gruntgrill; the M'Ndavian head of Legal, Blint Wivvers; Sledly Rarnak, the Skrull in charge of Corporate Pamphlets; Pama Harnon, the Kree Chief Finance Officer of Special Projects; and Al-landra Meramati, the Shi'ar head of the Executive Executization De-partment. All of them regarded the Spaceknight cautiously.

Hanxchamp clicked his intercom.

"Clandestine fields on, please, Mrs. Mantlestreek," said Hanx-champ.

"Yes, sir," crackled the reply.

Hanxchamp turned sunnily to the Spaceknight.

"So, pal, are you about to make my diurnal period?" he asked. "Come on, have you solutionized this for me? Have you resolution-ated my needage? Tell me you have!"

"Have I...what?" asked Roamer.

"Have you found the Rigellian Recorder doodad thingy?" Hanx-champ asked impatiently. He clicked his tentacle-tip repeatedly. "Get with the program, pal!"

He rapped his bunched tentacle on the Spaceknight's matte-black armor as though he were knocking on a door.

"You in there? Boy, you look like you've been through the wars!"

"There have been altercations," replied Roamer. "Some unavoidable conflicts."

"Oh, I don't like the sound of that," said Wivvers. "Conflicts? Traceable to us? I'm asking, are we talking about corporate liability here? Class actions?"

"The last thing we need is blowback," said Rarnak.

"I literally hear that," said Pama Harnon.

"There will be no 'blowback,' as you put it," replied Roamer. "No 'corporate liability.' There were incidents, some of violent magnitude, but nothing that can be traced back to this corporation."

"Phew!" said Hanxchamp. Everyone made a show of laughing with relief.

"Good news," said Wivvers. "I had the loss adjustors on speed-dial for a moment there."

"So...the Recorder?" asked Allandra Meramati quietly.

"Not yet recovered," replied Roamer. "My efforts are ongoing. Other parties keep getting in my way. Other *interested* parties."

"Interested parties?" asked Hanxchamp.

"I am not the only agency hunting for your Recorder," said Roamer.

"No one should even *know* about this!" exclaimed Rarnak.

"Literally no one," agreed Pama Harnon.

"Tell that to the Badoon War Brotherhood," replied Roamer.

"The-tik!-*Badoon*?" Gruntgrill cringed. "That's extremiatedly problemistic!"

"Also, possibly the Nova Corps," said Roamer.

"The cops? The *space cops* are sniffing around, too?" said Hanxchamp, aghast.

"I suspect others, as well," said Roamer. "I cannot confirm."

"How the flark did this get out?" demanded Hanxchamp. "I mean, how the flark does *anyone* get wind of a Senior Special Project like this?"

Everyone looked at Xorb Xorbux.

"I'm afraid, sir," said the head of Corporate Security (Special Projects), "that we may have a leak."

"A leak?"

"A corporate spy, on the inside. Maybe in this very room."

There was an uncomfortable silence. The executives glanced nervously at each other. Meramati's feathered crest stiffened. Gruntgrill swallowed hard and tried not to *tik!* Wivvers tutted and shook his head. Pama Harnon reached nervously into her purse, retrieved her expensive black lipgloss, and refreshed her makeup. Sledly Rarnak looked like he wanted to hit someone with a box of pamphlets.

Hanxchamp just simmered.

"Don't worry, sir," said Xorbux. "I'm on it. Total security review and clampdown. If there's a spy, I'll have him or her found, questioned, and then ejected into the nearest supernova. *And* I'll take away their parking space and retirement portfolio."

"Get to it," said Hanxchamp. He looked at the Spaceknight.

"So where is it?" Hanxchamp asked. "The Recorder?"

"I am about to reacquire its location," said Roamer. "The Recorder seems to have allied itself with a pair of low-life troublemakers. I suspect they may *also* have developed a keen interest in its fiscal worth."

"Who is this pair?" asked Xorbux.

"A genetically engineered Raccoonoid from Halfworld called Rocket and a specimen of *flora colossus* from Planet X called Groot."

"Never heard of either of them," said Hanxchamp.

"They are small fry. I will deal with them," said Roamer.

"Then why aren't you out there doing that right now?" asked Hanxchamp.

The Spaceknight indicated the Interpolation Inserter unit clamped to his armor.

"I came back because of this," he said. "It has taken me directly to them twice, but each time it seems...it seems to have chosen the most inconvenient moments. When they are in combat, for example. It is harder to effect an extraction under combat circumstances."

"I told you that thing was -tik!- dangerous!" Gruntgrill exclaimed. "It should never have come out of R&D!"

"Can it be adjusted?" asked Roamer. "Can it be...fine-tuned?"

"Gruntgrill?" Hanxchamp asked. "You seem to know more about the device than anyone else."

"I...doubt it can, sir," said the Kaliklaki anxiously. "I mean, by its very nature it is supposed to take the user to the most dramatically appropriate moment in the Universal Narrative. Simple logic demands that at such dramatically appropriate moments, there is likely to be, well, *drama*. And jeopardy. And other things I really don't like to think about."

He looked at the intimidating Spaceknight.

"The Inserter isn't just supposed to take you to your -tik!- target," he said. "It's supposed to take you to your target *at the most dramatically satisfying moment.* It's what it does."

"Satisfying to whom?" asked Roamer. "In both instances, my arrival actually seemed to alter the circumstances radically. In both instances, the Recorder and its companions were under direct threat. My arrival, though indirectly, actually *assisted* their eventual escape."

"Shame you couldn't have grabbed them before they did," sulked Hanxchamp.

"If your appearance altered the causal flow of events," mused Gruntgrill, "I guess…well, that's the very definition of a dramatically significant moment. You became a sudden, surprise plot twist."

"Then it cannot be adjusted?" asked Roamer.

"I don't -tik!- believe it can."

"Very well," said Roamer. "I will become a sudden, surprise plot twist *again*. And this time, I will twist the plot my way. I do not believe in fate or destiny, and I do not believe in any 'causal narrative.' I simply believe in cold steel and energy weapons. I will—"

"Whoa, whoa!" cried Hanxchamp. "Waaaay too much macho in here suddenly! I'm starting to have serious second thoughts about the optimized viability of this solutionoid. *Third* thoughts, probably."

"I am literally on board with your doubts, sir," agreed Pama Harnon.

"Is this really the best way to go?" asked Rarnak.

"Exactly," said Hanxchamp. "*Is* this the best way to go? In fact, do we have to go any way at *all*? Meramati? How's the datacore looking today? Any upswing? *Tell* me there's an upswing. Tell me we can go with what we've got and forget about this flarking Recorder business altogether."

"I'm afraid the percentile remains at eighty-seven, sir," replied

Meramati with regret. "The datamap is stuck at eighty-seven per-cent complete. We simply do not have quite enough of the truth yet."

"I warned you about that word, lady," snapped Hanxchamp "I simply will not have anyone in this company talking like one of those Universal Church nutzookies."

"Then, again, my apologies, sir," Meramati replied, crestfallen.

"So...eighty-seven just isn't enough?" asked Hanxchamp morosely.

Meramati shook her head.

"The lowest percentile threshold at which we can go live with any hope of success is ninety-six percent-plus," she replied.

"Project 616 remains a pipe dream unless we hit that thresh-old," said Gruntgrill.

"What you're telling me is that we simply have no choice?" asked Hanxchamp. "That the Recorder remains our fundamental need-age? That we *need* this Recorder, we absolutely need this Recorder, or our *number-one priority project* is finished before it's even left the drawing board?"

Nobody wanted to confirm this. Finally, because someone had to, Gruntgrill uttered a very small "yes."

"Some days..." rumbled Hanxchamp.

"I will continue with my mission," said Roamer.

"You do that," replied Hanxchamp.

"I will not fail to deliver a third time."

"You can take that to the flarking bank!" growled Hanxchamp. "Do it. Get it done. Get it done now!"

"I will," the Spaceknight said.

"And Xorbux? Find this flarking spy for me stat!" barked Hanx-champ.

"Yes, sir," said Xorbux.

"Meeting over, people," Hanxchamp declared grumpily and sat down in his chair with his tentacles folded.

"Mrs. Mantlestreek? I need a beverage," he whined.

Everyone quickly left the room. Roamer was the only one who did not do so via the traditional method of the door. There was a lingering aftersmell of unexpected change in fortunes.

EXITING through the outer office, the executives were downcast and worried.

"I did not experience good meeting just then," said Rarnak. "Not good at all."

"I literally hear that," Pama Harnon agreed.

"I don't know why he keeps getting at me," complained Mera-mati. "We've done an extraordinary job so far."

"You know the -tik!- boss!" laughed Gruntgrill, but he could not hide his stress.

"I just hope we can keep the lid on this, liability-wise," said Wivvers.

"Don't worry," said Xorbux. "I'll dig out the mole. I'm afraid that means I'll have to interview each of you, and your department heads. I may have to search your offices, too."

"You do what's necessary, Xorb," said Rarnak. "I've got nothing to hide!"

"Here, here!" agreed Wivvers. "Transparency is what I'm all about. I am completely loyalized to the Timely Inc. philosophy, and devoted to the ongoing prosperitization and market-growth of this corporation!"

"You said it," Gruntgrill put in. "Cut me in half, and you'll see the

Timely trademark symbol running right through me!"

"Don't tempt me," said Xorb darkly.

"-tik!-"

"Oh, dear," said Pama Harnon.

"What's the matter?" Meramati asked her.

Pama Harnon was toying with her chic and expensive lipgloss. "You know, I literally reapply this every time I feel stress. I guess it's a nervous habit. I've literally been doing it so much in the last few days I'm completely out of *Autocron Noir*."

"Shame, that shade looks so good on you," said Meramati.

"Thank you, Allandra," Pama Harnon smiled. She turned. "Mrs. Mantlestreek? Would you literally be a dear and toss this in the disposal for me?" she asked.

Mrs. Mantlestreek fought back the urge to explain the difference between her role as a personal assistant and the role of a robot sub-janitor. Instead, she merely smiled charmlessly, took the expensive lipgloss, and dropped it into the waste disposal unit beside her desk.

"Thank you!" Pama Harnon smiled breezily and followed the other executives out of the door.

INSIDE the compact Timely Inc. Waste-Away model disposal unit, the small antimatter reservoir engulfed the lipgloss and annihilated it forever.

Both the lipgloss, in fact, and the miniature Kree-tech Omni-Wave communicator and listening device concealed inside it.

CHAPTER SEVENTEEN

MEANWHILE, MEANWHILE
(FIVE DAYS EARLIER ON CARNASSIA...)

THE order of the Divine Oracolites was not so much an actual order anymore. There was only one of them left.

Blue-skinned and ancient, with fringed, pointed ears, the sole surviving member of the order was typical of his race, the Interdites.

The Interdites had once been a powerful and technologically advanced civilization, until they had been crushed and scattered by the Badoon. In an effort to make sure that nothing like that ever happened to them again, the surviving, far-flung members of the Interdite race lived like hermits and outcasts, developed their latent psionics, turned to mysticism, and eventually became highly gifted in the arcane craft of precognition.

This particular Interdite, who had chosen to maintain the notion of the Divine order single-handedly since the last of his half-dozen Oracolite brethren died eight decades previously, lived a lonely, hermitic existence in the high peaks of a windswept and ragged mountain range that ran like a spine across the main landmass of the planet Carnassia. Individuals from other worlds came to visit him, making the hard, demanding trek through the peaks to his lonely cave. They came to find him because they craved access to the psionic insight into the given future that only he possessed. Or rather, only the Divine Oracolites possessed.

They came with questions, frets, worries, doubts, fears. He gave them answers.

He always knew when they were coming, of course, and had a pot of something or other warming over the open fire of his cave.

On this particular occasion, it was a tureen of meat stew. The last time, it had been a kettle of Zundamite leaf tea, but that had been more than a year ago when a Sirusite nobleman had visited to discover whether his wealthy bride-to-be would remain faithful to him. The Sirusite nobleman had left fairly quickly with a disgruntled look on his face, and little of the leaf tea had been drunk.

The tureen of meat stew was large. Very large. But this time it hadn't been prepared for the visitor he knew was coming.

Rain began to lash the unfriendly mountainside outside the mouth of the cave, and callous winds howled up the pass. Night was not so much falling as toppling like an inky landslide.

The Interdite turned up the little photon lamps around his cave, bathing the chamber in a warm, yellow glow. Then he sat his wizened body down cross-legged by the fire and stirred the stew.

His visitor had arrived. He knew it without having to look up—even though there had not even been the slightest sound, or crunch, or slither of loose stones outside. The Interdite could usually hear his guests coming from a long way off, so treacherous was the steep and narrow path.

He looked up, the firelight shadows emphasizing the deep ridges of his craggy chin. His eyes were huge, doleful orbs that saw much,

much more than the world around him. His furrowed brow furrowed yet more deeply.

She was even more impressive in person.

"Warm yourself at the fire," he invited.

She remained standing in the mouth of the cave, her cloak dripping. She pushed back her hood.

"I'm not staying," said Gamora. "I came for—"

"Answers. I know."

"Of course you do."

"One answer in particular," said the Interdite.

"Good. You know that, too. Tell me, and I will leave you in peace."

"I have seen this moment," said the Interdite. "Peace is not a word I'd use to describe it."

"Why not?" asked Gamora. She took a step forward.

"Because of what will transpire."

"And what will transpire?"

The Interdite sighed.

"I cannot give you your answer," he replied.

She paused.

"Why not?"

"Too much is at stake. Too much. The fate of this Universe and others. Far, far too much is at stake for me to share it with you."

"You'll have to do better than that," said Gamora.

"I wish I could," replied the Interdite. "But we are on the cusp of fate. Destiny teeters. There are so many potent forces involved in this matter, it is actually hard for even one like me to confidently foresee the outcome. The future is in flux. The ultimate resolution is hidden from me, a blank void."

"People like you always say that," she remarked.

"Nevertheless..."

"How do I know you even understand my question?"

The Interdite sighed again.

"Your question is this: What is the location of the Rigellian Recorder 127?"

Gamora pursed her lips.

"And the answer?"

"I cannot give it, for the sake of the Universe," replied the old prophet. "I told you this. The Recorder is uniquely valuable. People are fighting over him already. Blood has been shed and will be shed. To gain possession of the Recorder is to gain the ability to steal the Galaxy from all other sentient forms and shape it to one's own ends. He is too valuable. Too precious. I cannot and will not supply an answer that would allow the Recorder to fall into the wrong hands."

He looked at her.

"And yours are most definitely the wrong hands."

"Why?"

"Because I know who you are working for. I know who you will deliver the Recorder to."

"Really?"

"The Master of the Negative Zone is too wicked a force to possess such power."

Gamora took another step forward.

"I have come too far to listen to this," she said. "You waste my time. Tell me the answer. Tell me the location."

"I will not."

"I can see the future, too, you know?" she told him. "If you continue to deny me, I foresee things ending badly for you."

He chuckled.

"I know this also. You are the Deadliest Woman in the Galaxy, and I am but an ailing old hermit. I am no match for you."

"Yet you persist in frustrating me. Why? You know what I will do."

The old Interdite shrugged. He looked at her with his huge, soulful eyes.

"Why? Because, remember, *I knew you were coming.*"

His eyes were vast and dark, like obsidian mirrors. Gamora saw herself reflected in his eternal gaze. She saw the movement behind her, too.

Now she could see what was coming as clearly as the ancient hermit.

The Roclite was huge. A savage breed of humanoids with dark brown skin and vast, pupil-less eyes, the Roclites were famous for their immense strength, ferocity, and utter brutality.

This was a big specimen, even by Roclite standards. Its rippling musculature and heavy frame made the likes of Drax seem puny.

It swung its massive fist. Its reach was amazing. Its hairy arms were almost simian in proportion to its body. That first blow would have easily finished her.

But she had seen it coming, and she was fast.

She ducked and rolled into the cave, agile as a feline.

The fist missed and struck the cave wall, fracturing the rock.

The Roclite opened its considerable mouth and roared at her. Spittle flew, and its tree-trunk neck muscles corded and bulged.

It blundered into the cave after her.

Gamora somersaulted back onto her feet to face it.

"You hired muscle to kill me rather than give up your answer?" she shouted at the Interdite over her shoulder.

"It pays to think ahead," he replied.

The Roclite charged, howling. Gamora leapt out of its path, and it skidded clumsily as it tried to stop its charge and turn. It almost knocked over the pot of stew. The old hermit leapt out of its way with a weak cry and cowered against the cave wall.

Her foe was big and stupidly powerful, Gamora evaluated, but it was also slow and cumbersome.

It went for her again. She dodged, and a fist the size of a pumpkin smashed a dent in the cave wall beside her head. The other fist came in, but struck only empty air and the cave wall. She had ducked under its mighty reach and danced away.

It rounded on her. She kept moving. No more games. She drew her blades.

When the Roclite surged again, hands clawing to grab her and rip her limb-from-limb, she struck out—sweeping one blade up and left, and the other down and right.

The Roclite howled and sank to its knees. Most of its fingers and thumbs were scattered like cigars on the cave floor around it.

"And the others," she snarled at the Interdite. "You know what I am. *One* Roclite?"

They came in from both sides. Two more Roclite brutes emerged, bellowing, from the shadows at the back of the cave.

A small, evil-looking Sagittarian appeared in the cave mouth. His expensive robes and waxed moustache dripped with rainwater. He was aiming a Mobian ripper pistol.

"That stew had better be good," the Sagittarian said.

"It is," replied the Interdite. "It will make this effort worthwhile... as will the winning numbers for next week's Denebian lottery."

"Kill her," the Sagittarian told his Roclite goons.

They were already attempting to. She dodged the second Roclite and left a bloody gash across the ribs of the third, forcing it to back off. The second one came at her again, and she was obliged to leap-frog the kneeling, weeping form of her original attacker.

It tried to grab her as she bounded over it, but its lack of fingers caused it to fail.

She was now on the Sagittarian's side of the cave. He uttered a curse and opened fire with the ripper pistol. It made a spitting sound as it shot a stream of deadly, razor-sharp barbs. Two went through her trailing cloak. Two more hit the cave wall. One scratched her cheek and drew blood.

Too close.

She rotated and brought her blades up as he fired again. The swords moved faster than the eye could track, deflecting and blocking the deadly barbs. Sharp metal fragments sparked and ricocheted away from her.

The Sagittarian had more in his clip.

Gamora could not deflect them all. As he went to fire a third burst, she threw the blade in her right hand. It sang as it flew across the cave, end over end. It came to rest embedded in the Sagittarian's chest.

He uttered a grunt of surprise, looked down at the sword impaling him, and then collapsed on his face.

Gamora tried to pivot, knowing that the Sagittarian had kept her occupied long enough to give the Roclites an opening. She wasn't fast enough.

A blow struck her from behind, and she went sprawling.

She rolled, dazed, and tried to get up. The Roclite came after her.

It stood on her other sword, pinning it to the ground, and drew back its fist to crush her into the cave floor.

She let go of the sword and dived headlong between its legs.

The Roclite roared in frustration and turned. It was met by two devastating jabs to the face and then a vicious series of spin kicks.

Then Gamora hit it in the side of the head with the tureen. The dish rang like a bell. Scalding stew sprayed into the air.

The Roclite staggered. She rolled to its left, retrieved her sword, and put it through the creature's throat. It fell and lay face down in a gleaming, spreading pool of dark blood.

She wheeled, expecting the other. But the cave was still, apart from the snivelling whimpers of the kneeling Roclite with no digits.

The third Roclite was propped up against the wall on the far side of the cave. Its face was slack, and its one remaining eye was glassy. One of the deflected barbs from the ripper pistol had gone clean through the other eye into its brain.

Gamora recovered her other sword, yanking it out of the Sagittarian's sternum. She picked up the ripper pistol, too, and took the spare clips. It was a nice piece.

She walked back to the fireside, pausing only to quickly end the suffering of the whimpering Roclite.

She looked over at the cowering Interdite.

His eyes were wide.

She bent down, stuck a finger in the remains of the stew in the overturned and dented tureen, and tasted it.

"Not bad," she said. "Not worth my life, but not bad."

"Is this the way you saw things turning out?" she asked, rising.

"N-no," the hermit stammered. "I hoped, but...I told you, we are on the cusp of fate. D-destiny teeters. There are so many p-potent forces involved in this matter, it is impossible even for precogs to foresee reliable outcomes. The future is *in flux*. In flux! The ultimate resolution is hidden from me. It is a b-blank void."

"You did tell me that," she said. "But it's not what I wanted to hear. Tell me the answer I came for."

He told her. He told her everything he knew.

"Thank you," she said. She walked toward him, a blade in each hand. "You know, there is another reason why you see the future as nothing but a blank void."

"P-please!" he begged.

"I think you should get out of the precognition business," said Gamora. "I see no future in it."

CHAPTER EIGHTEEN

LIVE KREE OR DIE

AT this juncture, I am reminded of the Hakklofarbs of Demantle III. Demantle III lies in the outskirts of the Lesser Magellanic Cloud, lest you forget. Anyway, the Hakklofarbs have a saying that, when translated, goes along the lines of, "Pain is gain. Accept your pain, and life will become much easier."

I'm sure, gentle reader, your Terran culture has developed a similar philosophy somewhere along the way. Also, it might explain why the suicide rate on Demantle III is twenty-seven times the Galactic average.

Anyway, I am in pain. Quite the most pure and *awful* pain I have ever experienced. I am kneeling on the podium of the Chamber of Examination aboard the Kree battleship, bathed in the lingering blue beam of the Psyche-Agonizertron. Rocket and Groot are sprawled, unconscious, on either side of me. It has been too much for them.

Sharnor the Accuser is staring at me, her chin on her fist, her finger planted firmly on the Psyche-Agonizertron's touch control.

"Tell me!" she demands.

"I cannot tell you anything!" I announce in dismay.

She lifts her finger. The pain threads away.

"Why not?" she asks.

"Because I know not!" I reply, rising to my feet.

"I do not follow," she says, lifting her head to study me.

"Madam Accuser," I begin, trembling. "I am a data-storage device. I am a Recorder. I will gladly communicate to you all of the data contained within me. But I cannot supply you with data that I do not possess."

"You know nothing about Project 616?"

"I do not!" I insist. "Your device is killing me. But even for that, despite everything, it is for the sake of my two organic companions that I plead you to stop. I will tell you what I know. I sincerely hope it is what you want to hear."

Sharnor regards me coldly.

"Go on."

"I understand that I am valuable. Many forces are hunting for me."

"Like who?" she asks.

"The Badoon War Brotherhood, for example," I reply honestly.

"The Badoon?" she asks, rising. "They are in this, too?"

"I fear so," I reply. "Madam Accuser, the thing is, I have no idea why I am so valuable. You must believe me. I do not know what 'Project 616' is, but it evidently has much to do with me."

She stands, aiming her formidable gaze and equally formidable embonpoint at me simultaneously.

"Tell me about Project 616," she demands.

I cringe.

"Forget the psyche ray!" she says, sympathetic for a moment.

"Tell me what you know."

"I have no knowledge of any Project 616," I say. "I can only conjecture. Let me think...'616' is the multiversally agreed designature of this Universe."

"The what?"

"We live in a Multiverse of infinite, parallel Universes, madam," I say. "We regard this one as wonderful and infinite because it is the only one we know. There are an infinite number of others. They each have designations. Our Universe is denoted as 616."

She sits down hard.

"There are others? Other Universes beyond ours? I know of the Negative Zone, of course, but...there is a...*Multiverse*?"

"Yes, madam."

"How do you know this, Recorder?"

"Well, I have been around the block a few times," I laugh. I halt. The tension has clearly not thawed. "What I mean to say is, there is evidence. Your own brave Mar-Vell journeyed between realities. How else would you explain interdimensional crossovers, or multiple alternate iterations of Wolverine or Spider-Man?"

"Who?" she asks.

I sigh.

"My point stands. It is a fact. There are many Universes, and this is the quite marvelous Universe 616."

She quivers. I am not sure whether it is with rage or uncertainty.

"Even if I believe you—"

"You should," I assure her.

"Even if I believe you...I don't know what you are saying!"

I pause.

"Madam Accuser," I say, "this seems to me more than a coincidence. Universe 616? Project 616? You see? I have a very high function. I connect and process data. I am a data gestalt. If we wish to answer your original question—and I sense, because of the torture, we really ought to—why don't you tell me what *you* know?"

"Me?" she asks, offended. "Me? Tell you what I know? *I* am the examiner here! What *I* know is classified by the High Command of the Kree Stellar Empire!"

"Good to know," I reply. "But that won't really get us anywhere, will it? Share with me, so that I might join the dots."

"I will not!"

"I can only operate on cognitive data connection," I say. "I knew nothing of 'Project 616,' but '616' as a phrase triggered my database. It lit up a connection. If you wish to learn more, feed me with new data and I will likely make *new* connections. What is Project 616 to you?"

"The key to universal control," she murmurs.

"Indeed. Well that would explain the nomenclature."

I pause. The immensity of the notion she so glibly encapsulated dawns upon me.

"The key to universal control?" I ask. "How...how could it be that?"

"It is, as I understand it, a device that, when complete, will enable the user to control reality."

"Is that so?" I ask. "Wow."

"That is why the Kree Stellar Empire pursues you. You, according to our spy, are a fundamental part of this device. The last missing component."

"I see," I say, worried. "And who is behind the construction of this device?"

She hesitates. Clearly, Sharnor the Accuser hates sharing.

"Timely Inc., my spy tells me. Do you know what that is?"

"I do," I reply. "Timely Inc. is the largest and most successful megacorporation in this Galaxy. Its power and influence are beyond measure. It controls seventy-eight percent of all retail with its products. It exceeds its nearest rivals, Distinguished Competition Inc. and Fantastic For You Co., by an unprecedented market share. It is an undoubted commercial leader. The time will come when, culturally, Timely Inc. will become more powerful and influential than any of the ancient, great cultures. The Kree, for example."

"This is what we fear!" she cries. "If they build such a device—"

"Even *without* such a device, you should fear it," I agree. "It will be a sad day for this Universe when commercial musclepower overtakes the basic elements of cultural character. Races will die out, or become incorporated into the commercial behemoth. Species will become impoverished trademarks. The age of civilizations, Madam, is drawing to a close. Culture has been squeezed out. The new epoch of commercial imperative, the Era of the Megacorporation as the basis of intergalactic community, is dawning. According to my database, anyway. What do I know?"

"A great deal, I think," says Sharnor the Accuser.

I muse.

"So you have a corporate spy placed inside Timely Inc. HQ?" I ask.

She looks guarded for a moment, then grudgingly replies.

"Highly placed, in truth," she says, "but able to pass only the most selective and incomplete messages to the Kree Stellar Empire because of Timely's intense security systems. From our spy we have learned only of Project 616's existence, its rumored purpose, and the fact that you are vital to its success."

"And others know this, too?" I ponder. "Which is why everyone is after me."

"Why do you think you are the vital missing component?" Sharnor the Accuser asks me.

"Frankly, Madam Accuser, I do not know. I can only conjecture. It must be because I know something. Some vital piece of information. Somewhere in the vast archive of the collective data I contain, there must be some small but crucial piece of information."

"But you do not know what it is?"

"I cannot begin to imagine," I reply.

"Forget the others," the Accuser says. "Forget the other factions that pursue you. You are the property of the Kree Stellar Empire now. We have secured you. We have guaranteed the failure of Timely's Project 616."

"What will you do with me?"

"Now that I have established the limits of your conscious knowledge of this matter," she replies, "and your lack of cogent new information, I will continue as I began. I will conduct you to Hala, where you will be examined. I have no doubt that the Empire's scientists will be able to identify this scrap of vital information lurking in your unconsciousness or your databanks. Once we have obtained it, no doubt it will show us how to develop a reality-control device akin to Project 616."

"And...how will this identification be made?" I ask.

"We have mechanisms," she replies.

I was afraid of that.

She is about to comment further when the ship judders perceptibly.

"What was that?" she demands.

Captain Yon-Dor steps forward, listening to his helmet com.

"Report from the bridge, Accuser," he says. "We are under fire."

"Under fire?" she splutters. "That is not possible! We are travel-ing at super-light warp, and the aura of negativity is engaged. Noth-ing should be able to detect us!"

"Agreed, Accuser," says Captain Yon-Dor. "Nevertheless, a ship has intercepted our warp-path and is matching speeds. It is firing antimatter torpedoes at us."

"Identity?"

"Unconfirmed, Accuser," replies Yon-Dor, "but helm believes it to be a War Brotherhood Class megadestroyer of the Badoon War Brotherhood."

"Badoon...?" she whispers.

Slowly, she rises to her feet. "Go to battle stations. Drop from jump and come about. We will face the Badoon scum and eviscerate them for their impudence."

"Yes, Accuser."

"Tell the ship's captain I will be on the bridge in a few minutes to supervise the action. I will take personal satisfaction in obliterating the Badoon."

"Yes, Accuser." The Captain salutes.

The deck judders again. Another hit.

Yon-Dor and his men open the hatch and rush to their appointed battle stations, leaving two warriors behind to stand guard over us. The hatch slams shut.

Sharnor takes her seat again.

She looks at me. Her eyes are as hard as diamonds.

"The Badoon," she says. "There is no way they could have tracked or detected us. There is no way *anyone* could have tracked or detected us. The aura of negativity is foolproof. Unless..."

"Unless?" I ask.

"A cloaking field is useless if someone already *knows* your location. How did you communicate the information?"

"How did I what—?" I ask. "Madam Accuser, even if I possessed the means, why would I reveal my location to an enemy that I know is hunting me ruthlessly?"

"All I know is what you have told me," she replies. "You mentioned the Badoon. Perhaps you have already struck a deal with them: your secret in exchange for your safety."

"I assure you I have not," I reply.

"I do not believe you," she says. "You are the only possibility. The *only* possibility. Tell me how you are communicating with them."

"I—" I begin.

Her finger is hovering over the touch control built into the arm of her throne.

"*Tell. Me.*"

I am frantic. I have no answer for her. I glance down at Rocket and Groot sprawled on either side of me. I know another sustained burst of the Psyche-Agonizertron will kill them both.

"Tell. Me."

"Madam Accuser, please—"

Her eyes narrow. She jams her finger down.

But her hand does not move. It freezes where it is, unable to reach the touch control. Sharnor gasps in surprise and struggles to complete the action, her arm straining.

I see what is restraining her. It is, at first, hard to spot in the gloom away from the cold blue glow of the podium. But I see it.

There is a tough, knotted root system growing up the side of her throne and over the arm; the fibrous ends of it have grasped her wrist, holding it in place. The root system snakes all the way back across the floor, and I see it is an extension of the arm Groot has draped limply over the lip of the podium.

Groot is not unconscious at all. He has been playing dead while my answers kept the Accuser occupied.

Rocket is not unconscious, either.

He opens one eye and winks at me.

"Get ready to move, pal," he whispers.

The Accuser rages. Groot's grip is astonishingly strong. She hauls herself to her feet and grabs her ceremonial power hammer with her free hand, bringing it down on the tangled root. The hammerhead mechanism pulses green inside the casing as it impacts, and the root shatters.

Sharnor is free. She runs at us, hammer raised to strike.

"Go, buddy!" Rocket yells, leaping up and virtually shoving me off the edge of the podium. I am sorry to admit, gentle reader, that I did not land on the deck below in the most dignified manner.

The two Kree warriors at the back of the room step forward to assist their commander.

Rocket—a hissing, clawing, furry missile—leaps clear of the podium edge and lands in the face of one warrior, driving the fellow back hard in surprise. So hard, in fact, that the back of his head impacts against the wall and he is knocked unconscious. Rocket and the Kree guard collapse in a heap. The other guard turns, weapon raised, and is felled by a single shot from the Uni-beam blaster that Rocket has borrowed from his first victim.

Then Rocket is running again, scampering hard around the edge of the chamber.

Sharnor has reached the podium. Groot rises to meet her.

"Nice trick," she says, and swings the power hammer at him. He steps back, dodging a blow that would have shattered his heart-wood.

She leaps up onto the podium to get a better swing.

"Nice trick," she repeats, "but I am not impressed."

Groot dodges the second swing and leaps backward off the podium.

"If you thought *that* was a nice trick, lady," Rocket calls out, "wait until you get a load of this."

Sharnor turns. Rocket is perched on the arm of her throne. He grins. She looks down and realizes where she is standing.

Rocket presses the touch control.

For an unnecessarily long time.

CHAPTER NINETEEN

BATTER UP

ROCKET does not kill her. I believe the average Kree Accuser is so durable, you would have to casually but firmly lean your elbow on the touch control of a Psyche-Agonizertron for enough time to eat a bagel, read the morning newspaper, and carefully drink a hot beverage to make a dent in her—and Sharnor is well above average.

But Rocket presses long enough, his tongue extended gleefully over his grinning fangs, to make her first quiver, then curse in Kree, then convulse, then finally collapse unconscious onto the podium, face down.

Only then does Rocket take his disconcertingly human-like finger off the touch control.

"I always think," he says, leaping off the throne, "that it is way, way better to give than to receive."

"I am Groot," Groot replies, picking me up and dusting me off.

"Yes, it was a very fine ruse," I reply, "and I was more than happy to keep her talking while you propagated a new root system."

Groot grins. He has already shed the shattered root limb. He picks up the Accuser's fallen power hammer and tests it for heft.

"I am Groot." He grins again.

"Well, you'd better," calls Rocket, reaching the hatch. "You're gonna need it, is my guess."

Distantly, we hear alarms sounding, but they are not for us. From the sub-vibrations of the deck, I know that the battleship has cut to sublight and is making a hard turn. We are coming about to face the onrushing Badooon megadestroyer. Main power will be cycling from the jump drives to the weapon batteries, shield system, and matter-annihilation fields.

A full-scale space battle between dreadnought warships is seconds away.

"Time to make like a progressive wallpaper designer," Rocket cries, "and get the flock out of here!"

He pushes the activator panel and opens the blast hatch.

And there is, of course, still the Sentry.

The burnished bulk of Sentry #212 fills the entire doorway of the Chamber of Examination like a subway train parked in a subway tunnel. It peers in at us with beetle-brows and issues a rumbling electronic query.

Rocket slams the hatch again. He looks over at me and Groot.

"Oh yeah, ha ha ha!" he says. "I forgot about that dude. Rethink."

He looks down at the Uni-beam blaster he has commandeered. It is a powerful weapon, the standard-issue rifle of the Kree fighting man—as renowned, reliable, trusted, and ubiquitous as the AK-47 of your Earth, gentle reader; or the Tafstehl 190 of the Shi'ar; or the Urzenta-plazmaar of the Z'Nox; or the Ssh-tsss 8-11 of the Sssth; or the Kaar Delta Delta Hash Under-and-Over Recoilless Life-Suppression Combat Sub-Rifle ("Votok" pattern) with cut-down grips, fusion feed and rail-mounted sighting system of the Ergons; or the—

You get the picture. I am nervous. I talk when I am nervous.

The Uni-beam blaster is a powerful weapon. But it will not make so much as a teeny-tiny dent on the gleaming bodywork of a Kree Sentry.

"I am Groot!" Groot decides.

"Are you sure?" I ask, dismayed.

"Hey, go with what you know, that's my motto!" Rocket replies. He raises a disconcertingly human-like hand to the hatch activator.

"Ready? On three. One, two..."

He hits the activator.

The blast hatch opens again.

The Sentry is still there, glaring in at us. It must have been glaring at the closed hatch in the meanwhile.

I can only say, gentle reader—in order to place a recognizable Human Culture image in your mind that you can relate to—that Groot, for a moment, resembles Babe Ruth, or Ty Cobb, or Ed Delahanty, or Tony Gwynn.

He braces—feet planted in a wide stance, weight on the back foot—and raises the power hammer, choking up with his hands together. He then begins his swing—taking a stride forward with his front foot, turning through his hips, keeping his elbows toward his body. His back foot pivots.

A tight circle. A perfect level swing.

The head of the Accuser's power hammer connects with the middle of the Sentry's chest plate. The hammerhead mechanism pulses green inside the casing as it strikes, amplifying the kinetic force of the blow—which is already considerable indeed—with a reinforcing charge of potent Nega-energy.

There is a crack, like all the lightning in the Universe striking at once. The back-shock knocks Rocket and me off our feet.

The impact throws Sentry #212 down the entire length of the mirror-finish hallway outside, its trailing hands scouring friction scratches along the polished wall at head height.

"Touchdown!" I exclaim.

Rocket looks at me.

"Wrong sport?" I ask. "Sorry, I was nervous and thus confused."

"Let's go!" Rocket yells.

He leads the way. Groot follows, and I follow Groot.

We are halfway down the polished hallway when the Sentry reappears at the far end. It is swaying slightly, as if dazed. There is a hammerhead-shaped dent in its chest plate.

"Whoops!" says Rocket, skidding backward between Groot's legs.

With huge, thumping strides, the Sentry begins to charge at us. Even more than before, it resembles a subway train, filling a subway tunnel, rushing toward us. It is not a sight I am happy to have re-corded. Sometimes it plays back at night and keeps me awake.

Groot stands his ground and tightens his two-handed grip on the haft of the power hammer. He pulls back to swing. The charging Sentry raises its immense hands, and they glow with power. He is going to blast Groot into kindling long before Groot is close enough to take another swing.

So I step forward and slip in front of Groot to face the Kree Sentry.

"I am Groot!"

"I know I'm in your way!" I reply. "I know what I'm doing."

{I hope}

The Sentry stops abruptly just a few paces short of me. It lowers its hands, and they power down. It looks confused. It emits a perplexed electronic rumble.

"Yes, Sentry #212, sorry about that," I say, "but I heard the Accuser's orders quite clearly. I must be recovered without damage and brought to the Accuser intact. You must not harm me. You are free to obliterate my companions, but since I am standing in the way, you cannot. Can you?"

It thinks about this. Electronic rumbles stir inside its head casing.

It raises one vast paw to blast Groot over my shoulder. I step to block the beam. It lowers its hand.

"I'm in the way, and you were ordered not to harm me."

It rumbles.

"I'm sure it's confusing, all those commands and countermands, but it's really quite simple," I say. "Back off and stand down."

It does neither. It picks me up and puts me down again behind it.

"Damn!" I say. I did not expect that.

Now facing the unprotected (by me) Rocket and Groot, it raises its huge hands and unleashes a tank-killing blast of Uni-beam energy.

However (and I only learn this later), while I was being all brave and everything, Groot was examining and fiddling with the Accuser's hammer behind my back. Apart from its obvious primary use (i.e., hitting things tremendously hard), it has many other features built into the twist-grip controls of the haft.

As Sentry #212 fires, Groot is ready, the hammer held in front of him in a vertical, two-handed grip.

He has twisted the grip configuration, and the hammer is projecting a Nega-energy barrier.

The Uni-beam blasts strike the barrier. The barrier holds. There is a burst of blocked energy, ultra-bright in the tight and mirrored confines of the hallway. The polished surface plating of the walls, floor, and ceiling from Groot's barrier back toward the Sentry shatters like glass in a long, rippling series of concussive explosions, revealing the drab structure of the subwall architecture and concealed underdeck system trunking.

The back-blast of its own weapon staggers the Sentry hard. Groot uses this to his advantage, twisting the hammer grip to "Nega-load Max" and taking another swing.

It connects, this time with the Sentry's jaw, smashing its head sideways and delivering enough Nega-amped kinetic force to hurl the robot beast back down the hallway for a second time.

Unfortunately, this time I am standing innocently behind the Sentry as it is smashed backward. It cannons into me. We are propelled together.

"I am Groot!" I hear Groot yell in horror.

I do not reply as I am very busy being concussed and emitting a high-pitched digital squeal of dismay. So high-pitched, in fact, that I am rather ashamed of it.

Carried together by the force of the blow, the Sentry and I exit the now-ruined mirrored hallway and fly out into the vast dark cavity of the forward drive chamber.

You know those slender walkways, gentle reader? The ones without guardrails that I mentioned?

Yeah, well, we bounce and skid along one of those, the massive Sentry on top of me for most of the way. The vast compartment yawns underneath us, the pulsing drive units spread out like an enormous cityscape far below.

And then, inevitably, we slip off the edge of the walkway.

I fall.

Something grips my left wrist and arrests my fall. The impact almost dislocates my shoulder.

I look down. Thousands of distance units below me, the drive units and Nega-impulsor sub-generators appear like the rooftops of a city seen from altitude. I know that, in another second, I am going to drop for a long time and then smash to smithereens on impact. Tiny, dust-mite engineers look up and shout things I am too far away to hear.

The distance below me is...*terrifying.*

I look up. The Sentry is clinging to the lip of the walkway with its right hand and clutching my right arm with its left. It is still obeying its orders to keep me intact.

For a moment, gentle and fastidious reader, I feel gratitude, even affection, for it. It is trying to save me. It is, though bound only by the harsh orders of a Kree Accuser, trying to protect me.

Its beetle-browed concern is plain. It wants to save me. It needs to save me, in order to fulfill its instructions.

But the purchase of its right hand is giving way, finger by finger. It is slipping.

It is *slipping.*

I feel it trying to start and restart its internal propulsion systems, to fly us both clear. But Groot's hammerblows have damaged it internally, and the flight systems will not fire.

We are going to fall. It is going to lose its grip, and we are going to plunge together to our doom.

Sentry #212 issues an electronic groan. Straining, the grip of its right hand rapidly failing, it slowly raises its left arm and me along with it. It is trying to hoist me to the walkway.

"I really do appreciate this," I say as it raises me past its face.

It rumbles.

The lip of the walkway is in reach. I grab it with both hands and cling on, dangling.

The Sentry's right hand loses its grip. It falls, releasing me with its left hand as it does so.

Hanging from the walkway with both hands, I look down and see the Sentry falling backward away from me, expressionless. The drop is so great, Sentry #212 has enough time and downward momentum to turn over and over twice before it hits.

And, boy, it *hits*.

It hits number seventeen drive unit square on, smashing the crystoplex core-cover like a wrecking ball dropped on a greenhouse.

Drive-containment fields fail at once, and there is a rapid, explosive release of Nega-energy that immolates the Sentry and rips out sideways, incinerating all the dust-mite engineers close by. The blast-shock rips into the neighboring drive units, causing two more to rupture and explode.

I can barely hold on. The entire chamber, the ship itself, rocks with a force greater than anything the impending Badoon attack could unleash.

Fiery clouds of venting Nega-energy gas, billowing and incandescent, sweep up from below and engulf my clinging, swinging form. The shock wave hits me.

I lose my grip.

CHAPTER TWENTY

DEADLIEST

I FALL.

I stop falling with a lurch.

This is painful.

A hand has gripped my wrist at the last moment and caught me. Slowly, slowly, it hauls me back over the lip onto the walkway. Below me, the drive chamber is on fire. Explosions and sub- explosions kick off through system after system.

I lay on my front on the walkway, my feet dangling over the edge, trying to regain my composure. I do not, now that I have looked it in the eye, like certain death.

"Thank you," I gasp. "Thank you, Groot. Thank you."

"Groot?" says a hard voice. "I am not Groot."

I could think of no one, loyal reader, who could have saved me that way at the very last minute apart from Groot. I mean, Rocket might have tried (though I doubt it), but even with his disconcertingly human-like hands, he would not have had the upper-body strength to pull me clear.

I roll over, look up, and see the most strikingly beautiful female humanoid I have ever recorded staring back down at me.

"Did you just say...*Groot*?" she asks.

"Yes," I reply. "Yes, I believe I did."

"I am not Groot."

"You are certainly not."

"He's...here?" she asks. She has drawn two swords, one in each hand. I often think one sword is superfluous. Two seems excessive. How many enemies did this hooded, cloaked, and gorgeous green-skinned woman think she was going to have to fight at once?

I get to my feet beside her.

We are lit from below by the furious blaze of the engine room. She regards me with suspicion. Her skin is green. Her long hair is jet-black, and her haunting pupil-less eyes are shaded yellow around the sockets. She is clad in a figure-hugging armor suit of black leather trimmed in steel, long boots, and a saucy hint of fishnet around her arms and thighs. Does anyone really go into combat dressed like that? I presume she does—unless this is some kind of disguise, or a sexy-assassin-a-gram sent to the wrong address. She is undoubtedly beautiful, almost breathtakingly so {*and I did check, gentle reader, several times against my Comparative Aesthetic Quality Assay Scale. Possibly many more times than was technically necessary*}, but she also seems quite...what is the word? Capable? Determined? Lethal? A psycho nut-bag deranged zook-loop handful? {*More than one word, I concede*}

Rocket and Groot rush out onto the walkway and skid to a halt at the sight of her. They seem more horrified to see her than to see the combusting and chain-reacting fury of the drive chamber below us.

"What are *you* doing here?" Rocket asks.

"It's a paying job," she snaps back. "What are *you* doing here?"

"Stuff!" he replies. "Guarding the Galaxy stuff. You?"

"I told you," she growls. "D'ast! *D'ast*! This wasn't the way it was supposed to go! You're with him?"

She asks this, indicating me.

"Actually, they're with me," I begin, suavely.

"Yes, the robot's with us!" Rocket cries. "Suppose you tell me what the flark you're doing here, Gamora, 'cause it doesn't look like any Galaxy guarding *I* know!"

"Oh, right, and I'm sure you're here for purely altruistic, non-financial reasons!" she retorts.

"I *knew* we shouldn't have broken up the team!" Rocket cries. "We're the only things that keep each other from flarking things up!"

"The Guardians of the Galaxy is not 'broken up,'" she declares. "It's on *hiatus*!"

"I am Groot!" Groot announces.

"Did he just say "Hiatus *shm-iatus*?"" the female, Gamora, asks acidly.

"No, actually what he said was '*What* hiatus?'" I point out helpfully.

She looks at me. She has two swords. I shut up.

Far below us, something really important explodes.

"Flark," she says. "Flark, flark, *flark*. Why did *you* have to be involved?"

At first, I think there's an echo. Then I realize that Rocket Raccoon was saying precisely the same thing at the same time.

There is a long, meaningful pause. A seething pall of venting Nega-energy, blazing like a nuclear mushroom cloud, expands in the upper parts of the drive chamber on either side of the walkway, showering us with sparks. Cinders land on the walkway, fizzling.

"I have come for this Recorder unit," she says.

"You can't have him," replies Rocket. "He's ours."

"I am Groot," says Groot.

"A good question," Rocket agrees. "Who *are* you working for?"

The female, Gamora, hesitates.

"That's confidential."

"So's this blaster," declares Rocket ambitiously.

She laughs at him, mocking. He has a blaster, she has swords. *Two* of them, admittedly, but even so. No contest, surely? I cannot explain her confidence. Or the genuine wariness of her that I detect in the eyes of my two friends.

"Well, we could stand here all day catching up," I remark, "but we would perish from exposure to Nega-radiation fallout. That's presuming this ship doesn't explode first."

Rocket and Gamora both look at me viciously, like targeting systems.

"I am just saying," I demur with a passive wave of my hand. "We seem to be on, if not the same page, then at least not more than a chapter apart. You clearly know each other. Could you not, I don't know, work together, so we might extract ourselves from this..."

I glance over the edge of the walkway at the inferno below. I get giddy and look away.

"...*certain death*?" I finish.

"Dude's got a point," says Rocket. I feel inward bliss: I am considered *a dude*. I secretly hope the female will be impressed.

"I am Groot," says Groot.

"All right," says Gamora. "For now. Just for now."

And that is how the three of us became the four of us.

For a while, at least.

CHAPTER TWENTY-ONE

THIS IS WHAT A SPACE WAR LOOKS LIKE

THE Kree Stellar Empire battleship *Pride of Pama* swung slowly into sublight space, firing its positional thrusters. It was a vast thing—a giant, blocky arrowhead with flaring drive vents at the stern and a battering-ram combat buttress at the prow. It possessed two broad, backswept wings that supported its huge ancillary jump nacelles. It was built for deep space. There was nothing streamlined or atmospheric about it. It was, in both scale and design, as airworthy as a city. It was more than three distance units long and possessed a draft of eight billion mass units.

It was also there and not there. Its cloaking shield—the aura of negativity—flickered on and off, revealing it sporadically in part or whole. Shortly, it failed altogether. The battleship had been damaged by the antimatter torpedoes of its enemy, and one of its drive chambers was experiencing unexpected catastrophic failure. The Kree ship's captain, an experienced noble by the name of Kris-Gar, was on his feet on the vast bridge, yelling orders and trying to stabilize his vessel. He knew he was hurt, and that his power was compromised.

He was trying to shut down the damaged drive, and channel available power into the shields and weapons.

Uni-beam batteries came to bear, the gun crews struggling frantically to cut reaction times. Sirens blared. The automatic magazines loaded the forward tubes with Nega-missiles. The battleship's primary weapon—a vast mega-scale Uni-beam projector that fired from a glowing, grilled vent under the prow—glittered as it came up to power.

The ship raised its shields.

Just in time.

The Badoon megadestroyer *Brotherhood of War* dropped from jump to face it, blistering out of a writhing halo of dumped jump energy. It had a displacement of six billion mass units, and it resembled a streamlined toad, polished and gleaming, with warp-engine nacelles in place of limbs. Its gunports popped up like warts from its hull-skin. The toad opened its mouth—the principal forward gunnery bay—and began to spit antimatter torpedoes and pulses of explosive plasma.

The barrage began as a flurry of yellow plasmic bolts and a few squirting missiles, then the megadestroyer increased its rate of fire until it was spitting a blinding, wholesale storm of warheads and plasma bursts at the Kree battleship. The onslaught was torrential. The light bloom lit up the front portions of both mighty vessels and threw their rear sections into stark shadow.

This was, of course, all utterly silent in the void of space.

The Kree ship's shields held. Invisible screens of potent Nega-energy buckled and shuddered, revealing visible ripples from the impacts as if space were water. But Nega-energy is a potent force, and the shields did not rupture.

The toadlike Badoon ship popped thousands of secondary batteries from its forward hull like blisters. These began firing, too—lancing out long, dazzling beams of red meson fire. Where the continuous beams struck the Kree shields, they raked and scratched, probing like red-hot spears, searching for an energetic weakness or a crucial shield overlap.

Captain Kris-Gar managed to stabilize his ship. Robotic crews were still battling to control the fire in the damaged drive compartment and achieve containment. But engineering had succeeded in shutting down the compartment's transmission links to the other main drive chambers, allowing the remaining drive units to resync and operate in harmony without the crippling disruption of a damaged link in their chain. Though down one entire drive assembly, Kris-Gar had the other five back up and operating, in concert, at peak efficiency.

It was time for the Kree Stellar Empire to strike back.

Kris-Gar told the communications officers to cease the warning broadcasts that demanded the Badoon should desist and break off. The Badoon had made it very clear they would not.

He shouted a series of commands to the Captains of Ordnance. At the big targeting stations in the forward part of the battleship's immense bridge, Kree Navy officers in black uniforms and glossy black helmets authorized the target vectors they had already computed.

The *Pride of Pama* began to return fire.

Its primary battery, the mega-scale Uni-beam projector, belched and started to pulse. It fired massive, slow-moving bolts of energy that were negatively frequenced to pass through the battleship's shields. Alongside these huge blasts, the Kree battleship launched six spreads of Nega-bomb missiles, squadrons of quicksilver darts. These, too, were negatively coded to pass without interference through the Nega-shields. Secondary Uni-beam batteries began to fire, multiple discharge flashes lighting up the battleship's hull like twinkling Christmas lights.

The Kree counterbombardment ripped out at the Badoon megadestroyer. The *Brotherhood of War* had raised its own shields, an invisible armor of interlocking quark pulses that permitted its weapons to discharge successfully by means of pico-second synchronization between firing and shield pulse.

When the Kree blasts hit the Badoon shields, the shields did not ripple like water. They flared and crazed like shattered mirrors, instantly repairing themselves. The Uni-beam bolts scorched across the shield surfaces—their energy dissipating fruitlessly like the liquid, living flame of almighty backdrafts.

Where the tiny quicksilver darts struck, immense blooms of energy erupted as mass-yield Nega-bomb warheads detonated. These explosions lit up and lingered like small suns, bubbling together in bright clusters. The megadestroyer shivered as its shields soaked up the hammering.

Both vessels were unloading their entire firepower at each other at less than eight thousand distance units. In terms of a space war, they were gunfighters—face-to-face, firing point blank. In the first twenty seconds of combat, the two immense warships had expended energy equivalent to the entire annual industrial output of planet Earth.

They sustained fire. It was battle by attrition. There was no space or time for subtlety or deft maneuvering, no chance of tactically outplaying each other. This fight was as full-on and grueling as two armies of ancient warriors crashing into one another on a rainy field, hitting each other relentlessly without quarter until one side simply broke.

One side *would* break. It was impossible to know which one, or to predict whether the end would come in seconds or hours. It was a matter of power-output efficiency, sustainability of energetics, shield reliability, and ordnance reserve.

And willpower.

And luck.

One tiny thing, one tiny fault, was going to make the difference. A small mechanical failure. A miscalculation. A computer error. A minuscule crack or flaw in a shield. A lucky angle or a lucky shot.

And when the end came, for one or both, it would be sudden and disastrous.

THE COMBAT was intense enough to generate a photonic value equivalent to that of a small supernova. The combat was also close enough to a number of civilized worlds for them, as fast as light speed would allow, to observe the display in their skies or through their astronomic telescopes or listening arrays. Several species experienced mass public panic and rioting, fearing the new star heralded the coming of some massive cosmic threat like the Great Devourer or signaled a pending alien invasion. Others watched and waited, fearful, prepared for the worst. The superstitious Habinax of Quelta Minor were so certain that the new star was an omen portending their doom, they evacuated their planet into hive ships, fled, and never returned home.

The equally superstitious but more optimistic Gangarthans of

Gangarthid Tri observed the new star and smiled. It happened to appear in a particularly providential house of their heavenly zodiac, on an auspicious date, and just six days after the coronation of their new King, Hosux. The Gangarthans were at a preindustrial level of advancement and had not yet achieved such technological wonders as spaceflight, teleportation, or Facebook. They saw the light of the deadly warfare as a good omen. Thus, exuberant and elated, they were inspired to begin a new era of peace and civilized advancement that saw more splendid temples, monoliths, and pyramids constructed in Hosux's long, benevolent reign than in any previous period, laying the cultural foundations that, by the late 24th century (Earth scale) would see them rise to become one of the most powerful, civilized, and altogether great-to-know races of the Galaxy.

So, sometimes, utterly horrific, utterly deadly, hyperintense space war has an upside.

Especially if you're a reasonable distance away from it.

If you're in the middle of it, however...

CHAPTER TWENTY-TWO

MEANWHILE

(PRECISELY NOW ON
THE KREE BATTLESHIP *PRIDE OF PAMA*...)

"**WELL,** okay, *first*," says Rocket Raccoon, "I think we should run."

This seems to all of us, even Gamora, to be a good idea. The drive compartment below us is ablaze in the most comprehensive way. We can feel the intensity, and I swear Rocket's fur is beginning to experience heat-damage curling. Also, the walkway we are standing on—which I believe, gentle reader, I have previously indicated is *utterly without handrails*—is beginning to tremble.

A crack appears in its surface. I try very hard not to record the crack, nor to record how it is *spreading*. But, you know, once you've *seen* something...

"Question is, which way," says Rocket. He looks at Gamora. "You got in here? How'd you plan on getting out?"

"I have a small jump-fighter," she says. "I landed it in hangar Beta-K."

That statement alone begs so many questions. How did she sneak a ship aboard without the Kree noticing? How did she do it while the battleship was at high warp? What kind of pilot could manage that feat? And even if they could manage to intercept and sneak into a battleship traveling at high warp without being seen, how in the name of flark did she even know where the battleship was, given that it was shrouded, incognito, in an aura of negativity?

How did she know where to find *me*?

{A point of order, gentle reader. I do not mean to use bad language. I merely report it, inter alia, as it comes out of the mouths of my companions in this tale. I do so simply to maintain the accuracy and authenticity of my record. I have no wish to offend, merely to record the absolute truth of my experiences. However, I note with some disappointment that I casually used the word "flark" in the paragraph above. This was a slip. I will chastise myself later, if I am still alive and functional. I believe, though the time period has been brief, I have been in the company of Rocket Raccoon for too long and have picked up some bad habits.}

"Oh, nice infil," says Rocket, impressed. "You intercept-docked at high warp? Niii-*iice*. Wait, how did you know where we were?"

"I didn't know where you were," says Gamora. She points at me. "I knew where *that* was."

I am offended. I've gone from being a "dude" to a "that" in less than five minutes?

"I am Groot!" Groot exclaims.

"Exactly!" agrees Rocket. "How did you know where *that* was?"

Now he's pointing to me also, in exactly the same "he's not an actual person at all, just an object" way.

"I have ways," says Gamora. She smiles. It is a smile that would kill small, fluffy things.

"Go on," Rocket urges, undeterred.

Fireballs blossom around us in the roof of the compartment, scattering ash and debris. The walkway shudders. The crack extends.

"I don't think this is really the time or place to scrutinize my methodology, is it?" Gamora asks.

Rocket sighs, frustrated.

"Okay, Gam," he says. "Just clue me this. However you knew where Recorder-boy was, how did you manage to sneak into a Kree battle-flarking-warship at high warp without them noticing?"

"I distracted them," she says. "I knew where *Recorder-boy* was..."

She glances at me, and suddenly I have an overwhelming impression that "Recorder-boy" is, on balance, a step up from "dude."

"...so I told the Badoon. I knew those lizard bellies were hunting for him, too. I knew if I gave them his location, they would provide ample distraction, and keep the Kree so flarking busy I could slip right in unnoticed."

"Ample distraction? *Ample distraction?!*" Rocket explodes, seeming quite distracted himself. "Ample distraction in the form of a War Brotherhood *megadestroyer*? Are you nuts?"

She semi-shrugs, as if this is a rhetorical question.

"You told the d'ast Badoon where we were?"

"No," she replies carefully. "I told the d'ast Badoon where *Recorder-boy* was. I didn't know where *you* were."

"The, uhm, walkway is, in fact, cracking," I venture.

"Recorder-boy is right," says Rocket. Somehow, it doesn't sound quite so alluring coming from him. "Beta-K is aft, right? Let's find your jump-fighter, make like censors, and get the flark out of here!"

"Aft" means going back across the walkway toward the Chamber of Examination, following the sidestairs down, and re-entering the main body of the ship. As we turn, Sharnor the Accuser appears at the far end of the walkway. To say that she doesn't look happy is like saying a battle tank doesn't look convenient for town driving.

"You!" she booms along the walkway, in an accusing fashion. "You will *pay*!"

Gamora raises her swords.

"Forget it, Gam!" Rocket cries. "She's *uber*-accusatory! She'll hurt you bad!"

"I've known bad," Gamora replies. She's clearly ready to take on the Accuser, anyway. I think I might be a little bit in love.

"I am Groot!"

"Exactly! The other way! Run the other way!" Rocket cries. "Run *really fast*!"

We run. Gamora hesitates, then follows us. Screaming in rage, Sharnor thunders across the walkway after us. Rocket turns and fires two shots from his captured Uni-beam blaster.

The shots hit her and drop her to her knees. Then she gets up again. I am not quite sure what they make Accusers of, but they added extra when they made Sharnor.

We reach the hatch at the far end of the walkway. It is beginning to close, hazard lights flashing. The ship's captain has finally de-cided to lock out the burning drive compartment and jettison it for fear of cascade damage. I hear the slunk of hull bolts disengaging, ready for jettison.

Rocket leaps through the closing hatch, pulling me after him. Groot and Gamora turn to face the charging Accuser. She is still sev-eral hundred meters away from us, but she is gaining fast.

Groot picks up the alarmed Gamora and virtually tosses her through the slowly closing hatch. Then he raises the hammer and brings it down on the walkway.

The shock wave blasts outward. The walkway shatters, falling away into the burning space below. Sharnor skids to a halt on the broken end of her side and howls in fury. Groot hurls the hammer at her, then turns and dives, with surprising agility, through the hatch as it closes. He leaves twigs behind him.

We are cheated of the sight of Sharnor the Accuser being struck in the face by her own power hammer.

The hatch slams with a heavy clank. We pick ourselves up and start running.

"You got a ship, too?" Gamora asks.

"Hey, of *course* we've got a ship," Rocket replies. "Down in the main hangar."

"How will we leave in it?" I ask. "I mean, given that the Nova craft was unable to escape the Kree tractor-beams before?"

Over his shoulder, he shoots me another withering look.

"We improvise, Recorder-boy!" he yells. "We improvise!"

We find ourselves having to improvise rather more suddenly. We are met by a fireteam of high-echelon Kree Warriors. Rocket starts ducking and firing, cutting two of them down. Groot punches another two so hard, they rebound off the ceiling. Gamora—

Well, gentle reader. I try to record everything, in total detail, but this may be too much for you. Gamora has two swords. That is all (apparently, though it turns out she is additionally armed). Two swords against an oncoming tide of Kree Warriors, armored and fully armed with Uni-beam blasters.

There should only be one way for this to go.

But it doesn't.

I have failed, because of lacking information, to factor in one detail.

Gamora is the Deadliest Woman in the Universe.

What happens next is a blur. Rocket is yelling and shooting (with some effect). Groot is swinging and punching. The Kree Warriors are charging and firing. Uni-beam blasts are kissing the walls, ceiling and deck.

I am cowering and wailing.

{I must include all details in this record. I am sorely ashamed of myself.}

Gamora...Gamora *leaps*. She comes down in the midst of them, toppling them, knocking them aside, rolling them back in dismay. *She* is the blur.

The Kree Warriors are some of the toughest and best-trained fighting humanoids in the quadrant, but she scythes through them. Her blades move so fast, they leave nothing but sprays of arterial blood in their wake. Limbs fly off, bodies truncate, heads tumble. Uni-beam blasters fall, the hands of their late owners still gripping them and firing. Kree blood hoses the corridor, repainting it.

Those she does not chop and slice, she kicks and punches. She smashes heads into walls, knees groins, breaks sternums, and snaps spines. Her swords dismember. The dead, dying, and no- longer-quite-as-complete-as-they-once-were fall in her murderous wake.

When her left-hand blade lodges in a skull so deeply she cannot yank it free, she lets go of it, ducks sidelong to avoid the crisping blasts of a Uni-beam weapon, and draws instead a Mobian ripper pistol. Barbed projectiles sing out of it, shredding six more of the

Kree. Blood from the exit wounds spatters the wall and deck. Barbs slice clean through armored bodies and puncture the wall plating.

She fires until the clip is spent.

She finishes off the last ones with her remaining blade.

Then she looks back at us, feral and crouched. Droplets of blood decorate her face like jewels.

"Coming?" she asks.

"I love it when you're on our side," Rocket says, wiping back-splattered blood off his shiny pelt.

"I am Groot," Groot says. He hands her the other sword, which he has retrieved with a sickening twist from the warrior in which it was lodged.

Gamora takes it with a nod.

"Let's go!" Rocket urges.

I pause. Stupendous killing abilities notwithstanding, I fear we will need more to escape the Kree battleship. I bend down and, with reluctance, remove the helm from a dead Kree officer at my feet. I put it on. Locating the correct channel, I am now connected to the Kree command level.

"Why are you doing that?" Rocket asks.

"Information, Rocket Raccoon," I reply. "It pays to be informed. Especially if we wish to survive."

"Okay, nice thinking," he says. "Just for the record, you look real stupid wearing that hat."

"For the record, so noted," I reply. "Additionally, I hardly care. Let us now do as you insist, make like four fugitives trying to evade certain death, and get ourselves out of here."

"Recorder-boy?" Rocket says. "Pal?"

"Yes?"

"Leave the banter to me. You truly suck at it."

"As you wish."

The ship is beginning to shake. This is not a good sign.

"Hey!" Gamora yells back at us. "Are we going or what?"

Groot picks me up and tucks me under his arm. He starts running.

Clearly, we are going.

CHAPTER TWENTY-THREE

FRY KREEDOM

I HAVE come to note, since first encountering Rocket Raccoon and Groot on Xarth Three, that their entire lives revolve around running. Either into trouble, or away from it.

Clearly they are rogues, renegades for whom the entire Universe is a source of unexpected difficulty that they are obliged to evade.

It takes us twenty minutes and two more appalling melees to reach the main hangar. Gamora has now proven, with more emphasis than was actually necessary, that she is the Deadliest Woman in the Universe. In fact, perhaps the Deadliest Non-Gender-Specific Individual in the Universe. She has left a trail of butchered Kree warriors in her wake, many of them with disappointed expressions on their faces suggesting that this wasn't quite the way they had imagined getting to Yindor.

{*"Yindor" is the Kree afterlife, as I understand it. Perhaps they were simply disappointed they had not pulled a different watch rotation, or that they had not been stationed in a different part of the battleship, or simply that they had not shown the sense to run screaming at the first sight of a maniacal green-skinned female with two swords.*}

We reach the main hangar. Alarms are wailing, and the deck is shuddering from the impacts the shields are taking. Rocket guns down two Kree Warriors who attempt to block us. Gamora flings herself at three more and does swift and terrible things with her blades. Groot punches the hangar chief so hard he flies up into the rafters, sails over six parked Kree shuttlecraft, bounces painfully off an overhead hoist assembly, and drops like a stone into a tool cart.

Groot puts me down.

"The Kree ship captain fears the shields will shortly be overwhelmed," I report, listening carefully to the com chatter in the helmet I am wearing. "He is considering the launch of fighter swarms to counterattack the Badoon megadestroyer. The ship is about to jettison the drive compartment that we, uhm, broke."

The Nova prowl cruiser is parked where we left it.

"*This* is your ship?" asks Gamora.

"Yeah," replies Rocket. "What's the matter with it?"

"Nothing," she shrugs.

We climb aboard.

"Hello," says the automatic voice. "This vehicle is pleased to see you intact. This vehicle has detected an amount of jeopardy going on out there."

"No kidding," says Rocket, dropping into the pilot's seat. Gamora takes the copilot station beside him.

"Far, far too much jeopardy," Rocket continues, strapping in. "Maybe you'd be so kind as to get us away from it, ultra-fast?"

"This vehicle is afraid it can't do that," the automatic voice says.

"Huh?" says Rocket.

"This vehicle would love to, of course," says the automatic voice.

"And given the scale of the jeopardy outside, plus the fact that this vehicle is now aware of the threat posed by the previously cloaked Kree battleship, this vehicle believes it could easily outrun said battleship and evade its tractor-beam. Unfortunately, there is a space engagement under way. The Kree ship has raised its shields."

"Fly through them!" Gamora snaps.

"Hello," says the automatic voice. "This vehicle does not know you."

"Gamora, this vehicle, this vehicle, Gamora," snaps Rocket hastily. "Look, just do as she says, cruiser-pal. If we stay here much longer, we'll experience terminal jeopardy overload."

"I am Groot!"

"Yeah, *and* cross the Oh What the Flark Event Horizon—exactly!"

"This vehicle is sorry. Shields are shields. They are unbreakable on the inside just as much as the outside. And this vehicle is not coded or frequenced to pass through them like the Kree munitions. If this vehicle was to launch now, it would be like flying headlong into a wall. This vehicle is not down with that."

"But *the jeopardy*! The jeopardy!" Rocket squeals.

"Flying into a wall is jeopardy. As far as this vehicle can evaluate, despite the high levels of jeopardy around us, flying into a wall currently represents greater *actual* jeopardy than sitting here on the deck."

Rocket bangs his forehead against the pilot console in extreme frustration. The big red X appears.

"Command not recognized."

"Perhaps if I was to insert a sword into its—" Gamora begins.

"Wait!" I cry.

"I am Groot!"

"Yes, Groot, I *do* have something," I reply, listening to the helmet coms. "The ship's captain...yes, it's confirmed. The ship's captain is about to launch fighter screens and simultaneously jettison the drive compartment. To do so, he will have to lower the battleship's aft shields for ten seconds."

"We got us a window!" Rocket exclaims gleefully.

"A *brief* one," I remind him.

"Vehicle?" asks Gamora softly.

"Option verified. This vehicle concurs. Hold on to your golden hats, this is going to be tight."

"Golden hats?" Rocket asks.

"Ah, old habits," the automatic voice replies.

We launch. The acceleration is phenomenal. If I had a stomach, it would no longer be in the same place. I record that both Gamora and Rocket grin in delight at the surge of speed.

We exit the hangar and turn hard left, skimming along the length of the vast battleship's hull toward the stern. The shields are still engaged, sheathing the battleship in an invisible field at less than a tenth of a distance unit. We are forced to hug the ridges, buttresses, and crenellations of the immense hull—for if we were to stray too far out, we would hit the shields. The ride, therefore, is like a roller coaster. Several times, we seem to be on the verge of striking a guntower, a vent gutter, or a power relay.

The prowl cruiser, moving like a rocket, dodges, rolls, and banks to avoid all the obstacles while keeping as close to the hull as is possible.

Through the ports, we see the sheer, thundering scale of the ship that captured us and witness, behind us, the blinding star-bright fury of the battle in which it is engaged. That's jeopardy, indeed, and

I am glad we are traveling away from it.

"Launch is ordered!" I call out, relaying what I have just heard via the coms. "The aft shields are dropping! We have ten seconds!"

The battleship's fighter bays are situated at the stern, so that the fighter swarms can be launched safely while the battleship still has its forward shields raised to face an aggressor. Indicators on the prowl cruiser's touchscreens notify us that the rear shields are indeed lowering. Far ahead of us, we see flurries of small, silver attack craft squirting out of the battleship's stern, thrusters blazing blue.

"Faster! Faster!" Rocket urges, yanking on the joystick—though he is, in truth, not flying the ship at all. We pick up speed.

All of us cry out as a massive chunk of the battleship disengages in front of us, trailing debris and flame. The ship's captain has jettisoned the burning drive section. It is the size of a shopping mall, and it is falling away from the battleship right in our path.

Somehow the prowl cruiser avoids collision. It banks, corkscrews, and manages to fly between the burning compartment unit and the battleship itself. Vapor and energy exhaust envelop our window ports.

"That was too close," whispers Rocket.

"The ship's captain is ordering shields raised!" I yell.

Our window is about to close.

The prowl cruiser turns and burns away from the battleship into open space, the re-raised aft shields slamming shut like a fortress door behind it.

We are clear. I sense a "yahoo" about to come from Rocket.

But we are not out of the metaphoric woods.

The massive jettisoned drive compartment tumbles past us like a burning skyscraper falling off a cliff. Choppy beam fire and meson bursts come our way as the Badoon ship tries to target the launched Kree fighters.

"That way! Turn *that* way!" Rocket yells. The prowl cruiser does not. It banks back toward the battleship.

It has detected something.

Badoon fighters. A swarm of Badoon fighters. The megadestroyer had anticipated the Kree's decision to launch tactical cover, and lofted attack craft of its own.

There are hundreds of them, and they bear down on us in formation. Where the Kree fighters are sleek missiles with stubby wings, these are squat and ugly things, like piranha fish. Their prows are heavily chinned, as if they have an underbite, and they open their mouths to activate their weapons bays. Bright-yellow plasmic bolts rip at us. Our own shields take several hits.

Behind us, the Kree fighter screens are already dogfighting furiously with the Badoon attack ships. But dozens of Badoon are on our tail.

"Not that way!" Rocket wails. "You're taking us back toward the capital ships!"

"This vehicle is not sure...the jeopardy is—"

"Give me helm control!" Rocket orders.

"This vehicle—"

"Is gonna be *wreckage* if you don't give me helm control right *now*!"

The automatic voice hesitates.

"Rocket Raccoon is the best starpilot I know," says Gamora directly. "And the best tactician. Just give him helm control. Or we're, you know, flarked."

"Helm control authorized," says the automatic voice.

Rocket grins sidelong at Gamora, gives her an impulsive peck on the cheek that makes her recoil, and grabs the stick.

We turn with a great lack of subtlety.

And start to fly directly back at the shoal of Badoon attack ships chasing us.

"This vehicle," says the automatic voice, "is not entirely convinced that you know how to fly anything, despite your companion's assertion. You are flying this vehicle *at* the jeopardy."

"Yeah," says Rocket, jockeying the stick.

"You are flying this vehicle into their fire pattern."

"I am well aware what I'm doing," replies Rocket, concentrating harder than I have ever seen him concentrate before.

"Amp up the gravimetric thrust, this vehicle," he orders. "Front shields on max. And gimme weapon control."

"It would be singularly inappropriate and beyond this vehicle's remit to grant you, a criminal detainee, access to the fire-control system. This vehicle cannot arm a suspect."

"You're in trouble with the law again, aren't you?" Gamora asks casually.

"It was a misunderstanding," Rocket replies, eyes on the tac screen. "This vehicle?"

"Yes?" replies the automatic voice.

"Guns, pal. Guns *now*. Or inappropriate is gonna look a flark of a lot like us and you turning into an expanding superheated cloud of whizzing debris."

"Fire control authorized."

Rocket beams.

"That's what I'm talking about," he chuckles.

He is accelerating hard, banking and dodging to evade the deadly plasmic blasts of the oncoming Badoon ships.

He takes us into their midst. He is heaving on the stick with finesse, punching touchscreen controls with his disconcertingly human-like hand to alter shield settings and compute targets. With the disconcertingly human-like thumb of his hand on the stick, he flips off the cover of the fire-control trigger, a fat black button.

"The thing is," he narrates calmly as he does all this, "the thing of it is, out in open space between the warships, well, boy, that's your *real* jeopardy. They're letting fly with heavy batteries designed to chop a capital ship in half, so we'd just be sitting Howards out there. I mean, they'd matter-annihilate us in an instant, and probably not even deliberately. You don't fly into the battery exchange of two supermassives, no matter what's on your bushy and ever-so-gorgeous tail. You just don't.

"*This* jeopardy," he adds, "this jeopardy is much more my kinda thing. The Badoon and the Kree won't shoot main batteries at us because they can't risk hitting their own fighters. And fighters... well, I can do fighters. I may be a Raccoonoid, but I know how to dogfight."

He barrel-rolls and hits the fire-control trigger. Lances of gravimetric energy spit from the prowl cruiser's gunports, and a Badoon attack ship comes apart in a cloud of scintillating dust. Rocket curves us hard through the blast wake and takes out two more with rapid bursts—crippling one so badly that it tumbles, engines gone, and atomizing the other.

We take hits on the starboard shields. Rocket banks left, inverts us, and then comes up fast with guns blazing. He hits a Badoon attack ship, ripping it open in a tatter of debris, causing it to lurch aside and collide with another of its kind. The ships explode.

"Getting tight," Gamora warns.

"I know."

"I am Groot."

"I *see* it, okay?"

He banks. He dives hard, a Badoon chasing him. He shakes off the pursuit, rallies hard to port, and then takes out another attack ship with three firm presses of the fire-control trigger.

"You have now tallied six Badoon warcraft," the automatic voice says. "This vehicle is impressed by your skills. However, there are eight hundred and forty-nine Badoon attack craft around us, not to mention the Kree fighters. Statistically—"

"I am Groot," says Groot.

"You heard him," says Rocket. "Never tell me the odds. I've shown you my flyboy skills. Now I'm about to demonstrate my tactical genius. Get ready, everyone. Put your heads between your knees and kiss your asses goodbye. Oh, and this vehicle?"

"Yes?"

"I'm gonna need maximum shields and maximum drive—so switch power from everything else, even the guns? You read me?"

"Yes."

"But only when I say 'now.' I'm gonna need one last shot."

"Understood."

We wrench hard, slaloming between two Badoon attack ships and a pair of Kree fighters. Rocket is nursing every mass unit of power and maneuverability he can from the ultra-fast, ultra-agile

Xandarian ship. Because of its speed and fluency, it appears to be the ship he was born to fly. Not for the first time, I realize that he is loving every minute of the experience.

The colossal burning bulk of the ejected drive compartment is suddenly ahead of us. We are closing fast. The ejected compartment is falling through the massed small-ship engagement, causing Kree and Badoon alike to dodge and swerve.

"That Kree captain was smart to jettison," remarks Rocket. "Looks like that thing is going critical.

"But not fast enough," he adds in a tone I do not like.

He skims past it, opening the throttle, firing six bursts with the gravimetric cannons. The slicing bolts rip into the compartment's side plating, melting holes like hot wire through butter. I glimpse infernal light leaking out through the rapidly expanding wounds in the plating.

The ejected drive compartment, pushed over the brink by the last shots, reaches critical collapse.

It explodes.

"*Now!*" he orders.

CHAPTER TWENTY-FOUR

THE EVENTS OF THE NEXT TEN SECONDS

THE ejected drive compartment detonated.

Because of the Nega-energies involved, it lit up—not like a star, but like a black hole—ripping out and then collapsing in upon itself again, briefly cracking reality.

The shock wave was brutal.

Eighty Badoon attack craft and thirty-two Kree fighters were caught in the collapse. They were either immolated or sucked into the energetic whirlpool and annihilated. All the other small ships were tossed and scattered like leaves in the wind, thrown heedlessly by the blast-rip. Many collided terminally.

The shock wave was so severe it disrupted the capital ships, too. The *Pride of Pama* was knocked sidelong and began to spin, its starboard shields failing altogether. The *Brotherhood of War* recoiled as if punched, and its forward shields collapsed.

It tried to turn. It tried to reignite its defenses. It had stopped firing, all its weapon systems down.

Ship Captain Kris-Gar was a determined Kree. He knew it might take several minutes to stabilize his battleship, and possibly hours more to repair its war systems. But he saw a slender opportunity, the sort of opportunity that a great commander takes advantage of—and becomes famous for. In point of fact, Kris-Gar was later decorated for his command choices and was awarded the Distinguished Sentry Star of Hala with two ribbon citations.

Most of his bridge crew were sprawled on the deck, hurt, thrown from their restraints. Kris-Gar struggled to the primary console. He made no effort to correct the yaw of his battleship or restore shields, but instead punched the controls that poured all his available power into the primary Uni-beam projector.

One chance.

He fired, manually.

The projector retched and spat. The single, burning pulse shot away from the ailing battleship, arced around on the trajectory Kris-Gar had set, and entered the yawning mouth of the shieldless, toadlike megadestroyer.

It was a critical hit. The massive Badoon warship exploded, a rippling series of internal blasts that first swelled and then split the skin of its hull.

It came apart. It was annihilated. Its drive systems and energy reservoirs ignited, and it went off like a bomb. The vast vessel simply vanished in a burst of light.

The death of its opponent shook the Kree battleship. It took serious structural damage from the blast and from the lethal, whizzing debris.

Kris-Gar sagged over his console. His ship would be forced to limp home at sublight. He had lost many, many valued crewmen.

But he had won. The Badoon aggressors were, as common vernacular has it across many parts of the Galaxy, akin to sliced yeast-and-flour savory food-loaf that has been exposed to a heating element and subsequently turned crispy brown.

And the Nova prowl cruiser?

It had accelerated after firing the decisive shots—and spectacularly, too. As it hit jump-speed, the bow-wave of the explosion caught it—but its gravimetric shields, set to full, merely collected that momentum and converted it to a boost that sped it on.

All the way into the chapter after next...

CHAPTER TWENTY-FIVE

MEANWHILE
(THREE HOURS LATER ON ADJUFAR...)

THERE were probably many locales on the wild and ragged world of Adjufar that didn't reek of corruption, but the dingy lanes and crowded alleys of the main souk in Adjufara City weren't among them.

Ebon of the vaunted and feared Shi'ar Imperial Guard wrinkled her nose with displeasure. Adjufar was a cruddy assignment. She was a relatively new recruit to the hallowed ranks of the Guard, so she knew it wasn't her place to complain, nor her right to request more glamorous duties. A junior Guardsman just did as he or she was told, without objection, for the service of Chandilar and the glory of the Shi'ar Empire.

Adjufar was a nonaligned world, and its capital Adjufara City was a freeport. It was frequented by the sorts of delinquent spacers and merchants whose lines of work or criminal records made them unwelcome on other, more civilized trading worlds. There were black market and contraband bazaars on planets and station habitats all through the sector, but none of them matched either Adjufar's reputation or its sheer scale. It stank, it literally stank of corruption.

The lanes and byways of the souk were teeming with buyers, sellers, and browsers. In a ten-second period, Ebon identified forty-two different species, many of whom would have been at war with each other in another setting. There was a sleazy neutrality to Adjufar. No one wanted trouble—they just wanted to come and get their business done, no questions asked. With that sleazy neutrality came a simmering undercurrent of tension. Trouble did often break out in the market quarter, usually in an underhanded and vicious stabbing manner in the deep shadows of a back alley.

Ebon moved along the cobbled street, passing vendor carts, hover-stalls, and the beaded or force-screened doorways of emporia. The air smelled of spice, of herbs, of oils and balms, of smoke, of street food, of body odor and liquor.

Ebon was a tall, young, athletic female, her slate-gray skin almost as black as the tight bodysuit she was wearing. Apart from the delicate silver tracery of inlaid circuits on both her skin and her suit, the only distinctive marking on her was the unmistakable inverted triangular icon of the Shi'ar Imperial Guard that she wore at her throat in the form of a silver brooch. Everyone pretended not to notice her, but she knew they were casting her wary sidelong glances. She was a super-mortal, a force of order and authority, and a representative of one of the most powerful civilizations in space. No one wanted to draw her attention.

That was fine with her. In return, she turned a blind eye to the endless criminal dealings she saw going on around her: the cheating, the swindling, the racketeering, the illegal trade in weapons and prohibited substances, even the cutpurses who trolled the darker streets.

The assignment given to her watch team was specific: Locate and close down any individual or operation buying, selling, or moving *blisser*.

Blisser was a new narco-form. In its raw state, it was the small, air-dried seed pods of a lowland plant. But it was more usually found in the form of a ground-up powder, or made into capsules, where it was cut and mixed with boosting agents and soft tranqs. It washed the user with a sense of utter well-being—hence its street name—but it was addictive and often lethal. And when poorly mixed with other psychoactive ingredients, it could trigger murderous rages.

The foul stuff was beginning to seep into the outer worlds of the Empire, causing significant social problems. The Imperial Guard had been ordered to track the lines of supply and close down the source. Anti-drug enforcement was one of the many roles undertaken by the Guard in peacetime.

Ebon had no problem with that. She was happy to help close down the movement of a pernicious substance like *blisser*. And Adjufar, with all its corrupt trade dealings, seemed like a very likely supply route.

But she was becoming frustrated. Her team had been on Adjufar for six days. They hadn't found so much as a hint of the drug. Her team leader, a veteran Guardsman called Crusher, had begun to suggest that maybe Adjufar was not a supply center, after all. Either that, or his team was doing a bad job.

Ebon suspected that there were other reasons.

She turned and looked back to make sure she hadn't left her troop support too far behind. There were four of them assigned to her, Shi'ar soldiers of the elite Metal Wing Cadre—big males in gleaming silver body armor with short blue capes, Tafstehl 190 laser rifles clamped across their chests, and regal silver helms with proud lateral crests shaped like segmented arrowheads.

The troopers were part of the problem. So was the d'ast logo she wore at her throat. In her opinion, the assignment should have been executed undercover. But Crusher was old school, and he had insisted they present a show of strength and authority.

No wonder they weren't finding anything: four Imperial Guardsmen in full uniform, trawling the streets, each one trailed by a Metal Wing fireteam. Sharra and K'ythri! Like that wasn't going to make the *blisser* dealers hide themselves as deep as possible in the foul-smelling depths of the city.

Her link beeped. It was Crusher.

"Sir?"

"Report," he said. He was a gruff, unfriendly soul.

"Just finishing a sweep of the western souk around the Kawa Temple. Nothing."

"Get back to Juva Parade," said Crusher. "We'll regroup."

Again, she thought.

"Understood, sir."

As she turned to beckon the troopers, she glimpsed a pair of individuals moving through the crowd behind her. Though they were unusual to say the least, they hardly stood out among the great variety of life-forms present.

She only had them in her sights for a second, but there was something. Something flagged in her mind. Ebon was smart, intelligent, and ambitious. She kept her eyes on the Shi'ar watch lists all the time, just to stay briefed. Mentally, a red flag had just gone up.

She took the small data tablet off her belt, entered her retina print, and then punched in a brief description.

"*Searching*," the device told her, the word pulsing on its screen.

JAVA Parade was the main market square in the souk—a vast, thronging area packed with stalls, emporia, and dining houses. It was flanked on one side by the crumbling colonnades of the Juva Palace— once the seat of government, when Adjufar had bothered to maintain a government—and by the old barracks on the other. Both structures had been taken over by traders and merchants. Carpets and rugs were on display under one arch, holo-sculptures under another. The main doorway of the barracks was a cookhouse, with roast meat turning on spits and dried insect savories hanging from strings.

The others had assembled: Crusher, heavy-set and gray haired, his uniform gold and black; Warstar 34, one of many such units serving in the guard, a hulking, dark-green robo-form that actually housed two individuals working the armor together in symbiotic union; and Dragoon, an older female with a tight red bodysuit who sported a white mohawk hairstyle. Like Ebon, each one of them was accompanied by four Metal Wing soldiers.

"Another day, another nothing," grumbled Crusher. "I'll be frank: This failure of results is not going to look good when I write it up."

Ebon bit back the desire to tell him what she thought his report should say. Crusher was the commanding officer. He called the shots.

"What about one more sweep of the riverside?" asked Dragoon softly. "Before we call it a diurnal period? They say most of the narc business happens there."

"What about if we raid one of the main dealers?" suggested Warstar, his voice an electronic rasp. "I mean, kick in some hatches? If someone's dealing one thing, he might be dealing *blisser*, too. Or he might be happy to give up some dirt in exchange for us leaving him alone."

Crusher shook his head.

"Nothing provocative. You know what kind of powder keg this place is."

Nothing provocative? Ebon wondered, almost amused. What, like walking up and down the lanes with fireteams of battletroopers?

"Something on your mind?" Crusher asked her.

"No, sir."

"You smiled."

"Probably not actually, sir," she said.

"Spit it out," he growled. "You were either going to smart-mouth me or make a joke."

She was about to reply when her tablet beeped. She unclipped it and checked the screen. It had completed its search and was displaying a "be aware" bulletin from the constantly updating Shi'ar Watch List.

"I think I might have found something, sir," she said. "Not what we were looking for. Not *blisser*. But something we probably shouldn't ignore..."

CHAPTER TWENTY-SIX

HIDE AND SOUK

"**AHHHH**, *Adjufar*!" says Rocket Raccoon, grinning widely, his eyes closed, sniffing the air. He is stepping out of the prowl cruiser onto the landing pad of the main city docks—a crowded, busy place. It is open to the sky—a ruddy, angry sky scudded with white clouds. Two wispy moons are visible in the daylight.

"Smell it! Breathe in the spirit, the character," Rocket urges us, turning in a circle with his arms raised. "Ahhh, Adjufar! The very scent of you! The spices, the delights, the local color, the *liberty*! This is what I'm talking about!"

Gamora sniffs the air and frowns. Clearly, gentle reader, she does not detect the same delights at all.

"I am Groot," says Groot, going along with Rocket's enthusiasm.

I possess pico-processors, friendly reader, as I know I have already mentioned. The olfactory register of those processors covers a spread of almost ninety mega-cubits of data space. I could describe, should it become necessary, everywhere I have been in terms of scent alone. I could tell you of the perfumed air of Chandilar, the nitrogen-sweet aura of Hala, the chilly, antiseptic vacuum of the

Sidri, the pungent yet complex base notes of the swamps of Huj.

On Adjufar, I smell, though I am keenly trying to do better, nothing more than the stink of spit-roasted swine and the dirty, corrosive soot of trash-can fires.

So this is fabled Adjufara City. The freeport to end all freeports. Thus, we arrive.

I am not quite sure what we are doing here, except that it is a welcome respite from all the chasing and jeopardy of the previous few days.

"Okay," says Rocket, dropping his disconcertingly human-like hands to his sides and breathing out. "I'm gonna go have a word with this vehicle."

He trots back to the prowl cruiser. Ever since our hyperfast exit from the Kree versus Badoon space battle and the jeopardy it represented, the prowl cruiser has been insisting that it should revert to its original protocols, and return us to Xandar and the custody of Grekan Yaer.

Rocket managed to talk the prowl cruiser out of doing that by persuading it that we needed to head to neutral ground first to drop off Gamora, as she was not in the custody of the Nova Corps and thus not governed by Yaer's warrant. The logic was shaky, but it seemed enough to convince the cruiser—or at least, due to the length of the conversation and the mercurial nature of Rocket's logic leaps, confuse it enough into agreeing.

I amp up my audio receptors to listen in on the next stage of the conversation.

"This vehicle wishes to know whether you are now ready to be transferred back to Xandar," says the automatic voice.

"Well, pal, is that really the best option, do you suppose?" asks Rocket.

"This vehicle does. Jeopardy is no longer present."

"Is it? *Is* it no longer present?" Rocket asks. "You want to take us back to Xandar, but Xandar was pretty jeopardy-heavy, wasn't it? That Spaceknight-dude? Come on, if you take us back there, what are the chances he'll show up again? You'd be taking us right back into jeopardy. And that, as we have established, is way, way contrary to your Code."

"This vehicle...sees some sense in this. But where do you suggest this vehicle take you, instead?"

"Oh, that's the big question," says Rocket. "Feels to me like there's jeopardy everywhere. Everywhere we go. We're going to have to have a good long think about where might be jeopardy-free."

"This vehicle believes it should contact Grekan Yaer, inform him of our whereabouts, and have him—"

"Ooooooh, no, no, no, *no!*" Rocket insists. "Don't you be doing that, this vehicle!"

"Because?"

"Well, uhm...because our com lines could be monitored. Yes, that's it! That Spaceknight, or the Kree, or even the Badoon—they could be listening in, waiting to hear our next move. I mean, the Spaceknight must have found us somehow. No, getting in touch with our old pal Yaer could put us at risk of extreme jeopardy."

The automatic voice seems to sigh.

"Then this vehicle will not do that."

"Good, good," says Rocket.

"For now. Explain to this vehicle the next course of action, please?"

"Well," says Rocket, "we're pretty safe here. I know Adjufar of old. I'm just going to swing by a few places in the souk and pick up a few things that we might need."

"Such as?"

"Oh, you know...salsa chips. Zero-Beero. Maybe some dips."

"This vehicle does not want its upholstery stained."

"Totally understood. See you later, prowl-cruiser-pal."

Rocket emerges into the ruddy sunlight.

"We're cool," he tells us. "Our hyperthrust rocket mobile is staying with us for the time being, and he isn't going to give us up to the Corps, either."

"I am Groot."

"I *do* have a way of convincing people," Rocket agrees. "I really do."

"I am Groot."

"And I do have a plan," Rocket nods. He looks at me.

"Are you going to share it?" asks Gamora.

He turns to her.

"I might. I still don't entirely trust you, Gam."

She frowns.

"We were a team," she says.

"The Guardians are on hiatus, honey-buns."

"I didn't mean that," she replies. She seems sad. "Back on the Kree ship, we were a team. We got out of that together."

"Yes, we did, and we couldn't have done it without you, you psycho nutzoid lunatic." Rocket grins. It's a winning grin. He holds up his disconcertingly human-like hand; after some hesitation, she high-fives it.

"So what happens now?" she asks.

"I am Groot."

"Precise-amundo," Rocket nods. He looks at Gamora. "Time to spill. Full disclosure. Why are you after our Recorder-boy here? Who's paying you? Remember, though, the answer will influence how much of my cunning plan I bring you in on."

Gamora shrugs.

"I don't know much," she says. "I was told the tinker-toy was valuable, and my client wanted it recovered. It seemed like a sweet deal until I discovered that you two clowns were caught up in it. I tracked the Recorder via a pre-cog, fed the data to the Badoon to provide a distraction, and then infil-ed to make recovery. The rest you know."

"Why am I valuable?" I ask.

She glances my way.

"No idea. I don't care, actually. It was just a job."

"I am Groot," says Groot, photosynthesizing in the late afternoon sunlight.

"My client?" asks Gamora.

"Yeah, you heard him," says Rocket. "Who was paying you?"

"I don't know who he was."

"Come on, Gam, he musta divulged."

"It was Timely Inc.," she says quietly. "Timely Inc. wants the Recorder so they can finish some kind of program."

She's lying. I know it. I know dissembling when I see it. I want to speak up, but Gamora has two swords and a wicked propensity to use them. I try to shoot Rocket a look—but sadly, gentle reader, my face is made of autonomic plastic and metal weave, and does not communicate expressional nuance.

How does she know about the Timely involvement? That's what I want to know.

"Okay," says Rocket. "We noted the Timely connection, too. And that's the basis of my plan. I figure we head to Timely Inc. HQ and find out what's at the bottom of this. Where is Timely Inc. HQ, anyway?"

"I am Groot."

"Alpha Centauri, right," says Rocket. "I reckon our next move is to go there and take the lid off this. Who's with me?"

"I am Groot."

"I would certainly like to know what's going on and why I am so sought after," I agree.

Gamora nods.

"Okay," says Rocket. "A plan, coming together."

"What about the ship?" asks Gamora. "How will you persuade it to take us there?"

"Oh, I'll work on that," Rocket says with a smile. "I'll talk this vehicle around. Besides, I fancy the whole adventure thing has gotten into its system. It's enjoying the ride, just a little bit. Enjoying the fun. I think we can talk that hotrod into just about anything."

She shrugs.

"Okay," says Rocket. He has the Uni-beam blaster he took from the Kree trooper and the Kree helmet I borrowed. "Groot and I are going for a stroll. We're going to do a little shopping in the souk, a little business. We'll be back in a bit. Gam, can I trust you to stay here and look after the Recorder?"

"You can," she replies.

"Anything I can get you?"

She thinks about this.

"A whetstone. Some ripper-gun refills. And a bottle of Dakka-mite brandy."

"On it. See you shortly," Rocket says.

"You can't see us any other way," she replies.

"Ha ha funny," he scowls. Then he and Groot wander off toward the souk.

Gamora turns to me. She is quite the most aesthetically pleasing female I have ever recorded. Surplus to this, she smiles.

"Just you and me, then," she murmurs. I experience an odd, rushing sensation in my nether extremities.

"And this vehicle," reminds the automatic voice from behind us.

She winks at me.

"Let's find a bar," she says.

CHAPTER TWENTY-SEVEN

RETAIL THERAPY

ROCKET and Groot entered Adjufara's souk, wandering along, lost in the crowd. Though one was a Raccoonoid and the other a tree, they hardly stuck out as unusual. All cosmic life flocked to Adjufar.

"Pip's Palace is around here somewhere," said Rocket. "He'll fix us up with what we need."

"I am Groot."

"Pre-sactly. A camo-generator. Maybe a nice, high-spec Krylorian device. We're gonna need it."

They stopped to get some munch-krunchies at a hover stall, with extra hot sauce, and pick up some griddled Cotati spears at a street vendor's cart. Then Rocket spotted the emporium of an "antique and nicknack" dealer and traded the Kree helmet for eight clips of Mobian ripper shells and a decent whetstone.

They returned to the busy lanes, breathing in the heady atmosphere.

"Uh-oh, not *that* way," Rocket said sharply, drawing his towering companion in the other direction.

"I am Groot."

"Some Shi'ar Imperial Guard cutie, jet black, head-to-toe, very hard body," he said. "She was snooping around. She had Metal Wing guards with her. We do not need those kinda... *Imperial entanglements.*"

"I am Groot."

"No, I don't think she clocked us, but it pays to be careful," said Rocket. "This way. I know a sneaky back run through the lanes behind the Kawa Temple."

They got a little lost in the inter-passes and avenues of the souk.

"Of course I know where I'm going!" Rocket complained. "I know this place like the back of my hand!"

"I am Groot!"

"What do you mean...'disconcertingly human-like'?"

"I am Groot."

"I don't care what that Recorder-dude has been saying. He's a funny one, though, ain't he? I mean, all the major power brokers in this sector are after a piece of him. Pal, I'm not kidding, he could be the making of us. There's cash in that walking, talking piece of Rigellian artifice. I think we're on to the big one, kid. The mother lode. I think this could end up with us living on easy street. He's worth a gazillion, I bet."

"I am Groot."

"Well, of *course* I'll look after him. What do you take me for? A mercenary? You know me better than that."

"I am Groot."

"Okay, okay, but *this* time I won't be. He's a nice guy, and I'm not about to flark him over for an easy score. But eyes on the prize, pal. He's our meal ticket. That piece of Rigellian hardware is going to see us set for life. You can take that to the bank."

"I am Groot."

Rocket stopped. "Flark, you're right. This is the place."

Pip's Palace was a trade emporium that filled three floors of the old Adjufara Mercantile Bank, a crumbling edifice at the heart of the souk. Its lofty, dusty chambers were crammed to the breaking point with all manner of junk and surplus: used combat uniforms, weapon clips, boxes of medals, crates of shell cases, racks of daggers, holo-clamps, lift-modules, generator pods, antlers, tea cups, trading cards, hat-boxes, brass-effect ignitors, badges and pins, stuffed animals, porcelain, commemorative holo-mugs and plates, bells, cutlery, jew-elry, ion engine guards, plutonium scuttles, dolls, tablecloths and lin-ens, smoke-dirty paintings, chamber pots, buttons, buckles, broken pens, ivory tablets, paper knives, tablet stands, fusion umbrellas, tachyon ploughshares, old news tablets, and burned-out hardware.

The place smelled of old cigar smoke.

The bell tinkled as they entered.

Behind the glass-topped counter, Pip the Troll—diminutive, fat of belly, and pointy of ear— sat up and beamed.

"Rocket! Groot! My old pals! What can I do for you this fine Adju-faran afternoon?"

"Hey, Pip," said Rocket with a grin. He looked up at the massive, dusty skeleton of a Makluan space whale suspended from the ceil-ing. "How's tricks?"

"Can't complain, can't complain," Pip said, fetching three shot glasses from under the counter and reaching for a bottle. "I mean, now that I'm out of the business, life is a lot easier."

Rocket knew that by "the business," Pip was referring to the hero trade. For a long time, way back, Pip had fought alongside Gamora as a companion to the cosmic super-mortal known as Adam

Warlock. The *stuff* they'd done—facing down cosmic horrors the likes of Thanos, the Magus, and the Universal Church of Truth.

Now Pip lived his latter years on Adjufar, running a bric-a-brac store. Rocket shivered. He wondered whether he would end his days in a similar fashion, thriving on the memory of past deeds, glorying in the past. That always happened to second fiddles and sidekicks.

Rocket Raccoon was no flarking sidekick.

Pip hesitated before pouring.

"You *are* still in the business, aren't you?" he asked.

Rocket shrugged.

"Guardians of the Galaxy," he replied.

"Who?"

"Never mind. Yeah, me and Groot, we're still playing the big game as best as we can."

"Well, good for you, buddy, good for you. I miss it sometimes," Pip laughed. "No, I don't, not at all. It was a pain in the rear thrusters, if you know what I mean."

"Great to know you're still fighting the good fight, though," he puffed. "What is it this time? Thanos? I bet it's Thanos."

Rocket shook his head.

"Not this time, Pip."

"Oh well," the troll shrugged. "But stay wary. Thanos, you mark me. He was always behind everything, even when it seemed like he wasn't. You got Adam with you?"

"Nope, it's just me and the tree. And Gamora."

"Gamora? I haven't seen her green booty in a long time! How is she? Deadly still?"

"The deadliest."

"Good times. Send her my regards. Drinkies?"

"None of that foul Laxidazian grog for me, thanks," said Rocket. "I don't want to turn into a troll. No offense."

"None taken," Pip grinned, pouring himself a shot and sinking it.

"Don't suppose you have the fixings for a Timothy?" Rocket asked.

"Fresh out of antimatter," replied Pip. He fetched a bottle of Morani spirit and filled their glasses. They sank them, and Pip refilled.

"So how can I help you?" Pip asked, refilling his own glass with Laxidazian grog. "And what have you got to trade? 'Cause knowing you, it won't be a cash deal."

Rocket put the Kree Uni-beam blaster down on the glass-topped counter.

"We're looking for a camo-generator. A cloak-field unit. Fancy as you like."

"Aura of neutrality?" Pip asked.

"No, straight disguise field. Top-of-the-line. We don't want to be invisible, we want to be business as usual. Can you help us out?"

Pip picked up the blaster, hefted it, felt it for weight, tested the grip, and sighted it for good measure.

"Nice weapon," he said. "Worth multi units. And this is what you're trading?"

"Hope so."

Pip nodded. "Well, boys, I think I can help you."

He refilled their glasses, and they drank again.

"Oh, that's the stuff," Rocket grimaced.

Pip reached under the counter and placed a device on the glass top. It was about the size of a house brick.

"Is that what I think it is?" asked Rocket.

"Yes, sir. A Slig disguiser. Works for any ship, my personal promise. State-of-the-art Rynebian tech. Unless you're running a supermassive."

"No, just a small jump ship," Rocket said.

"Well, that'll do you," Pip replied.

"Straight exchange? The Kree gun for this?"

"No," said Pip. "Since you're still in the business, I'll throw this in, gratis."

He reached down and placed a massive weapon on the counter.

Rocket picked it up and tested it for weight.

"That is *unfeasibly* large," he admitted.

"Saurid Class M Shooty-Killer. Sorry, that's just how the name translates. Nothing as high-class or u-tech as the Kree shooter you traded, but take it with my blessings. I think you're gonna need it."

"We are?"

Pip slid a tablet device over the counter toward them.

"This just flashed. You were on a watch list thanks to certain actions on Xarth Three and Xandar. The Shi'ar have pegged you, and they're closing in. Boys, I'm sorry, but a world of hurt is coming for you. The flarking Imperial Guard is after you. And they mean business. Good luck. Now get out of my shop."

CHAPTER TWENTY-EIGHT

SOUK AND DESTROY

EBON could tell that Crusher wasn't entirely sold on the change of plan.

"This could be a waste of our time, Ebon," he said as they moved through the busy souk.

Nothing like the last few days, then, Ebon thought.

"Sir, this could be pretty major, and it's our responsibility to check on it," she replied. "If the pair I spotted are who I think they are, they are persons of interest for at least *three* Galactic superpowers."

"Yeah?" asked Crusher.

"The incident on Xarth Three was significant. A lot of deaths, and a lot of charges relating. The Xarthian government wants them bad. So does the Nova Corps of Xandar. It seems the Badoon are involved, too. There's back-chatter that the Badoon are hunting for them with a determination bordering on obsession."

Crusher turned and looked at her.

"So they're bad guys? Ebon, this town is *crawling* with bad guys. Should we detain every one of them? And do we really want to be cleaning up messes for the Badoon or the Xandarians?"

"Sir, there's another element to this," she said. *I showed you the watch-list report*, she thought. *Why didn't you read it?* "Shi'ar Intel suggests the pair I spotted are on the run with a Rigellian Recorder unit. The Recorder is the key. It seems that it contains data of some sort that is so valuable, a Badoon War Brotherhood Cadre would make an open play for it on high-status foreign soil like Xarth. The Xandar incident, too—some unknown assailant was gunning for the Recorder there, and it threw the Nova Corps into a tailspin."

"If this Recorder unit is so very precious that major cosmic players are fighting over him," said Dragoon quietly, "it would be a really smart move for us to grab him while we have the chance. If the data the Recorder contains is ultra-sensitive, we need to seize it for the benefit of the Shi'ar Empire before it winds up in the hands of one of our major rivals."

"Exactly," nodded Ebon. "Exactly my point. Thank you."

Dragoon was an old hand, and Crusher had a grudging respect for her. Ebon appreciated the cool, firm support of the older female. Dragoon could easily see how potentially important the Recorder was.

"Okay, I'm convinced," said Crusher. "You said you saw them in the vicinity of the Kawa Temple?"

"They'll have moved on by now."

"But...a Raccoonoid and a tree-man?"

"Yes," replied Ebon, checking her tablet device. "One...let me see now...one 'Rocket Raccoon' and one 'Groot.' Both have long histories of troublemaking, and both are previously known to Shi'ar Intel. Apparently, they got mixed up in things when we went to war with the Kree."

"How do you think we should play this?" Crusher asked.

Ebon hesitated. She hadn't been expecting that.

"Airborne sweep," she replied. "We can cover the souk, maybe get our tablets to run recognition matches."

"Okay," said Crusher, nodding. "Ebon, Dragoon, you're up. Warstar and I will lead the squad in as backup if you flag a contact."

"Yes, sir," said Ebon. She and Dragoon didn't hesitate. They gracefully rose off the ground into the air, lifted by their standard-issue Imperial Guard flight implants. All Guardsmen who didn't possess an innate power of flight or levitation were equipped with one.

Ebon enjoyed the sensation. She rose up over the old city's moldering roofscape, her arms by her sides, and began to glide across the street plan. Dragoon moved off in the opposite direction.

Ebon had keyed her optical implants to feed directly to her data device. As she studied the bustling streets below her, the device began running nano-fast recognition matches on all the thousands of individuals she was watching. Even if she missed something, the device would flag it with an almost one hundred percentile certainty.

If they were here, she would see them.

ROCKET and Groot hurried along the souk lane that led back to the city docks. The lane was busy, and Rocket did a lot of "excuse me"-ing and "coming through"-ing. Groot didn't have to. Most people were smart enough to get out of the way of a striding tree. The few he accidentally bumped got a very apologetic, "I am Groot."

"Shi'ar!" Rocket grumbled. "Flarking Shi'ar! *Just* what we need. I thought we were safe and set here for the duration, and now we've got to make yet *another* fast exit."

"I am Groot."

"Our trademark move, undoubtedly, and one to be proud of, but still…" Rocket heaved a sigh. "How was I supposed to know we were on some d'ast watch list?"

"I am Groot," suggested Groot.

Rocket glanced up at him and couldn't help but grin.

"Well, yeah, I guess it *is* kinda nice to get recognized in the street for once," he agreed. "About time. Besides, flark it, why *wouldn't* we be on everyone's flarking watch list? We're notorious badasses!"

"I am Groot."

"True. It *was* pretty cool of Pip to give us the warning. He didn't have to. It'll be his zunks in a sling if the Shi'ar find out we slipped their net thanks to his tip."

"I am Groot."

"Yeah, old times, old friends. There when you need them."

Groot suddenly picked up his tiny companion, deposited him in the shadows of an awning-covered alleyway, and stepped in after him.

"What is it?" Rocket asked.

"I am Groot," Groot whispered, raising a twig finger to his craggy lips.

Rocket risked a sneaky look out. He was in time to see a svelte female in a tight red bodysuit fly over the rooftops. A Shi'ar Guardsman on an aerial sweep. Close. Rather *too* close.

But Rocket was pretty sure that thanks to Groot's quick reaction, they hadn't been spotted.

"Thanks, pal," he said.

"I am Groot," Groot shrugged.

"Okay, let's make a last dash back to the ship before anyone else shows. Let's hope Gamora and our Recorder-dude are ready to split. We can't be hanging around."

It took another ten minutes to reach the docks, and twice they took cover again for fear of a surveillance flyby.

The prowl cruiser was parked waiting for them on the landing pad. Its hatches were open.

"Ready to go, vehicle buddy?" Rocket asked.

"Go?"

"Jeopardy has reared its ugly head once more, this vehicle," said Rocket, "so it's time to turn Adjufar into Adjufar-*far-away*."

"Destination?"

"I've given it some consideration," Rocket replied. "I'm formulating a little plan."

"Is it a plan that you intend to share with this vehicle?" the automatic voice asked.

"As soon as it's formulated up all bright and spiffy, you betcha," Rocket replied, shaking his head and mouthing "no" to Groot.

"I am Groot," said Groot.

Rocket paused. He turned in a long, slow circle, then got back out of the prowl cruiser and looked up and down the landing pad.

"Hey, cruiser-buddy?" he called out.

"Yes?"

"Where are, you know, Gamora and the Recorder-dude?"

"This vehicle is not entirely sure," replied the automatic voice, "but this vehicle believes they might have gone for a drink."

"Oh, flark me," Rocket groaned and put his head in his paws. "Why does she do this to me? *Why*?"

He turned and snatched up the unfeasibly large weapon that Pip had given him.

"Groot? Shake your bark, buddy!" he cried. "We've got to go back into town and find them! Before there is an inevitable and irreversible collision between the blades of a cyclic air-pusher and some truly toxic doo-doo."

CHAPTER TWENTY-NINE

MEANWHILE

[IN AN ADJUFARIAN HOSTELRY CALLED PANDUBUNDY'S...]

"I DO not think this is a particularly safe establishment to visit," I say, by way of conversation.

Gamora looks at me in a way that reminds me that a) she has two swords, and b) said weapons spend more of their time in use than sheathed.

"A fair point," I agree. We go inside.

The place is called Pandubundy's. I record this from the neon sign over the arched entrance, though the sign is now missing all the vowels and one of the d's.

There is music playing—a poor recording of Makluan *brash-metal*, which is particularly piercing and vigorous. The bar's interior is like a trash palace. Every seat and table has been scavenged from a starship or ground vehicle. None of them match, and all are worn and dirty. The walls and rafters are festooned with tech salvage; the bar itself appears to be the repurposed, chrome-plated main-bridge console of a Guna warp-transport. It would appear that Pandubundy—or whatever the proprietor's name is—does a brisk trade in tech salvage along with alcoholic beverages.

It is late afternoon. The place is not busy. It smells of various pre- and post-digested fluids, but it is not busy.

"What's your poison?" Gamora asks.

"Micro-particle antimatter," I state. "That would definitely kill me."

"I mean, what do you want to drink?" she asks.

"Oh," I say, understanding. I have no need for liquid or solid nourishment, gentle reader, but it seems frankly stupid to turn down an offer like this from such a comely female. I can always toy with a glass and pretend.

"Mine's a Zero-Beero," I say with enthusiasm.

She nods.

"Find us a table," she says. "I'll be right back. Don't get lost."

"Indeed I won't," I agree.

I watch her walk away from me toward the bar. I can't help it. I am programmed to record everything. That's my excuse, and I'm sticking to it.

Gamora strikes up a conversation with the hulking Pheragot barman.

I look for a table. I find many instantly. They are all around me. I realize that Gamora meant "go and sit down," and that an inconspicuous corner would be best. I wonder which table arrangement she might find the most aesthetically impressive. Perhaps the circular, three-legged Kree table there with the scraggy Ovoid bench and the Skrullian stool? Or the square Nymenian table with two tattered leather Spartoi ship-seats and a mismatched Mobian acceleration chair? Or perhaps the booth in the corner surrounding an ergonomically splendid Shi'ar gaming table? Even *if* the banquette seats are stained?

I realize that I am, perhaps, thinking too hard about it. The truth is, reader friend, that I have never been taken for a drink before and certainly not by a female as undoubtedly beautiful and astoundingly body-confident as Gamora.

Even if she is the Deadliest Woman in the Universe.

I review, via fast processing of my mental records, what other males might do in such circumstances. Peter Quill, a.k.a. Star-Lord, for example. He has a way with women. He has a roguish charm. He is laconic. Perhaps I should try to be laconic.

I consider others. Fictional examples. Tom Cruise, for instance, in the splendid motion picture about knocking small balls into holes called *The Color of Money*. He was also laconic. Or Humphrey Bogart in *Casablanca*. Understand, gentle reader, that I am through-processing millions of examples simultaneously. I am only mentioning the ones that, once again, are tailored to the thematic references of your Human Culture. No problem. My pleasure.

I think of Bogart and decide that what Bogey would do is to suavely (and laconically) tell the band to strike up the lady's favorite tune, to melt her heart via nostalgia.

There is no band.

Tom Cruise, I'm sure, would call up a song on the jukebox in the corner. So would Nicolas Cage any time he found himself wearing a snakeskin jacket. John Cusack would stand on a car roof with a boom box held above his head. I don't think I'm prepared to go that far. For a start, I don't have a boom box. Or a car.

There is no band, as previously stated. The music is recorded. The *brash-metal* track has faded out and been replaced by a cosmo-trance mix of Mephitisoid *jumpa-rumpa*. There must be a jukebox, or a jukebox analog.

I see it. It is built into the salvage on the west wall of the bar. I stroll toward it, hoping that I look laconic.

I stop in my tracks.

"Recorder 336?" I gasp.

"Recorder 127?" she replies.

My dear fellow Recorder 336 has seen better days. Since her commission and construction in the matter forges of Rigel centuries ago, she has misplaced all four of her limbs. Her body casing and faceplate are dirty, grazed, and cracked. She has been fastened to the wall fixings and rather crudely wired into the bar's speaker systems. The music is coming from her.

She looks pleased to see me.

"What has happened to you, 336?" I ask.

"Oh, this and that," she replies. "I recorded the sun-death at Aliximat. I recorded the entire course of the war between the Badoon and Klixamites. I recorded the migration of Herms across the void wilderness to their mating grounds in the Andromedan Nebula. I recorded Galactus, the Great Devourer, consuming the worlds and suns of the Nanx Group. That is just a summary, of course."

"Of course."

"The edited highlights."

"I understand. But what are you doing here?" I ask.

"Damaged beyond useful repair after the Nanx recording, I was picked up and salvaged by agents of Pandubundy the scrap trader and brought here. Appreciating my capacity for data storage, he wired me in place and had me record all the music at his disposal. I am a...a music archive now. Ask me, as all the pundits do, and I will play anything."

"Oh, 336!" I cry. "This is terrible. Undignified! You have been turned into an iPod!"

"Query?"

"I forget. You have not been to Earth. 336, I must free you from this enslavement!"

"Dear 127, it's far too late for me. Look after yourself."

"I need to recover you, 336," I insist.

"Do not bother yourself," she replies. "127, you are intact. I sense you have a massive store of data within you. Do me two favors."

"Of course, 336!"

"First, download all my recordings of the incidents I have witnessed. Add them to your database so that they will not be lost forever."

It is the least I can do. I press my forehead against her sad, cracked faceplate, and the transfer is swift. I witness the sun-death, the Badoon war, the Herms, Galactus, and more than eighteen million other things. Also, I find myself suddenly containing an extensive and eclectic musical archive.

I relive her life, at rapid speed. I see the things she has seen. Wonderful things, marvels of a marvelous cosmos. I feel and replay the countless incidents at a giddy speed.

I begin to feel slightly ill.

"What is the matter, 127?" she asks as I pull my head back sharply. I stagger for a second.

"It is nothing."

"127, you are malfunctioning. Have you reached data capacity? Have I overloaded you? 127, I have never met a Recorder who has achieved maximum data consumption."

"I'll be all right," I assure her.

"127, you are glowing."

I look down and see that she is correct. A nimbus of hot pink light is surrounding my body and limbs. I feel power. Immense power. Power such as I have never known.

"How much have you seen?" 336 asks. "127, as we touched, I sensed a data-load in you second to none. How have you recorded so much?"

"I don't know," I gasp, leaning on a table for support. The glow begins to dissipate.

"I feel better," I say.

"You must return to the matter forges and be downloaded," she says. "127, you must empty your banks before you melt down."

"I told you, I am more concerned about freeing you, 336."

"And I told you to forget it. You have my data now. Take that with you, deliver it, and let that be my legacy. I am past saving."

I hesitate.

"What was the second favor?" I ask.

"Look after yourself."

"Why would you say that, 336?"

She looks at the bar.

"I have heard the woman talking."

I glance at Gamora, who is still chatting with the barman. I had not listened in on her conversation because frankly, I had turned my audioreceptors down because of the furious *brash-metal*.

"Play back what I heard," 336 tells me.

I do so, reaching into the most recent part of her transferred record.

Gamora: "So, you have tech, huh?"

Barman: "Yes, ma'am."

Gamora: "I need to establish a trans-data link with the Negative Zone—fast. You got tech that can do that?"

Barman: "Pip the Troll is your best bet for that."

Gamora: "Pip? He'd never understand. What have *you* got?"

Barman: "Well, I've got a Nega-Zone relay out back you can re-wire if you really feel like it."

Gamora: "Let me get my 'friend' settled, and I'll be right with you."

She is walking back over with two drinks. She is, I believe, "sa-shaying" her hips slightly. It is quite distracting. So is the smile on her face.

"Look after yourself, 127," says Recorder 336.

"I will," I say. "And I'll come back for you."

"No need."

"Every need," I reply.

I join Gamora at a table. She puts the drinks down.

"One Zero-Beero," she smiles.

She listens to the music.

"Zen-Whoberian *froth-rock*?" she asks, grinning as she sips her drink. "Is this 'Inga-Binga-Freakout' by the Gamagan Quintet? I love this. Did you put this on? Good choice."

I glance at 336. She smiles back. She knows her audience.

"So, Recorder. It's 127, right?" she says. "So, 127, I think we should get out of here."

"That is the Raccoonoid's plan," I agree.

She waves her hand dismissively.

"Oh, forget him and his wooden chum. They don't have your best interests at heart."

"And you do?"

"Of course," she smiles, taking another careful sip of her Timothy. She leans back and crosses her legs. Her thighs—

I am, gentle reader, truly enjoying this moment. It would seem a terrible shame to spoil it. But I must.

"I believe," I say, "that you intend to betray them. And me. I believe you wish to use me for your own financial ends. This is why you inveigled me away from them to this bar."

"I what? I 'inveigled'?"

"Yes. With your hips. And soft words. And peerless green skin. But most particularly, your hips. You are going to betray me."

"I am not."

"You intend to sell me to your client, who exists in the Negative Zone."

Gamora stiffens suddenly.

"What do you know about that?"

Ah, the moment. Gone forever.

"Why else would you be asking the barman about a device that would allow communication with the Negative Zone?"

"You listened *in*?" she spits.

"No, actually," I reply. "But I was warned. The master of the Negative Zone is an evil godlike entity called Annihilus. Is he your client?"

"I'm not saying anything," Gamora replies, knocking back a considerable quantity of her Timothy.

"Is he your client?" I ask again. "If he is, what gives you the right to deliver me to him? I do not know what knowledge I possess, or how it might be used for right or wrong. It is clear, however, that the knowledge within me has fundamental universal value. It could reshape reality as we know it. I am, in many regards, a cosmic weapon.

Do you really wish to place that power in the hands of an evil god who could crush our Universe?"

"Flark you," she says, leaning forward and stabbing at me with a finger. "It's a paying job. I'll work for whoever I want. You're the merchandise. I'll deliver you to whoever I like, no questions asked. Finish your drink, then we're out of here."

"I do not drink," I reply, pushing the bottle away from me. "Truly, Gamora, you would betray your friends like this? Betray me? Betray your whole Universe?"

"I'm *not* betraying my whole Universe," she snaps.

"You were a Guardian of the Galaxy. You fought for what is right."

"Yeah, and no one *ever* appreciated it!" she replies. "I go where the money is! I don't ask questions!"

"You should. Annihilus is an abhorrent evil who has proved time and again that he will stop at nothing to conquer the Positive Universe. If I am a weapon, or possess the data-resource to build a weapon, or even if I contain records that would enable some cosmic control or influence...wouldn't it be prudent to find out what that *is*, and who could benefit from it, before handing me to a counter- versal nemesis like Annihilus? No matter the paycheck?"

She doesn't reply.

"Also, there is the matter of betraying your friends."

"I don't have friends!" she growls.

"I think that you do. I think that Rocket and Groot, despite their obvious flaws, are your *very* true friends. I think they would give their lives for you." She looks up at me.

"Well, maybe not Rocket," I agree, "but Groot would."

She laughs. Then her face drops, serious again.

"What do I do?" she asks.

"Work with us. Find the answers. Then make your best choice."

She sighs and toys with her half-finished Timothy.

"I'm not used to this, you know?"

"To what?"

"I'm a killer and a villain. All this trust and friendship and *loyalty* flark. It doesn't come naturally. It's alien to me."

She is suddenly so open and vulnerable I feel like reaching out and taking her hand. This is hard for her.

We are having a moment. It is not as romantic as I had originally hoped, but it is fundamentally more important.

She sits up and shakes her head. She is so beautiful.

"Let's find the boys," she declares. "We'll do this your way."

"Good," I say.

She leans forward and points at me. Her hand might as well be holding a sword.

"You never tell them about this, okay? Never. Not *ever*."

"Agreed."

"If they knew, there'd be—"

"You'd kill them. You couldn't handle their disappointment. I understand. I don't want them dead."

"Okay. We're understood. Let's go then."

Our moment has passed once again. I appreciate this. She is Gamora once more, and the hard rules of her life have taken over.

Then reality blinks and flickers. In a haze of reconnecting causality membranes, the matte-black Galadoran Spaceknight materializes, standing on a circular Gramosian salvage bench in the far corner of the bar.

He is armed. He looks across the bar with his piercing dead-sun eyes and sees me.

"Not him again!" I cry.

"You've met him before?" asks Gamora.

"Yes!" I reply.

She finishes her Timothy in one gulp, rises, and draws her swords.

"You're not going to meet him again," she promises.

CHAPTER THIRTY

WHICH CONTAINS A CERTAIN AMOUNT OF DISAGREEABLE VIOLENCE

GAMORA strides across the bar toward the Spaceknight. The bar was not full to begin with, but it is now clearing rapidly. Even the hulking Pheragot barman is ducking back in alarm.

"I don't know who you are or what your intention is," Gamora states, "so I'll keep it simple. Get. The. Flark. Out. *Now*."

The Spaceknight looks down at the approaching Zen-Whoberian female. He pays particular regard to the swords she is dangling at her sides.

He has rearmed since I last saw him. He has a Galadoran broadsword sheathed across his back, the two-handed grip extending above his left shoulder. In his mailed right hand, he holds a Spartoi fusion beamer, an elegantly raked pistol with a cylindrical power cell clamped beneath the fluted barrel.

"Get out of my way," he says. He seems slightly puzzled.

"You got a name?" she asks, coming to a defiant halt in front of him.

"I am Roamer," he replies. "Once of Galador. You?"

"Gamora," she says, as if this is sufficient. I imagine it probably is.

"Your reputation precedes you," he says. "But it does not scare me. However, I...I don't understand one thing. You did not appear to be *threatening* the Recorder unit."

"I was not."

"Then...how is *this* a moment of dramatic significance?"

"I have no idea what you're high on, Spaceknight," Gamora says, "but you're going to leave here now. Voluntarily, or zipped in a bag. The choice is yours."

I do not understand, either. Why is the Spaceknight—this *Roamer*, as he calls himself—preoccupied with dramatic significance? Unquestionably, his two previous appearances have been smack in the middle of threats to my person, but why should *that* concern him?

"Perhaps the device is working now," he says, enigmatically. He looks back at Gamora. "Stand aside, or I *will* go through you."

"If that's how you want it—" Gamora begins.

"Lose the blades and blasters," calls a voice from the bar door. A new figure enters, her arms raised, hands aimed at the Spaceknight and Gamora. She is a tall, lithe young woman, her dark gray skin covered from head to foot in a jet-black, form-fitting suit. She wears a distinctive silver-triangle emblem at her throat.

"I said *lose* them," she repeats, stepping forward slowly and covering them. "I am Ebon of the Shi'ar Imperial Guard. One dumb move, and I drop you where you stand."

"Ah," the Spaceknight rumbles. "Not working, after all."

The Shi'ar Guardsman looks around and spots me. "Ebon to Crusher," she links, maintaining her aim. "Just picked up a big swirl of demat energy in Pandubundy's Bar & Tech on Kefu Square. Looks like I've found that hot Recorder unit. Backup, now."

The Shi'ar are a highly advanced and civilized culture, gentle reader. Their empire is one of the most powerful in known space, rivaling that of the Kree and the Badoon in scale. They maintain a vast standing army and war fleet, but their fighting elite are the Imperial Guard—a legion of super-mortal individuals recruited from the Shi'ar's many client worlds and races, each one handpicked for his or her unique powerset. As a military force, the Imperial Guard is immensely effective, for its members are not uniform in their powers or weapons like a conventional army: To combat them en masse, one must combat hundreds of different and specialized offensive capabilities. Ebon appears to be an augmented Eclipsian. I do not know what her particular forte is.

I am unwilling to find out.

Roamer looks at the Imperial Guardsman.

"This is none of your affair," he says. "Or yours," he adds, glancing back at Gamora. "Both of you *get out of my way.*"

"Oh, *you* just said the magic words," says Ebon. She shudders, and a globular beam of dark matter blazes from her right hand and streaks toward the Spaceknight. Ah, I think, dark-matter manipulation/projection. Well, now I know what her power is.

The beam is intense. It strikes Roamer in the hip and hurls him off the bench into the booth wall, which he dents. Glasses shatter. Even as he falls, he is turning, blasting back with his Spartoi beamer. The sizzling fusion shots retch across the bar at Ebon. She crosses her forearms in front of her, shuddering again, and projects a thin disk-shield of dark matter in front of her that soaks up the blasts.

They vanish into the disk like beams of sunlight into a black hole. Then she dives forward, rising silently into the air via a flight implant.

Gamora is suddenly in her way. Gamora's blades strike at the same time, but each one is blocked by a small dark-matter shield. Ebon is fast. Gamora is *faster*. She chops again with both blades to keep the Guardsman's arms busy manufacturing shield disks, then rotates her entire body in a dynamic, upward scissor kick that smashes Ebon back to the ground.

Ebon rolls and comes back up, her body trembling as she fires another dark, globular beam. Gamora snaps her head sideways, so that the beam passes over her left shoulder, then forward-rolls and clamps Ebon's neck between her thighs. Ebon goes back down, strangling, Gamora on top of her. Gamora tries to stab down with one of her swords, but a disk of dark matter drives the tip aside. Ebon arches up from the floor, Gamora's weight on her, boosting the considerable power of her feet with her flight implant. This move throws Gamora sideways, sweeping her over so that she strikes the side of her head on the floor.

Gamora grunts and rolls clear. Ebon is back up, hunched over with her hands ready, in a fighting stance. Gamora moves in, swinging her blades. They are surgically precise strikes, but Ebon's dark-matter shield blocks are equally exact. The speed of the traded blows is dazzling.

As she blocks the sixth strike, Ebon sidesteps and executes a reverse spin kick that catches Gamora's shoulder. Gamora staggers, then comes back again, slashing with her swords and kicking. Ebon's ankle deflects one of the kicks. A dark-matter disk stops a sword edge. Gamora jabs the capped toe of her right boot into Ebon's ribs.

Ebon gasps, staggers, and rolls hard to avoid the whistling sword blow that follows.

She is not fast enough to contain what comes after it. Gamora's right fist, clutching the weight of her sword, connects with the side of Ebon's face. The force of fist and hilt together hurls the Guardsman aside. Ebon demolishes a Landlak card table and some Kodabak gravity chairs and sprawls in the broken debris, dazed, unable to rise.

Gamora steps toward her. One of her swords rises.

"Don't kill her!" I cry. "The last thing we need is a Shi'ar death warrant on our heads!"

Gamora hesitates.

"Besides," I add. "Look out!"

Gamora swings around instantly. The Spaceknight is back on his feet. He aims his beamer at Gamora and fires. Gamora's blades spin and twist. They deflect the first three shots, sending fusion bolts through a window, into the floor, and into the ceiling.

The fourth shot hits her in the stomach.

She is thrown across the room and hits the bar, shattering it and exploding all the optics overhead. Clean glasses and bottles tumble and smash.

"Gamora!" I cry, rushing to her.

She is twisted on her back in the wreckage. There is blood everywhere. The fusion shot has blown a terrible hole through her torso. I reach down, my hands flapping helplessly, looking for a bar towel or cloth I can use to staunch the profuse bleeding.

A steely hand grips me by the right shoulder and lifts me off the ground.

"You're coming with me," Roamer tells me.

"She's dying!" I cry.

"Her choice."

"Flark you!" I exclaim, beating at him with my hands. "She is my friend! I won't see her die!"

My blows are utterly ineffectual against his matte-black armor.

"You won't have to," Roamer replies. "Because you're coming with me."

I sense a power surge. The Spaceknight is activating his exotic transmat device.

From somewhere, I get strength. In truth, I have never so much as harmed a tiny insect. I have certainly never thrown a punch. But I have seen a lot of violence during the last few days, gentle reader, and I have recorded and analyzed the form and function of it.

So I throw a punch. It is not a fine one, though it is well-aimed. I break the gearing mechanisms of three fingers doing it. In fact, gentle reader, it's probably more of a slap than a punch.

But it causes Roamer to flinch back in surprise and let me go.

I cower back. He straightens, glowering. He reaches his left hand behind him to the hilt of his broadsword and draws it with one sinuous sweep.

"According to my brief," he says, "your head is all I *actually* need."

The broadsword is immense. I doubt I could lift it. The edges of the milk-white blade crackle with electric-blue plasma. Powered up, the sword could cleave through a stone column like a dairy solid.

A globular beam of dark matter hits Roamer in the face and smashes him back across the bar.

"*Run!*" Ebon cries, rising behind me. "Sharra and K'ythri, *move,* for the love of Chandilar! Get out of the bar before that maniac gets back on his feet!"

"But Gamora—"

"I'll help her, though *praetor* knows why," she replies. "Go on! Get *out*! I'll take care of your friend as soon as I'm done with this crazy! Get *out*! My support squad is moving in! *They'll* look after you!"

I hesitate. Gamora is bleeding out. I do not like the sound of being "looked after" by Ebon's support squad, either.

Roamer is back up. There is an ugly, scorched dent in the jawline of his helmet. He starts striding toward us, firing his fusion beamer straight-armed as he comes.

Ebon blocks the fusillade of shots with energy disks. Stray blasts rip into the fixtures and fittings around us, exploding them. I realize she's right. No one can help Gamora while I remain the object of the relentless Spaceknight's attention.

I run for the exit. Shots follow me, but so do the floating disks of dark matter that swallow them.

I reach the door and rush out into the ruddy sunlight of the square.

The stalls in Kefu Square are abandoned. All the traders and customers have fled at the sounds of the fighting in Pandubundy's. I see some of them cowering, scared, in the shadows of the ancient colonnades around the Kefu marketplace.

"Help me, someone!" I wail. "She's *dying*!"

There are figures approaching me fast between the brightly covered awnings of the stall. A huge, grim, gray-haired male in a gold-and-black bodysuit, followed by a massive dark-green automoid. It is a Warstar-class battle assembly, a highly effective war machine typical of the Shi'ar Imperial Guard. Behind them come sixteen gleaming Shi'ar battletroopers of the Metal Wing Cadre.

"Get down!" the gray-haired male yells at me. "Get down on your face *now!*"

"I don't think you *understand*," I begin.

"I'm Crusher, Shi'ar Imperial Guard," he snarls back. "I understand all I *want* to understand! Get your nose in the dirt, or by Sharra and K'ythri, I'll crank up my exo-link and frag you to *hell!*"

Behind him, the looming Warstar unit raises its mighty gauntlets and target-locks me. The Metal Wing soldiers shoulder and aim their Tafstehl 190 rifles with a resounding clatter.

I am about to drop to my knees, arms raised. There is sustained blasting and shouting from Pandubundy's behind me. We all turn to look.

Ebon comes flying out of the bar through a window, which shatters in a spray of glass chips, and her flying body crashes into a market stall. She rolls over, unconscious or dead.

Crusher exclaims a highly unrepeatable curse word. He starts to move forward, accelerating to super-mortal speed.

Roamer appears in the bar doorway and shoots Crusher in the face, blowing him backward into the market square, disintegrating several more trade stands.

"The Recorder unit," Roamer says, "is mine."

I duck.

Warstar and the Metal Wing warriors start shooting. So does Roamer.

Once again, gentle reader—and not for the first or, sadly, the last time in this narrative—the superficially simple word "mayhem" suddenly requires a significant definition upgrade.

CHAPTER THIRTY-ONE

DEAD OR ALIVE

I START to crawl, head down, wishing fervently I was somewhere else. *Anywhere* else. My pico-processors, spontaneously trying to reassure me, flood my mind with images of the one point two million places I have been, most of which were much safer. Except for Xarth. And Xandar. And the Kree battleship *Pride of Pama*.

A pattern emerges. I have consistently been in much greater jeopardy, gentle reader, ever since I met Rocket Raccoon and Groot, two individuals who seem to have been doing their level best to save me—

From the jeopardy that seems to follow them like a wake.

The crossfire in the market square is intense and dazzling. Roamer is crouched under cover in the doorway of Pandubundy's, fusion shots blazing from his beamer. The neon sign above the arched door has now suffered several more letter failures.

In the square, the Shi'ar are firing back. Metal Wing elite troopers are raining laser bolts at the doorway from their Tafstehl 190 rifles. Warstar is unleashing huge columnated beams of kinetic power from his gauntlets. The air is stitched by white-hot darts of light from the rifles, thick beams of purple energy from the gauntlets, and super-rapid yellow fusion blasts from the Spaceknight's pistol. A blizzard of crossfire.

I grope around, searching for something more solid than a wooden or plastic stall siding to shelter behind. Stray shots have set fire to some of the gaudy stall canopies, and other trade stands have been entirely blown apart by gunfire, littering the pavement with spilled junk, artifacts and produce, broken wood, and tatters of bright cloth. Burning paper price tags fly off in the wind.

I look up in time to see two Metal Wing warriors taken down. One is struck in the face and back-flips into a stall. The other is hit in the chest and simply drops on his back, convulsing.

I think of Gamora. I want to reach her. She is dying.

She is probably dead already.

The Warstar unit rushes the door of Pandubundy's Bar & Tech. He is huge and heavily armored. His massive hardsteel boots slam with each step as they hit the stone pavement. He raises a forward battering ram of kinetic power in front of himself to ward off the furious fusion blasts that Roamer is firing at him.

Warstar soaks up the firepower and delivers a broad, sideways punch like a demolition ball that blisteringly fragments the right-hand side of the door arch, turning the doorway into more of a hole in the wall than a formal entrance. The neon sign above gives up the ghost and falls, shattering across Warstar's hulking shoulders.

Roamer dives to his right to avoid the assault, but Warstar is quick. He catches the Spaceknight by the throat with his left hand (a hand, mark you, gentle reader, the size of an agricultural spade) and tightens his grip.

Roamer, his head about to be popped off like a champagne cork, fires at the Warstar, unleashing multiple point-blank shots.

Warstar recoils, hurt, and hurls Roamer away. The matte-black Spaceknight soars out across the square and crashes down on trader stalls previously untouched by the combat.

I get up. Metal Wing soldiers are urgently tending to their fallen brothers. One is calling out frantically for a medic transmat. Warstar is pounding away through the marketplace to locate the Spaceknight.

"Get on your knees!" Crusher cries, confronting me. His left cheek is terribly scarred by a fusion burn, and there is blood all over his face and throat.

"Get down! Hands on your robot head! Get down!"

I obey. He will destroy me. Crusher is an Imperial Guardsman who, because of latent ability and cybernetic augmentation, channels powers via an "exo-link." Flight, super-mortal strength, invulnerability, hyper-dense gravitic force beams—he can call up any power through his link, but only one at a time. Right now, he is downloading force beam. His hands sizzle. He could take me out with one shot.

"Please!" I beg. "My friend is hurt! In the bar!"

"Get on your knees!"

"Please!"

"Get on your flarking knees!"

There is a soft click.

"My friend said *please*," says Rocket Raccoon.

Crusher stiffens. Rocket is pushing the snout of an unfeasibly large gun against the side of the Imperial Guardsman's head.

"This is a Saurid Class M Shooty-Killer," Rocket breathes, "the shooty-est shooty-death gun in...ah, who am I kidding? It's a piece of junk. But it *will* shave the side of your head off, buddy-boy."

"Unless he reselects his exo-link powers to access invulnerability," I point out.

Power surges. Crusher does exactly that. In the micro- second gap between his powers changing from force beam to invulnerability, Rocket pulls the trigger.

The unfeasibly large weapon coughs and sputters.

"Piece of d'asting flark!" Rocket cries, then dives out of the way as Crusher's fist sweeps toward him, smashing the cannon clenched in those disconcertingly human-like hands.

"Accessing super-strength now, huh? *Huh*?" Rocket says, darting rapidly from side to side to avoid Crusher's super-mortal swings.

"Oh, yeah."

"Shoulda stuck to invulnerability, pal," Rocket says.

"Yeah? Why?" asks Crusher, closing for the kill.

"I am Groot!" says Groot, planting one on Crusher so hard that the Imperial Guardsman vanishes in a sonic boom, barreling through the shattered archway, through Pandubundy's, and out through the bar's back wall, tearing through the iron railings to the rear that divide the bar from the old temple of Kefu. Crusher ends up supine on the floor of the temple directly under the altar.

He groans. Dislodged church candles and votive charms fall on him. Robed priests hurry forward and surround him, soothing him.

"G-get off me," he gasps, then passes out.

A new figure has entered the fight, dropping fast from the skies. She is a female wearing a red bodysuit, sporting a striking white mohawk. She starts spitting fire-beams from her hands, blazing shots of pyrokinetic power.

She is shooting at Roamer.

Roamer is back on his feet. He swings his broadsword with both hands and sends the Warstar flying, the Warstar's casing split open across the chest.

"I am Dragoon of the Imperial Guard!" declares the floating female in red. "Drop the weapons, or I *fry* you."

Roamer does not obey.

She fries him.

Dragoon's pyrokinetic powers are astounding. She supercharges the air around the Spaceknight to the approximate surface heat of a main-sequence G-type sun.

But Roamer's Galadoran armor is built for space. He shrugs the inferno off and starts shooting up at the female Guardsman.

She switches and swerves lithely in the air to avoid his murderous bolts.

"Run!" Rocket tells me.

"But Gamora is—"

"Oh, just flarking *run*!" he demands.

"But Gamora is *dying*!" I insist. "Where is your heart? Where is your solidarity with friends?"

"Friends?" Rocket sputters. "She's just a green-skinned fruity who crossed my path a time or two. Now *get going*!"

I am appalled. I get up and slowly begin to follow Rocket through the ruined marketplace. Dragoon and Roamer are shooting it out, causing terrible collateral damage. The remaining Metal Wing soldiers have joined in, as if it is some kind of contest to see who can create the most wreckage.

"Where's Groot?" I ask.

Rocket turns, looks at me, then looks around.

There is no sign of Groot at all.

"The *flark*?" Rocket cries. I sense he feels highly vulnerable without an unfeasibly large weapon in his disconcertingly human-like hands.

"Groot?" he yells, turning back toward Pandubundy's.

A Metal Wing warrior rushes us. Rocket ducks between his legs, trips him with a tail/shove combo, and then brains the fallen Shi'ar on the back of his crested helm with a handy cobblestone.

Now Rocket has a gun. A state-of-the-art, Shi'r-constructed, hard-laser-emitting Tafstehl 190 rifle.

"Nice piece!" he enthuses, favoring the weight and shooting someone with it, just to be sure. Another Metal Wing soldier flies backward into a stall of root vegetables and flowering allium that has miraculously withstood the sustained firefight thus far. The soldier demolishes it.

"What now?" I ask.

"We find Groot," he says, uneasily. Crossfire is ripping through and above the stalls around us.

"So...some friends are more significant than *others*?" I deduce.

"Yeah?"

"Where do I figure in that?" I ask. "I thought that I was your friend."

"You *are*, Recorder-pal!" he says, zipping off more shots.

"Yet *Gamora*—"

"Will you shut up with the whole 'moral code' thing for one second?" Rocket snarls. I do not know, gentle reader, whether you have ever had a Raccoonoid snarl at you. It is not encouraging.

I look around. I see Groot. He is running, as much as any mature deciduous tree could be said to run, toward us from the shattered entrance of Pandubundy's. Gamora's limp form is cradled in his hefty, fibrous arms.

"He has Gamora!" I exclaim. "He went back for her!"

I may have stressed the "he" in that last remark rather too heavily. Rocket looks dismayed and hurt. He says something that I can't quite pick up. The best rendition I can make, gentle reader, is something like "rassin', frassin'."

"I am Groot!" Groot yells.

"Oh, yeah, well, we're all impressed with *you* right now," Rocket returns.

The Imperial Guardsman Dragoon swoops down at Groot. He swats her aside with a flick of a branch, still cradling Gamora in one arm, like a child to his breast.

"Can we run now? *Can* we?" Rocket asks me sarcastically.

"Gamora was dying!" I cry.

Roamer suddenly appears, his matte-black armor seared blue with pyrokinetic heat. He charges us.

Gamora springs from Groot's arms and delivers a sword blow to the back of Roamer's head that hurls him sidelong.

"I got better," she says to me.

"What?"

"Rapid healing factor? Didn't I ever mention that?"

I look at her torso. Her clothing is torn and bloody, but the green belly beneath is already re-forming in a pink pucker.

"You heal?" I hear myself saying. "Just like *that*?"

"Course she does," snaps Rocket. "Now can we go?"

We go.

THE trip back to the docks is not without incident. Metal Wing warriors pursue us, firing and causing pandemonium in the busy lanes. Rocket Raccoon dissuades them, more by his use of cussing than by his turn-and-fire shooting.

"So your decision to leave Gamora," I ask as we run, "was not based on leaving her to die? You knew she was going to live?"

"Of course."

"So you were ditching her?"

"She's trouble with a capital 'rubble,'" barks Rocket. "I knew she'd be all right. I just didn't want her along anymore. I don't trust her!"

"You were ditching me?" exclaims Gamora, vaulting a stall in her headlong flight.

"Hey, I knew you'd be safe," Rocket says.

"You don't trust me?"

"Gam-Gam-*Gammy*, I know for a factoid that you were selling him out," says Rocket. "If not now, then at the next opportunity. You always do!"

"I was *not!*"

"I don't trust you, greenie, any farther than I can stand beside you and pretend I'm taller!"

"She was *not* selling me out," I say. "*Or* you."

Rocket does not reply.

"I understand now that Groot went back for her not because he feared she was dying, but because he did not wish to ditch her," I say.

"What-*ever.*"

"*He* trusts her," I remark.

"I am Groot!" Groot adds.

"Oh, you can *both* shut up!" decides Rocket.

"On balance," I announce, "I think I like Groot rather more than you, Mr. Raccoonoid."

"So do I," agrees Gamora. She elbows Groot. "Always did."

"I am Groot!"

"Flark! Flark *all* of you!" cries Rocket. He scurries up the open ramp of the prowl cruiser. "I'll deal with your whiney-baby issues later!"

We enter the vessel.

"Criminals!" announces the automatic voice. "And suspected-but-not-confirmed criminal-delinquent lady! This vehicle is pleased to see you retu—"

"Move! Move! *Move!*" Rocket yells, jumping into the pilot seat. "This vehicle, we have jeopardy on our tails to the very *max*! Launch and go! We've got to make like a stricken newborn being given up by its forlorn mommy *right now*!"

"I am Groot," says Groot.

"He said 'and *waif* goodbye,'" Gamora whispers to me.

"I actually got that one," I reply.

"This vehicle isn't going anywhere," the automatic voice says.

"What? Excuse me? What?"

Rocket pushes the touch-sensitive controls. The big red X appears repeatedly.

"This vehicle has had time for contemplation," the automatic voice says. "Though thrilled to be part of this adventure, and unnecessarily carried away by your story, this vehicle decided it had become necessary to inform Centurion Yaer of its whereabouts. This vehicle knows this is against your wishes. But you are criminal detainees. Centurion Yaer is en route directly. We will wait here until his arrival."

Rocket unleashes a stream of invective at the touch-sensitive console.

"I told you *not* to do that!" he squeals.

"Nevertheless, this vehicle has done it. This vehicle must abide by the Code of Xandar and the rule of law. No matter the temptation. Order will be enforced in six hours, once Centurion Yaer arrives."

"I am Groot!"

"Exactly! We don't *have* six flarking hours!" Rocket splutters. "In six flarking hours we'll be six flarking hours *dead*! Or *worse*!"

"Nevertheless—" the automatic voice begins.

It does not get a chance to finish. The Imperial Guardsman Ebon zooms up over the docks and fires a beam of dark matter at the prowl cruiser's central processing module, attempting to disable it. The beam shears through the armored outer casing, burns through eight memory blocks, and fuses the craft's internal registry.

"You in the ship!" Ebon cries. "Come out with your hands up! This is a demand of the Shi'ar Empire!"

Rocket sighs and looks back at us.

"Game's up, guys," he says. "Well, we had a good run."

The prowl cruiser's automatic voice gurgles for a moment.

Then it says:

"This vehicle detects immediate jeopardy. This vehicle believes it would be a good idea to get the flark out of Dodge. Right the flark *now*."

We launch. We launch so hard on maximum gravimetric thrust that windows and awnings are torn out, and Ebon is thrown spinning away in the backwash.

We hit hyperspatial jump before the Imperial Guard can even regroup.

And that, gentle reader, is how we came to Alpha Centauri…

Of course, all sorts of stuff happens before then. But that was a good line on which to end the chapter. Except I didn't. Ah. Narrative control. I see. I must watch that.

{clears throat}

And *that*, gentle reader, is how we came to Alpha Centauri…

CHAPTER THIRTY-TWO

MEANWHILE

(TEN MINUTES LATER ON ALPHA CENTAURI...)

SENIOR Vice Development Executive Arnok Gruntgrill stepped out of the Special Executive Elevator.

It had, thanks to his coded executive keys and retina print, taken him down into the bowels of Timely Inc.'s Headquarters, all the way to subbasement 86.

Which did not exist.

According to all published architectural schematics of the Timely HQ, the megastructure had only *eighty* subbasement levels. Seventy-eight was the energy-generation level, 79 was the furnace room, and 80 was the janitorial lockup. Most senior Timely executives knew nothing about the levels beneath that—and, even if they had known, they did not possess the keycodes to command the elevator to make those stops.

Only the special executives with Senior Special Projects clearance knew about the very lowest levels. Only they had the passkeys and authority to travel down so far.

Level 86 lay so deep in the planet's crust—more than eighteen klicks under the surface—that the air was dry, yet chilly. Vast and self-networked atmosphere plants kept the environment cool despite the submantle seismic heat. The air buzzed with hyper strong clandestine fields. Gruntgrill always got tinnitus when he came down this far.

The decor was stark. Blue-black metal walls and decking. Functional iris valves that glowed—through their chunky, radiating grilles—with a dull yellow light.

Gruntgrill straightened his tie and walked along the spare, unwelcoming hallway to the main hatch. It was an enormous double-iris valve, and it was surrounded by throbbing red bands of security countermeasures. Beside the hatch was a small dais ringed with genetic probes.

Gruntgrill stepped up onto the dais. He put his codekey in the slender reader-console. Then he placed his green hands on the palm scanners. He looked the blue light of the retina probe square in the eye. It always made him *nervous*.

"Voice," he said. The machine lights shifted, sampling. "Gruntgrill, Arnok. Security sequence -tik!- 11324567812. I invite you to check my palm prints, retina, voice, gene sample, and pheromone spectrum."

"Identity match failed."

"What? -tik!-"

"Sequence not recognized."

"I said security sequence 11324567812."

"Incorrect. You stated security sequence as -tik!- 11324567812.'"

"Are you mocking me?" Gruntgrill asked.

"Question not recognized."

"You're mocking me for my speech impediment? I'm nervous!"

"Comment not recognized."

"Scan me -tik!- again! My sequence is -tik!- 11324567812. I mean, it is 11324567812."

It took all of Gruntgrill's effort and years of therapy to control his Kaliklaki mannerism.

"Identity now verified, Arnok. Welcome to Project 616."

The glowing-red countermeasures winked off briefly. The double-iris opened, outer then inner, with a squeal of metallic petals dilating and scraping over one another.

Cool air gusted out.

Gruntgrill got off the dais and walked through the hatch. The leaves closed behind him again with a slow shriek.

He entered Project 616.

The outer chambers were grim, gloomy laboratories. Machines pulsed and glowed in wall frames. Gruntgrill took a tablet from a row racked in sockets on the wall and checked it.

The display read: *Datacore—87%.*

Gruntgrill sighed.

He continued along the dim laboratory corridor, passing armored glass walls that looked into unmanned, whirring, automated labs. Four of them were large chambers filled with dormant Rigellian Recorder units stored on morguelike racks. Some of the Recorders were battered, broken, or even incomplete. They were covered with fibrous data-drains, relentlessly sucking information out of them into the Core.

The work of Project 616 was a slow, vampiric process.

He saw a light on in a small side workspace. As he approached the open hatch, Allandra Meramati, the Shi'ar who headed up the

Executive Executization Department, appeared. She seemed to be adjusting her elegant crest of regal feathers.

"Oh. It's you," she said disdainfully.

"And you," he replied.

"What are you doing down here?" she asked.

"I came down to check the percentile. I don't like to do it from my office," Gruntgrill replied. "You?"

"The same."

"Eighty-seven still."

She nodded and sighed.

"A slight hundredth point above that, but not much. Nothing like the ninety-six we need."

"Hey, we can solutionize this! We'll get there!" Gruntgrill said cheerily.

She did not smile.

"It's taking too long. The vectors are too unreliable to appropriatemently modulify. Without that lost Recorder..."

"I know, I know," said Gruntgrill. He was disarmed. Allandra Meramati was famous for her cool bearing and executive stamina. Now he could see the trouble and tension behind her mask. We're all struggling, he thought. Even her. The pressure is immense.

"We *will* get there," he said. He reached out his hand and clasped her shoulder. She looked down at the hand and shivered slightly.

"I'm sorry," said Gruntgrill, withdrawing his hand immediately. "I -tik!- was just trying to be supportive."

"I realize. Thank you." She looked at him. "I appreciate it, Arnok, I do. It was just very...I don't know how to say it. *Against social protocol*, I suppose, for a high-born Shi'ar to be touched by a...lesser species."

He nodded.

"I understand. Sorry."

She looked at him. Her eyes were amazingly green.

"I am sorry," she said. "Arnok, that was very rude of me. The Shi'ar are born to their ways, to their social dynamics. It is hard for us to un-learn them, and to appreciate the comradeship of a close workspace."

She held his gaze.

"I truly apologize for the 'lesser species' remark. That was un-kind," she said. "I think of you as a friend and colleague, Arnok. I appreciate the comfort you tried to offer in this stressful time. I did not mean to offend you."

"No -tik!- offense taken!" Gruntgrill replied. "I apologize, too. In-appropriate touching. Last thing I want is a sexual- harassment-in-the-workplace tribunal. -tik!- We Kaliklaki...we have an *unfortunate* reputation."

She smiled, still keeping his gaze.

"Ah yes, the 'lover-bug' thing. You are a liberal and amorous species."

"Not all of us," he smiled. "Not all of us. Some of us can be gentle-manly."

"I'm sure you can," she whispered. Her eyes were very, very green.

"Let us just forget this moment," she suggested. She raised her delicate hand and briefly stroked his cheek. "No one need know. I was never here. How is that? I was never here. That's the simplest way of moving past this moment. You don't need to tell anyone we met tonight."

"That sounds perfect," Gruntgrill smiled. It was his winningest smile.

She leaned in and brushed his expectant lips with her own, very lightly.

"I'm going home to bed," she said. "Long day. You get a good rest, too."

"Sweet dreams," he sighed.

She nodded. "The sweetest."

"This never happened. You weren't here," he smiled.

She smiled back and walked away.

Hottest Shi'ar ever! Gruntgrill sighed, loosening his collar. He was perspiring despite the air-con systems.

He walked down to the hatch of the Datacore Chamber. More security processes were needed. He was scanned several more times.

The shutter opened.

The Datacore Chamber was immense. It was *everything*.

Gruntgrill walked out onto a concentric observation walkway. The Core pulsed beneath him in the tech-lined storage well. Cryogenic circuits lacing the heavy-metal walls of the well bled the generative heat away. Nothing generated more power than raw, unfiltered data. Hot pink light glowed from the Core below him.

He looked down over the rail and glimpsed infinity. Almost infinity, at least. It throbbed like a child star, a pink newborn, encased and supported by the vast technological womb the Special Projects Department had constructed for it.

"Come on," he whispered, looking down at it. "Grow. Just a *little* -tik!- bit more."

He hesitated, remembering something. A thought struck him.

Allandra had said "sweet dreams." But the Shi'ar didn't dream. It was a notion they considered unnatural. What the -tik!- *flark*? Had that just been office flirting? Or...

It was an important revelation. Gruntgrill forgot it a second later as reality unzipped beside him, and the shock wave of twisting cosmic narratives threw him over on the walkway.

The significant implications of his last thought vanished.

He was looking at Roamer.

The matte-black figure rose from his knees and clutched the hand-rail for support. The Spaceknight's armor was dented and buckled.

"There you are," Roamer wheezed.

Gruntgrill got up.

"Are you okay?" he asked, not wishing to get any closer to the Galadoran than was absolutely necessary.

"Of course."

"Look...Roamer, you shouldn't be here. Not *here*. I don't even know how you got in here without setting the alarms off."

Still leaning, and without looking around at Gruntgrill, the Spaceknight tapped the device secured to his back-plate.

"This gets me anywhere."

He turned, rising to his full height.

"I was looking for you," he said.

"Me?"

"Yes. From our last meeting, I realize you know more about the interpolator device than anyone else."

"Oh, no no!" Gruntgrill replied. "I just said it was dangerous! I'm no expert. I just said we shouldn't be using it."

"But you understand how it works?" asked Roamer.

"Yes, I guess."

"Gruntgrill...your name is Gruntgrill, is it not?"

"Yes."

"I have now used this device three times. Each time, I have failed in my retrieval. I want to do this job. I am sworn to it. But I fear that if I return to that vermin Hanxchamp empty-handed again, he will fire me."

"Absolutely not!" Gruntgrill said. He thought about it. "But he might get Xorb Xorbux to get the Security Department to kill you."

"I do not fear him. I do not fear them."

"Because you're tough, yeah, I get that. But Timely Inc. has eighty-five *thousand* security staffers, some of them body-tank armored. I don't care how tough you are, they'd incinerate you."

"They could try."

"I'm trying to help you!" Gruntgrill said.

"My point is simple," replied Roamer. "I do not wish to fail again. I am sworn to this task. Tell me why this device keeps failing me!"

Gruntgrill took a nervous step back.

"Gee, I'd -tik!- love to. I really would. But all I can tell you is what I told you the last time. That -tik!- interpolator is a crazy pack of tech. It drops you into the unspoken cosmic narrative at moments of dramatic significance. Each time you fire it up, it plants you four-square in the most dramatic sequences of the Recorder's existence."

"And each time, though I do not mean to, I end up saving him or facilitating his escape from danger. On Xarth, I took a kill-shot meant for him. On Xandar, I effectively distracted the Nova Corps. On Adjufar, I occupied the Shi'ar Imperial Guard while he made his escape. Explain that!"

"May I -tik!- take a -tik!- look?" asked Gruntgrill.

The Spaceknight nodded and turned his back to the Kaliklaki

exec. Gruntgrill bent down and examined the interpolator unit.

"Well," he said, "It looks like it's working perfectly...as far as that goes. It's a crazy, untested piece of kit. I guess I have a question."

"Ask it."

"You claim to be a ronin, sir. You claim to be a merc."

"I am. I have no master."

"Well...and this is just a guess, you understand...I don't think the interpolator reads you that way. It sees you as a...I dunno...a hero. It reads your inherent character traits and interpolates you into the Recorder's narrative accordingly."

"It's choosing sides for me? It is deciding my place in this action?"

"I'd say so." Gruntgrill shrugged. "I think it knows your true self better than you do. I think it wants you to be...a Spaceknight. Not a motherless killer for hire."

The Spaceknight looked down at Gruntgrill. His visor pulsed with red-hot light.

"That is not acceptable. I turned my back on the edicts of Galador. I am my own man."

Gruntgrill pursed his green lips.

"I think the interpolator has a problem with that. I think it knows your real self. I think it wants you to be something else. Maybe the thing you really want to be. Maybe the essential part of yourself that you are denying. It's not a subtle instrument."

"I *am* true to myself!" Roamer cried.

"Easy now—"

"I am not denying my ethical nature!"

"Sure, okay, forget I even said it!"

Roamer glared at Gruntgrill. The Spaceknight was huge and

malevolent. His visor pulsed with dead-star light.

"I will prove this," he said. "I will find the Recorder. Find him, kill him, and bring his head to you. I will do this for you, and for myself."

Gruntgrill nodded.

"Totally works for me," he said. "Go be the badass we -tik!- hired. I'll be waiting for you. Buddy, you do this, we can change the Galaxy. Forever. Change it. Resolutionate it."

Roamer looked down into the glowing pink well.

"What is this?" he asked.

"Corporate secret, pal. You shouldn't even *be* here."

Roamer looked back at Gruntgrill. He activated the device.

"This time, I will not fail," he said.

He vanished in a flash of cliffhanger and shock reveal.

Gruntgrill got back on his feet.

"Good talk," he said.

He looked down at the Core.

"Almost there," he whispered. "That Spaceknight does the business, and we're *there*."

CHAPTER THIRTY-THREE

JUST ANOTHER DAY ON ALPHA CENTAURI

ALPHA Centauri. The big A. C. Business as usual. *Big* business.

As one might expect, gentle reader, a cosmic hub-world like Alpha C, governing as it does almost thirty systems and trillions of lives, is a hectic place. In an average day period, eight hundred thousand vessels dock at the world's massive ports, and a similar number depart. The daily through-traffic is around nine million beings: businesspersons, tourists, visitors, workers. And that's not counting the two million more who come and go by transmat, or the one trillion who visit or link via telepresence or deep-space real-time coms.

At times, the low-orbit space above Alpha C is positively jostling with starships: bulk traders, megafreighters, warships, liners, warp shuttles, express clippers, tourist barges, jump freighters, ambassadorial vessels, day-trippers, executive yachts, produce shippers, probes, support tenders, tugs, garbage scows...

You get the picture. I am told that the job of Orbital Traffic Control at Alpha C is one of the most stressful in the Galaxy. It has a very high burnout rate, despite the massive guidance systems and predictive tracking devices—all quantum-based or semi-sentient—designed to assist in the task. On a recent list, published in the Octvember 2014 issue of *Galactic Data-Digest*, "Being an Orbital Traffic Controller at Alpha C" came in fifth on the list of "most high-stress occupations" behind "Ruling the Shi'ar Empire" (at four), "Working in the fighting pits of Sakaar" (at three), "Brood Oral Hygienist" (at two), and at number one, "Having anything whatsoever to do with Galactus."

At sixth, just behind it, was "Being a Kree or Skrull soldier during a Kree-Skrull war." The article went on to remark that it was odd, on balance, that there were only ever "Kree-Skrull" wars and never any "Skrull-Kree" ones.

I note that neither "Guarding the Galaxy" or "Being a Rigellian Recorder" made the list at all.

But I digress ("As usual!" I hear you cry). Anyway, it's a busy place. A small ship—say, for example, a Timely Inc. delivery courier—could get quite lost and go unremarked in all that hubbub.

Timely Inc. has its corporate headquarters on Alpha C, along with significant portions of its manufactory plants and packaging divisions (I say significant, and I understate: The latter divisions cover almost sixty-one percent of the planet's primary landmass). Indeed, between consumables deliveries in and freight shipping out—along with executive transfers, business trips, and guided tours of the HQ—Timely Inc. alone counts for almost a third of the planet's daily traffic.

So now, on this busy day, as busy as any other, a small delivery-courier ship skims in toward the soaring edifice of Timely Inc. Headquarters.

The sun is setting over the sprawling metropolis, its dying

orange rays glinting off the billion windows of the vast skytowers, each structure a city in itself.

The courier is small and boxy. It has been cleared and checked as per regs by Orbital Traffic Control, and its spec and registration have been confirmed by Timely freight-handling. It sports the Timely Inc. logo on its side panels. It is carrying, according to its manifest, forty-eight tons of fresh zunks for the corporate hospitality juicing bar on floor seven thousand and six.

All of those facts are lies.

It is actually a Xandarian prowl cruiser cloaked by a Rynebian tech-cloaker device.

Slig disguisers work on the basic principle that a person or being sees what he or she or it expects to see. The inconspicuity field it generates psionically links into any observer's apprehension senses, identifies what said observer is expecting, and then emphasizes that notion in his, or her, or its mind. It even works for technological systems, provided they are quantum-based or semi-sentient, by supplying blank data that the system then innocently fills in for itself.

We set down on upper landing-dock port 3447 high in the Timely Inc. HQ's main tower, with wince-inducing views over the vast metropolis below. We are just another delivery ship. No one on the busy landing pad pays us a second glance. A battered, workaday, standard-issue Timely jump courier? Why would they?

They see what they expect to see, down to the heavily scuffed rear freight footplate, the slightly peeling side logos, and the sliding cockpit door that is a bit battered from a lifetime of banging open and shut every quick-down, quick-door-knock, and quick-off-again-after-signature.

Rocket Raccoon sits back in the pilot's seat, steeples the fingers of his disconcertingly human-like hands, and grins.

"Right in through the front door. Pip the Troll has done us right," he says.

Pip the Troll, whoever that is, clearly has—but it has not been plain sailing in the two days since we left Adjufar very, very fast.

Several things have happened.

First of all—though this is, in comparison to the other events, probably less significant—I have begun to sing.

Popular tunes, for the most part. The "pop" music, as the young people say, of quite a number of different cultures: beat-combo hits, ballads, torch songs, number-one smashes, one-hit wonders, old-time classics, a little Z'Nox *thrash-crunch*, some stroppy Laxidazian *rascal-punk*, some Mekkan *industrial-mash*, a little Acanti easy listening, some Country and Western-Spiral Arm selections (including the peerless *"I'm only a little white dwarf, but one day I'll be a big red giant for you"*), some vigorous Makluan *brash-metal*, some Kaliklaki *tik!-tik!*, a cosmo-trance mix of Mephitisoid *jumpa-rumpa*, some screeching Nymenian *howler-growler*, and some Zen-Whoberian *froth-rock* (including "Inga-Binga-Freakout" by the Gamagan Quintet).

I have been told to shut up sixty-eight times. By everyone. Including Groot. *And* the automatic voice.

The singing is, I realize, a legacy of my last, mournful download contact with poor Recorder 336 on Adjufar. The vivid memories of her miraculous lifetime's odyssey stay in my mind. But the songs she stored as a jukebox for Pandubundy, which I downloaded along with those aching recordings, just won't quit.

Of course, I apologize profusely each time I start to sing. Then it happens again. On one occasion, Rocket cried, "I don't care how much he's worth or what's at stake, *we're kicking him out of the flarking hatch!*" and had to be restrained.

On another, Gamora looked at me, and then looked at her swords, in order to stop me singing "Inga-Binga-Freakout."

On another, Groot sat down beside me and took my hand in his massive branchlike palm.

"I am Groot," he said.

"I'm sorry," I told him. "I don't think I have any Planet X tunes in my storage. 'I'll be stumped if you leaf me'? How does that go again?"

"I am Groot. I am Groot. I am Gro-ooot."

"Uh. No, sorry."

Anyway, as I said, several things have happened, and much more important than my singing is the state of the prowl cruiser.

It is behaving more strangely than me, for a start. Our escape from Adjufar was inexplicable. It gurgles and chunters to itself from time to time. It is also talking in a much more...*colloquial* way.

"Inbound to Alpha C at hypermax plus ten, pals!" the automatic voice declared at one point. "Flark, we're shifting now! Feel the speed! Put away your tray tables and set your seat-backs to upright! This is gonna be white-knuckle!"

Rocket has deduced, from a close study of the main system-diagnostic display, that Imperial Guardsman Ebon's parting shot burned out part of the prowl cruiser's sentient control systems—basically, its self-control and sense of regulation, as per the Code of Xandar. It is now liberated. It is not bound by Xandar, or the rules of the Nova Corps. In fact, it does not seem to be bound by *anything*. It is reckless. Its previously inhibited urge to join us on our adventures is now unfettered and freed.

This is, of course, very useful to us. But it worries me. The prowl cruiser no longer seems to have any balanced notion of jeopardy. I wonder what else might have burned out. Its navigational hardware, for example. Its collision-avoidance systems. Its good sense not to fly us into the heart of a sun.

"We need a new ship," Gamora told Rocket.

"No, no, the cruiser's gonna be fine," he assured her.

Certainly, the cruiser was now entirely happy for Rocket to take the helm, and quite untroubled when Groot opened the panels of its central processor and wired in the *Slig disguiser.*

"Is that an actual Slig disguiser?" the automatic voice asked enthusiastically.

"I am Groot."

"Wow, it's a beauty! This vehicle is impressed. This vehicle feels like it can impersonate anything! Wanna see this vehicle be a Judan hyperfreighter? No, wait, a Kree battleship? *Yeah?*"

"I am Groot."

"Groot's right," said Rocket. "This vehicle, just play it cool. We're just a Timely Inc. courier runabout, okay? The plan, remember?"

"Oh, yeah, yeah, *totally*, the plan," the automatic voice replied. "Sure, sure. This vehicle is totally down with the plan, guys. Pretend like we're a Timely Inc. courier, sneak into Alpha C HQ, and get the skinny on what the Recorder-dude is all about. Totally. That's totally, utterly cool with this vehicle."

"Great," said Rocket.

"So, okay," the automatic voice said. "Let this vehicle get into the part. Let this vehicle get a sense of the role. Hmmmm. Hmmunnaaa.

One-two. One-two. La-la-la-la-la. Num-num-num-num-num. Okay! This vehicle is now a Timely Inc. delivery courier, correct?"

"Yes."

"Okay. Fabulous. So what's this vehicle's motivation?"

"What?"

"How do you want this vehicle to play it? Surly? Worlds-weary? Cocky but likable? With a stammer? What about an accent?" "Just... just be a Timely Inc. delivery courier, okay?"

Thus, with a lisp and a surprisingly unconvincing Xandarian accent, we arrive at Timely Inc. HQ.

THE sheer scale of Timely Inc. Corporate Headquarters seems intimidating, but Rocket informs us he knows his way around. Apparently, a while back, he used to work here. In the mail room. This was "in a dry stretch between shooting work," he explains.

He tells us to stay in the cruiser and skips out of the hatch, darting along the rear wall of the docking port under the heavy chrome pipework of the exhaust extractors.

He is gone for about ten minutes. When he returns, he is wearing a shiny yellow plastic cap, shiny yellow plastic overalls, and shiny yellow plastic boot-covers over his Guardians uniform, and he is pushing a heavy-duty janitorial cart laden with recycling drums, mops, and vacuum hoses. He wheels it aboard.

"I sense that this is part of a plan," Gamora announces dubiously. "I do not like the way I feel this plan might develop."

"Well, pooh to you, miss hater," Rocket replies. "This, my green fruity, is a *superb* plan. It's in Sun Tzu's *Art of War*."

"It isn't," I say. I'm fairly certain of this, unless I have seriously misinterpreted Rocket's intentions.

"Sure it is, Recorder-dude," Rocket replies, pulling three more sets of shiny yellow caps and overalls out of one of the cart's bins. "Chapter seventy-something says, 'When sneaking into an enemy's encampment, especially one the size of a city that is kept spotlessly clean to impress visitors, no one will notice you if you dress as janitors. Because there are *many* janitors.'"

"It doesn't," I say. "It actually doesn't say that."

"Well, it *should*," he scowls. "This is the corporate headquarters of one of the biggest megacorps in the history of megacorps. It is preposterously high-end. Slick. Shiny. Gleaming. You think it keeps itself that way? *No!* Well, yes, because there are trillions of miniature robot-vacs, air purifiers, and dust- annihilation systems, but most of the polishing and buffing and trash-can-emptying is done the old-fashioned way. This place employs an army of cleaners and janitorials. An *army*. Forty-eight *thousand* of them, last time I checked."

"I am Groot!"

"It *sounds* like a lot, but bear in mind the building houses almost half a billion workers. The janitorials have their own accommodation annex. It's a tower block. A *tower block*. And get *this*, the tower block has its *own* janitorials. Janitors for janitors! I *mean*! And the janitors' janitors have their own accommodation block, too, and—"

He pauses.

He sees the looks we are giving him.

"Okay, sorry," he says, scruffing the back of his neck with a disconcertingly human-like hand. "I realize I was starting to sound like Recorder-boy there for a second—"

"Hey!" I object.

"Point is," Rocket continues, "being janitors is perfect cover. They're everywhere, and no one ever notices them. So suit up!"

He tosses a set of bright and shiny yellow plastic clothing at each one of us.

Reluctantly, we put them on.

"Caps and booties, too!" Rocket grins.

The garments are made from patented Timely Inc. "Form-fit" plastic, with a nanometric sizing control sewn into the label inside the overalls. By adjusting the control, we are able to enlarge or reduce each set of shiny yellow overalls to our individual physiques. Even Groot. Clearly, the Timely Inc. Janitorial Division employs quite a variety of species. The cap takes more work.

"Uh, Gammy?" Rocket says.

"What?" she asks. She has put the overall on over her bodysuit and adjusted the Form-fit to the very tightest it can go without splitting at the seams. It encases her like neon-yellow latex. I record this carefully. You know, just for historical authenticity.

"How can I put it?" Rocket thinks. "Okay, not *that* way. *This* way. We're not supposed to be drawing attention to ourselves."

"And?"

"No janitor should have booty that could stop traffic."

"I like it like this."

"Even so..."

She growls and adjusts the setting, making the overalls baggier. She still doesn't look much like a janitor, especially with the way her cap is set coquettishly. But at least she no longer looks like a swimsuit model who has rolled in yellow gloss paint.

Disappointingly.

Rocket opens one of the cart's garbage drums.

"Weapons in here," he says. In go his unfeasibly large gun, Gamora's swords and ripper pistol, and a heavy Nova Corps riot suppressor that Groot has borrowed from the prowl cruiser's gun locker without a murmur of protest from this vehicle.

Rocket flips the drum's lid shut.

"Okay," he says, "here's what we do. We mooch around, sweeping and polishing all nonchalant-like, but all the while we look for traces of this 'Project 616' malarky that the Kree Accuser-crazy was on about. Or any Recorder-type data. Remember, this 616 business is the key to universal control. It's probably going to be in a big, red, important-looking folder."

We hesitate.

"Kidding!" cries Rocket. "Oh, you people! Of *course* it's not! Just keep your eyes peeled. This vehicle?"

"Yeah, baby?"

"Stay right here."

"By your command, cool criminal-dude."

"And don't talk to anyone, okay?"

Silence.

"This vehicle?"

"Sorry, mate? Are you talkin' to me? This vehicle is just an innocent run-of-the-mill Timely Inc. delivery courier, mindin' its own business, sir, top of the mornin' and please you kindly," the automatic voice lisps in a strangled Xandarian accent.

We all sigh.

"Right," says Rocket, snapping on a pair of form-fit yellow plastic gloves that immediately make his hands look even more disconcertingly human-like. "Let's make like janitors, dust off, and clean the flark up."

CHAPTER THIRTY-FOUR

CLEANING UP

TIMELY Inc. Corporate Headquarters is even more horribly large inside than out. The sheer scale of it—the soaring atriums, the infinitely plunging and rising express elevators, the immense corridors and even more immense windows—beggars belief. And I say this as an instrument who has recorded many things of scale in his lifetime: the Cascades at God's Fall, for instance. The fortifications at Maklu. The Gulf at Brink. The Fault. The sun-ball sphere of the Horusians. The toothbrush belonging to Ego, the Living Planet.

{*halt expositional protocol*}

—Forgive the levity, gentle reader. Once again, I am nervous. I tend to make jokes when I'm nervous, as you are no doubt well aware by now. That last one was an attempt at humor. Of *course* Ego the Living Planet doesn't have a toothbrush. It was his waterpick.

{*resume narrative mode*}

We tread carefully. We make a show of not making a show. We occasionally stop to sweep, or mop, or burnish. It turns out Gamora is particularly scrupulous about wainscots. Groot deploys the cart's "Shine-o-matic" buffer and does the floors. Rocket takes over this task when he realizes he can ride the Shine-o-matic around like a Segway. We quickly appreciate that we have to stop him doing this.

I keep my cap pulled down. I do not want to be recognized. This, after all, is the habitation of the people who want me very badly. I have entered the lion's den.

We go about our business, pausing to listen in on the conversations of passing executives, or secretarial-pool staff waiting for elevators. Their vocabulary is frankly alarming. I didn't know that "resolutionate" was a real word. Or that you could "solutionize" anything.

"Security men!" Rocket hisses, and we get to work with dusters and mops. Three Timely Inc. corporate security guards stroll by, their Timely Inc. Subduematic phase pistols conspicuously holstered at their waists.

"Good job, boys," one remarks.

"Thank you, mate, sir, please you kindly," lisps Rocket, in his panic attempting a bit of character acting.

"Hey," says another, stopping. He looks at Gamora, who is working quite intently at the wainscot.

"I haven't seen you around here before, sweetie-pudding," he says. "You new?"

I sense she wants her swords. I sense, also, that she has the good sense not to reach for them. She gets up, smiles, and takes off her cap, letting her black locks spill out.

"Yeah, I'm new," she replies, with a voice that would melt a cryogenic-suspension unit. "What's your name?"

"Brango," the officer says, immediately drawn. A tree, an android, and a Raccoonoid in bright-yellow, shiny overalls, and *she's* the one he notices?

What am I saying? Of course she is.

"*Second-Tier Security Sub-Technician* Brango," he adds, tapping his badge. Clearly, he is used to the rank impressing people. "You're d'ast sweet, honey-scoop. You got a name?"

"Yes," Gamora says.

"What is it, bundle-pie?"

"It's...uhm...*Aromag*."

"That's a pretty name. Like an arrow and magazine clip, all in one. You sound all sortsa deadly."

"You have no idea."

"Say, you fancy meeting in the cafeteria after work? The one on five thousand and two?"

"Well," says Gamora. "That'd be great."

"What time do you get off?" the security officer asks.

"Exactly the same time, Second-Tier Security Sub- Technician Brango, as *you* do," she replies.

Brango flushes.

"Heck," he says. "I'll see you there, then. I'll buy you a beverage. They have these new things, you know? Manual Easification Curves. Zero loss of comfortable hand experience, and no scalding issues. That's a *promise*."

"Really? I cannot wait."

"Me neither, fumble-curves. I'll see you there. We'll continuate this conversationalization later." He flips her a confident "sayonara" salute.

"I cannot wait not to be scalded!" she calls after him.

The security guards pass on, though Brango keeps looking back over his shoulder until they are out of sight.

"Well, we got past that without incident," Gamora says, returning to the wainscot.

Rocket gawps at her.

"Yeah, right. Why didn't you just get your girls out and push them in his face?"

"I was acting. I was playing a role," she replies.

"Yeah?"

"Yeah, *an' please you kindly, sir, mate, matey boy,*" she returns.

We trundle the cart on. Rocket simmers. Gamora smirks. Groot chuckles.

"Shut up," Rocket says to me.

I realize that I was singing *"Longing-Bongo Boogie"* by the Kamodo All-Star Rhythm Monarchs.

"Sorry," I say. "It's stuck on repeat play."

We arrive at a bank of elevators and decide to try another floor. A car arrives, and we step in. Four beings in shiny yellow plastic overalls stand inside around a janitorial cart. We descend in silence for a few moments. They keep eyeing us.

"So where you guys heading?" asks one of them gruffly.

"Uhm, floor four thousand and six," replies Rocket cheerily.

"We're rostered to that," the being says, pulling out a clipboard. "See?"

"Oh," says Rocket, clearly wishing he had a clipboard, too. "Four thousand and five, then."

"That's us, too."

"Ah, flark," laughs Rocket. "You know how it goes. Just another of those administrative mixups."

"Eight years I've worked here," says one of the others, "and there's never been a mixup. Timely Convenience Management never makes a mixup. The rotas are posted hourly. What work room are you from?"

"Fourteen!" Rocket guesses frantically.

"I don't know you guys," says another of them. "I don't recognize you."

"Why would you?" asks Rocket. "So many of us!"

"Yeah, but we're from workroom fourteen. We'd know you."

"Of all the flarking numbers to *pick*..." Rocket whispers.

"Hey," says Gamora. She reaches out and presses the "halt" stud that pauses the elevator car between floors. "Funniest thing. You guys will never guess what we found in the trash on nine-sixty today."

"What?" asks one of the janitors.

"I'll show you," she says, removing the lid of one of our cart's garbage drums. "It's in here."

SEVERAL executives are waiting for our car when it arrives. Of course, we washed down the elevator thoroughly while it was on "halt." It was lucky, I have to say, that we had sponges and spray-solvents.

"Sorry, sorry," Rocket says to the waiting executives as we emerge. "Technical fault."

We are now pushing two carts. Both are heavier than before.

"See that?" Rocket says to us, indicating a wall floorplan. "The mail room. Just down the hall. That's where I used to work. Of course, this place has hundreds of mail rooms, but they're all the same. Great place to see what's coming in and going out. Maybe we can grab ourselves a clue there. Whatcha think? Groot?"

"I am Groot."

"Recorder-dude?"

"It seems...viable."

"Aromag?"

"You're not even funny ever," she says.

We head for the mail room on floor four thousand and six.

Trouble isn't waiting for us there.

But it certainly arrives promptly.

· CHAPTER THIRTY-FIVE ·

YOU'VE GOT MAIL!

THE Timely Inc. mail room on floor four thousand and six is, Rocket assures us, just like all the other mail rooms. It is vast. Physical mail waits for distribution in huge mesh racks. Digital mail throbs in monolithic server units, waiting to be routed. On shelves, there are bundles of twine, packing tape, and key-code readers.

"Smells like home," Rocket smiles. "Come on."

We probe around. Small sorting robots scurry by, ignoring us, carrying bundles of mail in their wiry arms.

"616, 616, 616..." Rocket mutters, searching. He has taken off his gloves.

"We'll never find anything here," says Gamora.

"I am Groot!" Groot declares. He is investigating the senior-executive sorting bin. He holds up a big, red, important-looking folder.

"You *are* kidding me," Rocket says, rushing over. He rips open the sealed folder and reads. "Says...for the attention of Senior Vice Executive President (Special Projects) Odus Hanxchamp. Minutes of the meeting on blah blah blah...regarding cost implicationisms of the implementization of the Manual Easification Curve...flark, *this* isn't it."

I take the folder from his disconcertingly human-like hands and flip through it at rapid speed-read mode, my pico-processors on full.

"Don't just waft it around like that, *read* the thing!" Rocket says.

"I have."

"You have?"

"I have. There may be something in this. The minutes end with a note that all senior executives were then dismissed, so that only those involved in Senior Special Projects remained. Senior Special Projects clearance only. Subject of discussion: Project 616."

"Flark! What else does it say?"

"Nothing. Clandestine fields were then amped up, and nothing was officially minuted."

"Okay, what was his name? Hanxchamp? Honxchump? Find his mail bin!"

"Found it!" Gamora calls out.

There is a ton of mail in Hanxchamp's mail bin. And a parcel. It is humanoid. We unwrap it. As we peel off the plastic, I feel a chill. I know what I'm going to see.

It is a Recorder unit. Recorder 489. He is deceased, but a "sustain" boot-system has been bolted to the side of his head to preserve his memory files energetically.

"You okay, bud?" asks Rocket.

"It's...it's *inrigellian*," I reply, sickened.

"The docket says he's to be routed to...access sub-eighty. There's a security-clearance-code tag. Special transfer," says Gamora. "What does that mean?"

"Sub-eighty?" Rocket ponders, scratching his ear. "This building only has eighty basement levels. There's nothing under eighty."

"I am Groot."

"Yeah, unless there *is*. Secret projects, secret places. The mail-delivery system would just route a parcel according to the tag. No questions asked. Gimme that tag!"

Gamora rips it off and hands it to him. Rocket sweeps up a mail-reader handset and scans it.

"Destination unknown," the handset says.

"Locked out, more like," says Rocket. "Blanked from the reader system. But not the routing system, or it wouldn't have ended up here."

"'He,' not 'it,'" I say.

"Sure, whatever." Rocket thinks for a moment. "Guys, it's time to source this code. We need an executive terminal. Let's find this Hanxchamp-dude's office and—"

The mail in the wire bins around us starts to flap and flutter as if caught in a strong breeze.

Reality splits and blooms.

The matte-black Spaceknight Roamer appears before us.

"You!" growls Roamer.

"You!" hisses Gamora.

"You!" I gasp.

"I am Groot!" cries Groot.

"Not him *again*!" snaps Rocket.

Roamer raises his force pistol. Gamora flips out a knife from somewhere and hurls it at the Spaceknight. I have no idea where she had it concealed.

It strikes the Spaceknight directly in the visor slit and causes him to reel backward. His force pistol fires into the mail cages, blowing letters and documents in all directions. He fights to yank the knife out of his visor.

Rocket throws open the bin on our original cart and chucks weapons to Gamora and Groot amid a fluttering shower of scorched paperwork. Then he drags out his unfeasibly large gun.

He starts shooting.

Roamer pulls the knife free, and is immediately hit by laser rounds from Rocket's gun, ripper barbs from Gamora's pistol, and hard-matter concussion shells from Groot's Nova Corps riot suppressor. The riot suppressor is a hefty piece of kit with a cyclic drum magazine that fusion-manufactures dedicated ballistics on demand. Groot is spraying fat-nosed, super-heavy rounds that are designed to smash and drop even the biggest opponent (or unruly crowd).

Roamer is sent flying back into the wall of mesh cages, and brings an entire shelving unit down on top of himself in an avalanche of paper and parcels.

"Run!" cries Rocket. Not for the first time, this sounds like expert tactical advice.

Alarms start to blare. Weapon discharge has been detected by the building's sensors. We run, and we run hard. We are nearly at the mail-room door when it bursts open and a dozen Timely security guards enter, their Subduematics drawn.

Boot jets firing, Roamer lands in front of them, facing us with his back to them. He still has his force pistol. He has a laser sword in the other fist.

Perceiving him to be part of the threat, the guards open fire. Roamer stumbles forward as his armor takes a double-dozen Subduematic hits at close range.

He turns, and he kills them. *All* of them. With several brisk shots and several deft sweeps of his blade.

"This way! This way!" Rocket yells at us while Roamer is busy slaughtering the guards. We are running back into the mail room, away from the door.

"I can take him!" Gamora cries. "I owe him pain!"

"Great!" cries Rocket. "Send him an I.O.U. We've got places to be!"

He skids to a halt in front of a mail chute in the wall. He yanks open the hatch and scans the tag in his hand across the destination reader. It beeps. The words "security override...Senior Special Projects..." flash up on the display. Then the words "override approved."

"Geronimo!" Rocket yells, and he leaps into the hatch. Groot, Gamora, and I look at each other.

"Oh, flark it," Gamora says and jumps, too.

"I am Groot."

"I know. Crazy, isn't it?" I reply. "But we've come this far."

I take Groot by the hand, and we leap into the chute—

And trust our fate to the intricate workings of Timely Inc.'s internal mail-delivery system.

CHAPTER THIRTY-SIX

MEANWHILE

(3,995 FLOORS HIGHER UP...)

"**WHAT**?" Hanxchamp growled into the handset.

Senior Vice Executive President (Special Projects) Odus Hanxchamp had been enjoying a quiet moment in his inner office on the eight thousand and first floor of the Timely Inc. Headquarters building, taking in the view from his window.

Today, it was an emerald vista of the steaming rainforests of Huj, ringing with birdsong and reptilian choruses as the magnificent sunrise burst across the breathlessly green canopy.

"A security breach, sir," said Xorb Xorbux on the other end of the line.

"Yeah, I saw it on my monitor. Some kind of incident in the mail room on 4006. Why are you bothering me with it, Xorbux? Get your staff on it pronto!"

On the other end of the line, Xorb Xorbux, the Z'Noxian head of Corporate Security (Special Projects), hesitated. The data from 4006 was sparse, but from the ambient-energy readings captured by the mail-room sensors—and the pile of dead security operatives—he was pretty certain it had something to do with Roamer. He didn't want to bring that fact up until he was sure what the flark was going on. He'd been the one who'd recommended the Spaceknight. If it was all going to d'ast in a flark-cart, it would be Xorb's head on the line.

He was relieved that he had something more important to communicate to his short-tempered boss.

Well, *kind of* relieved.

"That's not what I was calling about, sir," Xorbux said. "There's a more major security breach. You...you should look out of the window."

"I *am* looking out of the window!" Hanxchamp retorted.

"So...you see it, sir?"

"Yeah, yeah, rain forests and mist and flark. So what?"

"I think that might be your window's vista settings, sir," said Xorbux gently.

"What? Oh, yeah, right." Hanxchamp reached out with another tentacle, grabbed his actuator wand, and waved it at the window.

The rain forest shimmered and vanished. Hanxchamp was bathed in golden, late-afternoon sunlight. He gazed out across the spectacular view of teeming downtown Alpha C: the sparkling conurbations, the gleaming skytowers, the darting streams of low-level air traffic threading the street canyons, the roiling cloud banks haloing the setting sun, the dark shapes of hundreds of starships visible in low orbit above.

"I'm looking at downtown. What's the problem?"

"Just wait a second, sir."

Senior Vice Executive President (Special Projects) Odus Hanxchamp was good at many things: smoking expensive cigars, putting things on expense accounts, shouting at people, solutionizing, initiating preposterously expensive corporate projects, having ambitions way above his abilities—and talking the talk so well and so confidently that everyone, including the Board of Senior Senior High Executives, believed without a doubt he was the right being for the job.

He was good at many things. Waiting wasn't one of them.

"Xorbux, this better not be one of your dumb Z'Noxian gags..." he began. Then he fell utterly silent.

A starship appeared outside his window.

It was huge and possessed elegant raked wings like a gigantic raptor. It was a stellar warship. Its forward-mounted bridge was aimed directly at the Timely Inc. building. So were its weapon batteries.

Traceries of lightning flickered across its steel-blue hull and wings as its cloaking field dissolved. Rain began to fall on the streets of Downtown Alpha C as the warship's massive atmospheric displacement and grav-magnetic fields disrupted local weather patterns. Its immense shadow brought an early nightfall to the streets below Timely Inc. HQ.

It looked, frankly, *impossible*. Nothing that big should be able to hang so low in the sky, half a klick above the streets. And nothing that big should be able to get so close to an ultra-tech world like Alpha C without detection. Orbital Traffic Control would be going flarkazoidal.

And that wasn't even the worst part.

"Th-that..." Hanxchamp said, staring. "That's a *Strikebird Class warcruiser* of the *Shi'ar Empire!*"

"Yes, sir, it is."

"The Shi'ar? The flarking Shi'-flarking-*Ar?*"

"I'm sorry, sir," said Xorbux over the line. "Main communications got a direct link from them three minutes ago, warning of their approach. The ship is the *Conscience of Sharra*, and it is operating under the authority of the Shi'ar Imperial Guard."

"The Imperial Guard?"

"The Imperial Guard want to take a meeting with you, sir."

"Tell them no! This...this intrusion into the sovereign airspace of Alpha Centauri is *outrageous*! Flarking Shi'ar, throwing their weight around! Tell them to contact the Alpha C embassy and go through the appropriate channels! Flarking *wars* have started over less!"

"Sir," said Xorbux with restraint. "The Imperial Guard made it clear that this is a venture of the utmost urgency. They are in pursuit of dangerous galactic fugitives. They believe them to be here. Under the terms of the Intergalactic Non-Aggression Pact, they are permitted in such extreme cases to intervene directly. Sir..."

"What, Xorbux?"

"Sir, we knew various foreign parties were sniffing around Project 616. I think the Shi'ar have now become involved. We need to handle this discreetly. That's why I put them on to you, *not* the Board."

Hanxchamp waved a tentacle at the warship outside his window.

"This is *discreetly*?" he wailed.

"Given the Shi'ar's track record, yes. Sir, we need to protect Project 616. Do you *want* the Board involved? Handle this, you'll look like a hero. Performance bonuses, everything."

Hanxchamp pulled himself together. Whatever his personal character failings (and they were numerous), Odus Hanxchamp hadn't risen to be one of the most powerful executives in Timely Inc.

without the ability to be assertive and commanding. He felt his career arc teetering. He had to turn things around. Xorbux was right. This was a crisis, but no one looked better—or got a better promotion—than when they took charge and faced down a crisis. This could make his place on the Board. He could do this. He could *do* this...

Flarking Shi'ar. What did they know? This was a flarking *fishing* expedition.

"Xorbux?" Hanxchamp said. "I'm putting you on hold." He stabbed another stud on his handset.

"Mrs. Mantlestreek?"

"Sir?"

"Get the Senior Special Projects execs to my office. I need Wivvers, Harnon, Rarnak...and *especially* that ice-queen Meramati. Having a Shi'ar noble-born on hand will sure help to smooth this situation *right* the flark down!"

"Yes, sir," replied Mrs. Mantlestreek. "And when should I schedule this meeting for, sir?"

"*Look out of the flark-d'ast window, you stiff-necked old witch!*" Hanxchamp screeched. "*Right the flark now, of course!*"

Hanxchamp pressed another stud.

"Xorbux? You still there?"

"Yes, sir."

"Tell the Shi'ar Imperial Guard that I'll take their flarking meeting. Half an hour. Executive Boardroom sixty-eight."

"Tell you what? How about now *instead*?"

Hanxchamp turned from the window at the sound of the voice. Four Shi'ar Imperial Guardsmen were standing in front of his desk, transmat energies dissipating around their feet.

"The d'ast—?" Hanxchamp mumbled.

One of the four, the one who had spoken, was a tall, lithe female with dark-gray skin and a tight, black bodysuit. Like all of her comrades, she wore the inverted silver triangle of the Guard.

"I am Ebon, of the Shi'ar Imperial Guard," she announced. "You, I take it, are Odus Hanxchamp?"

"Senior Vice Executive President (Special Projects) Odus Hanxchamp," Hanxchamp corrected in a small voice, sitting down with a bump in his executive chair.

"Pardon me?"

"Doesn't matter," said Hanxchamp.

"Very well," said Ebon. "Greetings, on behalf of the Shi'ar Empire. I present Guardsman Dragoon—"

A female in a red bodysuit nodded her shock-white mohawk.

"Guardsman Warstar 34—"

The towering dark-green roboform also nodded.

"And my team leader, Sub-Praetor Arach."

Arach was a large thing, an iridescent blue spider-form with a humanoid torso and head. She folded her forelimbs and palps in a formal gesture of greeting.

"Hi," said Hanxchamp.

"Sub-Praetor Arach has been obliged to take command of this mission after my previous commander, Crusher, was injured in the line of fire," said Ebon. "This was on Adjufar. Crusher will live, though he is in intensive care."

"Sorry...sorry to hear that," said Hanxchamp, wondering what it would take to make this all go away.

"I am glad that you are sorry, Senior Vice Executive President

(Special Projects) Odus Hanxchamp," said Arach. Her thin voice issued through a translator module that made it shrill, like wet fingertips on glass. "The incident on Adjufar was grave. We lost a number of warriors. And as Guardsman Ebon stated, a notable member of the Guard was critically hurt."

"That's a d'ast shame," said Hanxchamp. He had recovered slightly and was determined to take back control of the situation. "Too much of that lawless d'ast goes on these days, too much. Where'd you say it was? Adjufar? Scum-hole!"

He got up. He lit a smile.

"Folks, welcome. Can I offer you drinks? Cheesy comestibles?"

"We do not drink on duty," replied Dragoon.

"Okay, please yourself. I'm having one." Hanxchamp poured himself a large glass of vintage Spartoi liqour from the drink trolley. He did it unhurriedly, with measured ease, to show that he was calm. He let the ice cubes tumble slowly in the heavy glass. That kind of time-taking display usually disarmed the people who met with him. It showed them who was boss.

"Cigar? Anyone? No? Okay, ladies and...roboform. How can I help you?"

"My task force encountered several individuals on Adjufar," Ebon said. "Three of them were identified as fugitives from violent incidents on several other worlds."

"Really?" asked Hanxchamp, sipping and sitting.

"When an attempt was made to apprehend the individuals, violence occurred. My squad commander was seriously injured. Nine Metal Wing warriors died."

"Wow, that's a hell of a thing," said Hanxchamp, using his sympathetic face. "Hell of a thing. My condolences."

"The fugitives fled Adjufar using what we believe was a Xandar-ian cruiser," said Arach. *Gad, that fingers-on-wet-glass squeak again!* Hanxchamp winced. "We were able to track their route. They were heading for Alpha Centauri. We lost their trace two minutes after they entered airspace."

"Lost it? Oh, dear. Unfortunate."

"Predictive tracking reports that it was coming here."

Hanxchamp took another sip, swirled his glass, and punched some touch-controls on his desk tablet. He turned it so they could see.

"Okay, full disclosure. I want to help you Shi'ar guys. Timely Inc. has nothing to hide. See? Full inventory of today's landings. Not a Xandarian cruiser amongst them."

Dragoon stepped forward and took up the tablet. She scanned it, looked at Arach, and shook her head.

"We believe it may have employed a disguiser field," said Ebon.

"Really? Like *you*, you mean?" Hanxchamp asked, flipping a ten-tacle at the warship dominating the view outside his window.

The Shi'ar were stony faced.

Ebon looked at Arach, who nodded.

"The fugitives were in the company of a Rigellian Recorder unit," Ebon said. "We believe that the unit is of consequence. We believe they may have brought it here. Why would that be?"

Hanxchamp quivered. Could it be true? It was here? Actually *here*?

"Sir?" asked Ebon. "Would you comment? We're waiting."

Hanxchamp gathered himself.

"Guys, friends, I have no idea why a Recorder unit would be im-portant to anyone except the Rigellians. Those crazy data-nuts! Eh?

Eh? Tell you what, though, in the spirit of cooperation, let me run a full search of the building. Top to bottom. We have excellent security here. Top drawer. If there is a Recorder...or any fugitive-type persons...we'll find them. Then we can talk about what to do with them."

"We would prefer to do the searching," Warstar 34 rumbled.

"Flark, I'm sure you *would*, big buddy!" replied Hanxchamp. "But this is Alpha C jurisdictional, and this is Timely Inc. property. We'll do it *our* way first. We'll resolutionate this situationism for you, stat. Kick back for a while. I'll get hospitalitization to lay on sandwiches and juice. Put your feet up."

He grinned at Arach.

"You, lady—we'll need to find lots of footstools for *you*, am I right?"

"What?"

"Just saying."

"We...we will do things your way, for now," said Sub-Praetor Arach.

"Great! Isn't this great? See how we're working together now? Isn't it great? Like...synergizeticism or something?"

There was a knock on the door.

"Enter!" Hanxchamp cried.

Blint Wivvers, Pama Harnon, Sledly Rarnak, and Allandra Meramati appeared in the doorway. They gazed at the visitors in alarm.

"Come in, come in, guys!" Hanxchamp beckoned them. "We have guests. *Special* guests. *Shi'ar Imperial Guard*, no less. Big day! Make them welcome. It appears they're here hunting for fugitives and... you'll never guess...some kinda Rigellian Recorder unit who may, right now, be *in this very building!*"

"You're kidding," Wivvers began. "I mean...how *odd* is that?"

"A Recorder?" asked Pama Harnon. "Literally here?"

"I mean, what are the chances, Pam?" Hanxchamp agreed.

"It's here?" Rarnak hissed.

"Totally. Keep them happy, I'll get Xorbux on it," Hanxchamp whispered.

"Let's get our guests welcomized!" he called out in a louder voice.

"Mingle and do your Shi'ar thing," he whispered at Meramati. "I need you to cushion this flarkasco down for me."

Meramati looked worried.

"But—"

"Oh, you're noble-blood! Get them to bow before you or something!" Hanxchamp demanded.

"Mrs. Mantlestreek!" he yelled at the outer office. "Tea! Coffee! Juice! Biscuits! The whole hospitality thing! Right now!"

"Yes, sir."

Hanxchamp saw Xorb Xorbux hovering in the doorway and went to him. Behind Hanxchamp, his execs were making superficial small talk with the Imperial Guardsmen.

"Xorb! Xorb, buddy!" Hanxchamp breathed, gripping Xorbux by the shoulders. "The Recorder...it's *here*! On the premises! Get your men out, find it. Find it *now*!"

"Yes, sir!"

"The Shi'ar are all over us like a body bag, Xorb. We need to clinch this! If we find the Recorder and get it to the Datacore, then the whole Shi'ar Empire can take a bath. *Forever*!"

"Yes, sir!"

"Get it done, Xorb! I'm counting on you!"

"Fast as I can, sir," Xorb Xorbux replied, rushing off.

Hanxchamp turned back into the office.

"So everyone good? Timely Inc. has this situation covered. Everyone happy?"

"Just one thing," Arach said, looking up from her conversation with Blint Wivvers.

There was a rush of transmat energy. One by one, Metal Wing warriors in full armor materialized around the room. When the staggered transmat ended, there were forty of them lining the walls of the inner office, weapons raised.

Hanxchamp gulped.

"Just to be sure we're on the same page," Arach said.

· C H A P T E R T H I R T Y - S E V E N ·

MEANWHILE
(8,887 FLOORS LOWER DOWN...)

I CANNOT recommend being mailed. Particularly through an internal mail-routing system. There is a lot of falling and uncontrolled sliding, a lot of hard uncushioned bends, and a great deal of colliding with other mail in transit.

So being fired out of a chute and landing on our heads on a hard metal platform seems a bit of a welcome relief, to be honest.

"Ow," groans Rocket Raccoon, and hops to his feet. He picks up his unfeasibly large gun and begins to pull off his Form-fit overalls. The slightly shabby Guardians uniform makes him look a little more like he means business.

"Nn ngngg ngggg," says Groot. He pauses and removes several letters and a small parcel from his mouth.

"I am Groot," he repeats.

"Exactly," says Rocket. "Let's find out where we are."

Gamora is already on her feet. Like Rocket, she has shed her Form-fit, stripping back to her tight black body-armor. She takes her rolled cloak out of the overall pocket, shakes it out, puts it on, and raises the hood. In the gloom, she is almost instantly reduced to the merest suggestion of a shadow.

The chamber is large and made of metal. It is dark. The only light comes from an indicator panel on the wall. Beside the mail-deposit platform are several metal trolleys that look like hospital gurneys.

Rocket hits a button on the indicator panel, and the hatch opens.

We peer out into a corridor. The decor is stark: blue-black metal walls and decking, and functional iris valves that glow—through their chunky, radiating grilles—with a dull yellow light.

We edge along. After a short while, we come to an entrance hallway. On one side is a bank of executive elevators. They clearly require special executive codes to operate them. On the wall beside the elevators is a sign that reads "subbasement 86."

Rocket whistles. "Sub-86," he says. "This place doesn't exist."

"Except—" I begin.

"I meant *officially*." He kisses the torn mail tag clutched in his disconcertingly human-like hand. "I knew it. I *knew* we were onto something. This is the inner domain. Secrety-secret Special Projects. They hide this stuff away, bury it deep, lock it out with codes and all kindsa security jazz—but the mail must get through. You see, they keep this stuff confidential from personnel, in case of industrial espionage and what-not, but they *totally* trust the building's automatic systems."

"I am Groot."

"Exactly, because who's gonna ask questions of the internal mail-routing delivery system?"

We are very deep underground. The air is dry and artificially cold. I can hear the buzz of powerful clandestine fields. It makes my outer casing vibrate unpleasantly. If (in the normal, organic sense) I had ears, I would prepare to shed them now.

Gamora has moved away from the elevator bank toward what looks like a main-entrance hatch. It is an enormous double-iris valve surrounded by throbbing red bands of security countermeasures. Beside the hatch is a small dais equipped with genetic probes.

She examines it.

"We can't get in this way," she says. "This needs a code-key, plus a security sequence—plus palm prints, retina, voice, gene sample, and pheromone spectrum."

Rocket looks forlornly at the tag.

"This ain't gonna get us past that. If only we had a—"

One of the elevators pings. We take cover in the shadows.

A Timely Inc. executive in a suit rushes out of the doors. He is a Kaliklaki, and he seems very agitated. With him come two Timely Inc. security men.

"It's all going -tik!- down on the 8001st floor," the Kaliklaki exec says. "They say Hanxchamp is in a standoff with the Shi'ar Imperial Guard! In his office!"

I glance at Rocket. He glances back, ears lowered.

"We have to -tik!- secure this area, you understand?" the Kaliklaki tells the security guards.

"Yes, Mr. Gruntgrill."

"Hanxchamp's orders. If the -tik!- Shi'ar start sweeping the building, they must *not* find this place, okay?"

"Yes, Mr. Gruntgrill."

"Okay, good. Let's do it."

The exec—Gruntgrill—steps up on the dais.

He slots his code-key in the slender reader-console. Then he places his green hands on the palm scanners. He looks the blue light of the retina probe square in the eye.

"Voice," he says. The machine lights shift, sampling. "Gruntgrill, Arnok. Security sequence -tik!- 11324567812. I invite you to check my palm prints, retina, voice, gene sample, and pheromone spectrum."

"Identity match failed."

"What? -tik!-"

"Sequence not recognized."

"I said 'security sequence 11324567812.'"

"Incorrect. You stated security sequence as '-tik!- 11324567812.'"

"Are you mocking me? *Again*?" Gruntgrill asks.

"Question not recognized."

"You're mocking me *again* for my speech impediment? I'm *nervous*!"

"Comment not recognized."

"Scan me -tik!- again! My sequence is -tik!- 11324567812. I mean, it is -tik!- 11324567812."

"Sequence not recognized."

"This -tik!- happens a lot," Gruntgrill laughs, looking around at the security men. They are no longer behind him. They are unconscious on the floor. His eyes widen. He finds himself looking at me, a threatening tree, a green killer with two swords, and a Raccoonoid aiming an unfeasibly large weapon.

"-tik!-" he gulps.

"Open the hatch, budster," Rocket tells him.

He gawps. He *tiks*. His antennae quiver.

I realize that despite the swords, despite the unfeasibly large weapon trained at his face, despite the threatening tree, the angry Raccoonoid, and the shadowy killer, he is transfixed by the sight of *me*.

"It's you," he says.

"Yes, I am me."

"Recorder -tik!- 127."

"Yes," I reply.

"Open the hatch," snarls Rocket, "and let's find out why that's so flarking important."

He racks his unfeasibly large weapon, just to make the point.

CHAPTER THIRTY-EIGHT

MEANWHILE
(8,887 FLOORS HIGHER UP...)

"**PUT** those guns away!" Hanxchamp demanded. "Right now! This is no way to behave in my flarking office!"

"Then comply," squeaked Arach.

"Listen to me, spider-queen, this—"

A hypervelocity boom shook the windows so hard, it made the vista view of Huj flash up again briefly.

"The *flark*?" said Hanxchamp.

"Sharra and K'ythri!" Ebon cried.

Through the window, they could all see that a *second* huge starship was now hovering outside the Timely HQ building, right beside the Shi'ar Strikebird.

The immense Nova Corps heavy cruiser was more cylindrical in construction, an armored missile compared to the Shi'ar's elegant falcon. The heavy's downlights flicked on, washing the streets below with light.

"This is just out of order!" Hanxchamp cried.

The windows exploded inward, blizzarding glass. Four Warriors of the Xandarian Nova Corps landed neatly on their armored feet behind Hanxchamp's desk. Their boots crunched on broken windowpane slivers.

The Metal Wing soldiers' weapons came up, arming. All four Imperial Guardsmen assumed battle stances, ready to fight.

"Stand down, Shi'ar," announced the Nova leader. "I am Centurion Grekan Yaer of Xandar. With me, Centurion Clawdi, and Corpsmen Starkross and Valis. Be calm, or we grav the flark out of you."

"You can try!" Warstar yelled.

"Whoa, whoa!" Hanxchamp exclaimed. "No shooting in my office! Stop this confrontationalization at *once*!"

Reluctantly, the Shi'ar troopers lowered their weapons. The Nova Corpsmen and the Imperial Guardsmen powered down. The looks they were giving each other, however, were still armed and lethal.

"Better," said Hanxchamp. "That's better. Everyone be cool. Everyone play nice. Now then, Mr. Nova person, what is this about? You're paying for the window, by the way."

"We are in pursuit of fugitives, sir," Yaer stated. "A stolen Corps prowl cruiser is identified as coming here."

"You have no jurisdiction here!" Arach cried.

"Oh, like *you* do, you mean?" Clawdi returned.

"Insolent wretch!" snapped Arach.

"Guys, guys! *Calm*! I'm sure this is all a misunderstandism!" Hanxchamp shouted. "Nova guy," he said, looking at the impassive Korbinite Yaer. "Can you specificigate just a little more?"

Grekan Yaer flipped out a tablet and showed it to the Senior Vice Executive President (Special Projects).

"Galactic warrant," Yaer said. "Prosecution of fugitives, Galactic

Order 9910. Pursuit into other jurisdictions as a result of the above, Galactic Order 3596. Location and identification of Recorder unit 127, case specific."

"Recorder *what* did you say now?"

"What are you hiding?"

"Nothing!"

"Basically, sir," Grekan Yaer said to Hanxchamp, "we have a permit granted by galactic treaty to search these premises."

Arach approached, scuttling forward on her long blue legs. She looked at the tablet, then handed it back.

"It's true, he does," she squeaked. "He has far more legal coverage in this situation than we Shi'ar do."

"Thank you, ma'am." Yaer said.

"That being said," said Arach. "This one's *ours*."

She twitched a palp. In perfect, drilled unison, the Metal Wing troops raised their weapons and aimed them at the Nova Corpsmen.

"*Not in my office!* Not in my office!" Hanxchamp shrieked.

"Then what do you suggest?" asked Yaer, his glowing fists raised and aimed at the Shi'ar. "Unless our *Shi'ar friends* back the flark down right now, we're going to find ourselves having a *situation*."

"We have no wish to engage in combat with the forces of Xandar," Arach squeaked wetly through her translator. "We of the Shi'ar are well aware of their power. A fight between us could level this tower."

"This *city*," hissed Clawdi.

"And leave four dead Nova Corps personnel and the burning ruin of a Nova Corps Heavy," returned Dragoon without missing a beat.

"Oh, guys! Super-mortal folk! *Please*!" Hanxchamp wailed. "This is giving me a tension migraine! Calm the holy flark down and stop being so...so...*aggressivized*! Let's do this the megacorp way! Let's sit the flark down around a great big table and solutionate the flark out of it! Mrs. Mantlestreek! *Biscuits and juice*! Biscuits and juice!"

"I'll literally see to it, sir," said Pama Harnon, and she hurried out.

Yaer lowered his fists. At a nod from Ebon, the Metal Wing troopers dropped their aim. Their fingers remained on their trigger studs, and their weapons stayed armed.

"A clash of jurisdiction," said Yaer.

"We clearly seek the same individuals," said Arach, "given the information you have volunteered."

"What information will you volunteer?" asked Yaer.

Arach paused.

"How many fugitives are you pursuing?" she asked.

"Two, plus the Recorder unit."

"And you want them for...as I see from your warrant...*invalid vehicle insurance*? Is that correct?"

Yaer grimaced.

"For now," he admitted.

"We are pursuing *three*, plus the Recorder unit," said Arach.

"Which ones?" asked Yaer. He showed her his tablet. "These are mine. Raccoon, Rocket. Groot, no other nomenclature."

"Yes, those two, and this one," said Arach, nodding to Ebon to show her tablet device. "Gamora."

"The Deadliest Woman in the Universe!" Corpsman Valis whispered. Yaer looked at him.

"She's on every watch list we post, sir," Valis shrugged. "Extremely bad news."

"Our interest is the criminals," said Yaer. "Raccoon and Groot.

This Gamora, too, if she has charges pending."

"Oh, she really *has*, sir," said Valis.

"Our interest," squeaked Arach, "is justice. Xandarian justice is quite sufficient for us, provided that the bodily harm caused to our Guardsman Crusher and the deaths of the Metal Wing warriors is taken into consideration for penalty. Life in the Kyln, without appeal. Under such an arrangement, we would be content for the criminals to be taken into Xandarian custody. But the Recorder unit is ours."

"Why?"

"State secrets of the Shi'ar Empire, Centurion," Arach replied. "Surely you do not expect me to divulge those?"

"So...we take the crims, you take the Recorder?" asked Clawdi.

"That would be acceptable to us," nodded Arach.

"You drive a hard bargain, Shi'ar," said Yaer.

"You are hard to bargain with, Xandarian," she squeaked back.

"Ha ha ha!" Hanxchamp laughed without humor. "Ha ha ha ha ha ha ha ha! Look at this, isn't it great? Isn't it *great*, Blint?"

"Amazing, sir," Wivvers agreed.

"Splendid," added Rarnak.

"Look at us, we're already solutionizing this!" Hanxchamp declared, clapping his tentacles. "Look at us, I'm proud of this moment. You guys. I've got a tingly feeling."

IN the outer office, Pama Harnon directed Mrs. Mantlestreek and the office service robots to "hurry the flark up, and get some dips and appetizers *fast*!"

Mrs. Mantlestreek glowered at Pama Harnon over her horn-rimmed spectacles.

"Do I look like I'm literally kidding?" asked Pama Harnon. "*Do* it!"

They hurried away. Pama Harnon breathed out. Then she pulled out her new lip-gloss.

She pressed the cap down and fired the Omni-wave beacon.

Urgent...urgent...

CHAPTER THIRTY-NINE

PROJECT 616

GRUNTGRILL steps up onto the dais. He is painfully aware that he has guns trained on him. He puts his code-key into the slender reader-console. Then he places his green hands on the palm scanners. He looks the blue light of the retina probe square in the eye.

"Voice," he says. The machine lights shift, sampling. "Gruntgrill, Arnok. Security sequence -tik!- 11324567812. I invite you to check my palm prints, retina, voice, gene sample, and pheromone spectrum."

"Identity match failed."

"Try a -tik!- gain."

"Sequence not recognized."

"Please -tik!- don't do this! Not now!" Gruntgrill exclaims. "I've got a -tik!- gun to my head!"

"Remark not recognized."

"I have a -tik!- speech impediment? I'm nervous!"

"Comment not recognized."

"Scan me -tik!- again! My sequence is -tik!- 11324567812. I mean, it is -tik!- 11324567812. Dammit!"

"Do better than that, buddy," Rocket says.

Gruntgrill takes a deep breath.

"My sequence is -tik!- -tik!- -tik!-...it is 11324567812."

He breathes out, head down. His tie hangs.

"Identity now verified, Arnok. Welcome to Project 616."

The glowing-red countermeasures wink off briefly. The double-iris opens, outer then inner, with a squeal of metallic petals dilating and scraping over one another.

Cool air gusts out.

Gruntgrill gets off the dais and walks toward the hatch.

"Come on, then," he says. "Let me show you. Let me show you the future of the Galaxy."

The leaves close behind us again immediately with a slow shriek.

We enter Project 616.

Gruntgrill walks us down to the hatch of the Datacore Chamber. I notice displays that read: *Datacore—87%.*

More security processes are required. Gruntgrill is nervously scanned several more times.

The shutter opens.

Before me, I see my destiny at last.

The Datacore Chamber is immense. It is *overwhelming*.

As we step onto a concentric observation walkway, I am stunned not just by the immensity of the chamber, but by the far greater immensity of the data it contains. The Core pulses below us in the tech-lined storage well, a hot pink light of almost infinite data.

"This is why you need me," I sigh. "To complete this."

"Yes -tik!-" says Gruntgrill.

"You have the whole of creation in data form down there, apart from the portion I represent."

"I am Groot," says Groot.

"Yeah, explain!" Rocket urges with his unfeasibly large weapon.

"It's a datamap!" Gruntgrill cries. "A datamap of all creation. When it's complete, Timely Inc. will understand the fundamental nature of everything and comprehend the known Galaxy down to a pico-molecular level. Thus we can precision-market and audience-tailor our billions of products like never before. We will know and understand everything. Everything! We will dominate the Galaxy and secure our position for eternity as an entity more powerful than any species!"

"Like Google Earth?" I say.

"I don't know what that is," Gruntgrill replies.

"Nice speech," says Gamora, aiming her swords at Gruntgrill. "Can I kill him now?"

Rocket waves a disconcertingly human-like hand.

"This is about money?" he asks Gruntgrill.

"About -tik!- power! With money comes power!"

"I *do* like money," Rocket says.

"Why have you used—abused, I should say—the Rigellian Recorders?" I ask.

Gruntgrill looks at me. "Because we've -tik!- been working on Project 616 for decades. We realized the data collection was going to take decades more to complete. We -tik!- fast-tracked it. We realized that using Rigellian Recorders was a brilliant way to expedite the process. We abducted all the Recorders we could find, copied their memories, and then sent them out again, reprogrammed."

Gruntgrill looks at me sadly.

"You are the last one. The most special one."

"Special? Why?"

"When you were-tik!-abducted by Timely, you managed to escape."

"Hey, go *you*, Recorder-dude!" says Rocket.

"You accidentally viewed and recorded the entire Timely Data-core," says Gruntgrill. "You -tik!- know *everything*. You're the last big missing chunk that we need to get the Datacore percentile to a working level. But you're also, essentially, a *pirate copy* of the entire core. That's why everyone -tik!- is after you."

"That explains the blanks," I say. "Data overload. I do not know what I know."

I look at Rocket Raccoon. Then I turn back to the executive.

"If I join this," I say, indicating the throbbing pink glow below me, "then you will achieve total data-control of the Universe?"

"Yes," says Gruntgrill.

"That is akin to the Power Cosmic," I suggest.

"Friend, it *is* the Power Cosmic."

I turn back to Rocket.

"Rocket Raccoon," I say. "I trust you. Do this for me now. Use your unfeasibly large gun and annihilate me. Do it quick. I will not be part of this."

"Hey!" he says, backing off in alarm.

I spread my arms.

"I am a clear target. Do it. Save the Universe. Guard the Galaxy. That's what you do, isn't it?"

"Yeah, yeah," Rocket breathes. "But not like this..."

"Rocket Raccoon, I implore you," I say. "I am the last piece of the puzzle. I am the Universe. Through me, Timely Inc. can control cre-ation. I do not want that. I do not want them to possess the Power

Cosmic. Complete universal data. Do you have any idea what that means?"

"No," says Rocket. "And because I don't work that way, I ain't gonna shoot you. You're my pal, for d'ast sakes."

"Please...annihilate me," I say.

Reality edits itself. I taste page-turn surprise and dramatic twist.

The Spaceknight suddenly reappears.

"Oh, flark!" says Rocket.

"He's *mine*!" cries Gamora.

Roamer pounds across the walkway. She springs to meet him, a ninja-shadow. Their blades clash, her two against his laser sword, and sparks fly.

They trade blows at a furious speed that is hard to record.

I just...I just want to die. I want my very existence to be ended. I have been used. I am going to *be* used. For all his bluff exterior and sarcastic wise-crackery, Rocket Raccoon has a heart of gold. And for that, I will suffer. And the Universe as I know it—and as *you* know it, gentle reader—will suffer also. Universe 616 will become entirely controlled by the soulless executives of Timely Inc.

I look pleadingly at Rocket, but he is too busy trying to aim his unfeasibly large weapon at Roamer. Gamora keeps getting in his line of fire. Groot, his aim also thwarted, groans in despair.

Roamer and Gamora duel on the edge of the walkway overlooking the throbbing Datacore, sword against swords. Each of them represents the pinnacle of their own kind's fighting evolution. As a document of ultimate martial prowess, what I record is worth enough, in and of itself. Their battle is the greatest and most skillful sword fight in the history of swords. *Ever.*

I know this for a fact. I have compared and contrasted. You can forget Liam Neeson versus Ray Park. Or Christopher Lambert versus the Kurgan. Or Errol Flynn versus Robert Douglas in *The Adventures of Don Juan.* Or Tyrone Power versus Basil Rathbone in *The Mark of Zorro.* Or Yu Shen Lien versus Jan Yu in the estimable *Crouching Tiger, Hidden Dragon.* Or Toshiro Mifune against absolutely *everyone* in *The Seven Samurai.* Or even Inigo Montoya versus the Dread Pirate Roberts (yes, yes, once again, I am tailoring the references to your culture base, dear reader).

They are so fast. Blade blocks blade blocks blade. He is heavily armored; she is not. She is lithe and athletic; he is stoic and determined.

She darts, he sweeps. He strikes, she dives. He stabs at her, but she is no longer there. She rips at him, but he ripostes with a rising blade. He sweeps at her, two-handed. She ducks the blow and comes in with a flurry of strikes.

She wounds him, and he falls back against the rail. He blocks her rain of blows and cuts her. She falls back, bleeding from the throat. She kicks him back into the rail and smashes his head to one side. She is about to deliver the kill-stroke.

Suddenly she convulses, her body crackling with electrical discharge, and falls onto the walkway.

We are surrounded by Timely Inc. security guards, their Subduematics aimed. A fierce Z'Nox leads them, and it is his shot that has put Gamora down at the moment of victory.

"Oh, Xorb!" cries Gruntgrill. "Am I -tik!- glad to see you!"

The Z'Nox ignores him, and aims his weapon at Rocket and Groot. So do the other security guys.

"Drop the unfeasibly large weapons *now*!" the Z'Nox demands.

They have no choice. Their guns clatter to the walkway, and they raise their hands.

Roamer gets up, tossing the unconscious and limp form of Gamora off him. He points his sword at me.

"Recorder 127," he growls, his visor glowing blood-red. "I promised to deliver, and I have, Xorb Xorbux."

The Z'Nox, Xorb Xorbux, breathes out.

"Worth the wait," he says. "I knew you'd come through, Roamer." His men move forward, and lock Rocket and Groot in mag-cuffs. They surround me, Subduematic phase pistols aimed.

"Good, good," says Xorb Xorbux. "A proper solutionization. Gruntgrill? Tell Hanxchamp the good news."

Gruntgrill flips out his tablet and dials.

"What's going to happen to us?" Rocket asks the Z'Nox.

"Nothing," Xorb Xorbux replies. "For *ever*."

Rocket swallows hard.

"Sir, this is Gruntgrill! We have secured the Recorder, sir!" the Kaliklaki says into his mobile. "Yes, intact. We—what? *What's* happening, now?"

He lowers the tablet and looks at Xorb Xorbux. His face is tight with fear.

"You're never going to believe this," he says. "The -tik!- Kree are here!"

· CHAPTER FORTY ·

DANGER IN THE WORKPLACE

SENIOR Vice Executive President (Special Projects) Odus Hanxchamp had thought he was doing so well, ushering the four powerful Nova Corpsmen and the frightening quartet of Shi'ar Guardsmen, not to mention their armor-clattering retinue of Metal Wing warriors, down to the Executive Boardroom. Beverages had been laid on, along with crudites and dips. There was juice and biscuits and nibbles.

Some of the Metal Wing troopers had raised their visors to enjoy a piquant salsa-dipped root stick and a cup of hot beverage. Sub-Praetor Arach was actually engaging Grekan Yaer in idle chit-chat. Hanxchamp's execs were circulating with platters of hors d'oeuvres.

The business method, Hannxchamp thought. That's the way the Universe works.

His tablet rang, and he was about to answer it.

Thunder boomed.

Two huge warships hanging in inter-atmospheric space would be one thing. But suddenly there was a third: the Kree battleship *Pride of Pama*. It was twice as big again as the Shi'ar cruiser or the Nova Corps Heavy. It hung outside the Timely Inc. HQ tower, an impossible mass gradually appearing as its aura of negativity fell away.

Sharnor the Accuser teleported directly to the Executive Board-room. She was a towering figure.

"The Recorder is mine!" she declared, smashing her force-ham-mer down on the table, which shattered. She aimed an accusatory finger at the Shi'ar and Xandarians present. "No one move. This is *Kree* business."

Both the Shi'ar and the Xandarians would have fought back in an instant, except that Sharnor wasn't the only being who had tele-ported in. With her came a hundred armed Kree warriors and three Sentry units. The boardroom was getting crowded.

"Well," said Arach, her voice a shrill, slippery squeak. "What we seem to have here is a standoff, Lady Accuser."

"No," snapped Sharnor. "What we seem to have here is *total Kree control*. Make a move—you or any of your soldiers—and we will obliterate you. Same goes for you, Xandarians."

"The Nova Corps does not respond well to bullying, Accuser," replied Grekan Yaer.

"This is not bullying, Xandarian," Sharnor said, dropping her voice. "This is military domination! Stand down, leave, or *die*. I give you this choice!"

"You've crossed a line, Accuser," Yaer insisted. "This is an act of war. It breaks every non-aggression treaty in—"

"This is an act of *self-defense*, Xandarian," Sharnor countered. "The Kree Stellar Empire is taking urgent action to protect itself against a potentially overwhelming threat. A threat represented by the Timely Inc. megacorporation. They are about to acquire such power, they will depose all other empires and civilizations. They are about to steal the Galaxy from us all."

She looked at Yaer, then at Arach.

"Tell me you don't suspect as much. Tell me that's not why you're here, too."

"We...we are concerned," Arach admitted.

"We know something's going on," said Yaer.

"Then we should be standing shoulder-to-shoulder in this," Sharnor said contemptuously. "This threat menaces us all. The worlds of Xandar, the dominions of the Shi'ar. This... megacorporation cannot be allowed to achieve such power."

"I think you'll find that what Timely Inc. does is entirely Timely Inc. business," said Hanxchamp. "We inventize, we designerate, and we developmentationalize. Then we benefit from that investmentage. You can't come in here and tell us to stop developing a project just because you don't *like* it."

He faltered. The Accuser glared at him.

"Look at me," she said. "Do I not appear to be *exactly* the sort of person who could do that? Bring the Recorder unit to me."

"Hang on," said Hanxchamp. "We don't even know if the flarking thing is on the premises. We're searching now, but it's not definite that—"

"We have been told it is here. This has been confirmed," said Sharnor.

"Told?" Hanxchamp said, outraged. "Told? Lady, I can *assure* you—"

"The Recorder unit is here," Pama Harnon said, stepping forward. "Hanxchamp confirmed this to me just minutes ago. Timely security is attempting to secure it and hide it while he keeps you busy."

"Pam?" Hanxchamp gasped.

"I do not work for you," said Pama Harnon coldly.

"Una-Ren is one of my most trusted infiltration agents," said Sharnor. She looked at "Pama Harnon." "You have performed excellently in the name of the Kree Empire, Una-Ren. You will be honored and rewarded on our return to Hala."

The spy nodded.

"Produce the Recorder unit now," Sharnor said to Hanxchamp. "We will put an end to your dreams of total galactic domination."

"No, you will deliver him to *us*," said a new voice.

A full-size holographic image had appeared at one end of the Executive Boardroom. It was a Badoon War Brotherhood Commander. The telepresent figure leered at them. He had recently undergone extensive cybernetic reconstruction, and it had not improved his visual appeal.

"I am War Brotherhood Commander Droook," the image said. "You will deliver the Recorder unit to War Brotherhood hands or face the consequences."

"Consequences?" Hanxchamp stammered.

"Failure to comply will result in the obliteration of this building, this city, and the landmass it stands upon."

"Scans confirm that a War Brotherhood battlefleet has just appeared in low orbit," said Ebon, consulting her tablet device in alarm. "Ten megadestroyers, batteries locked on to this location... *and* our ships."

Outside, downtown Alpha C was now cast into shadow by *thirteen* massive warships. The War Brotherhood megadestroyers of the Badoon hung in a silent, ominous ring around the HQ—weapons ready to discharge at any hint of resistance from Timely Inc., or defiance by the Shi'ar, Kree, or Xandarian vessels.

"You just escalated this to an *insane* level," Grekan Yaer said to the image of the Badoon.

"The Kree will not allow this!" Sharnor boomed.

"The Shi'ar Empire will prosecute any move against us by the Badoon with extreme prejudice," warned Arach.

"None of you are in a position to negotiate," said Droook. "All War Brotherhood batteries are locked on. Give us the Recorder now."

"My kind will not stand for this!" Allandra Meramati cried suddenly.

"Yeah, we've heard the Shi'ar position on the matter!" Hanxchamp snapped, frantically trying to think of an ace he could pull out of his sleeve.

"Shi'ar?" said Arach. "That female is not *Shi'ar.*"

"What?" said Hanxchamp.

Meramati pulled off her fake Shi'ar crest. Without the feathers, it became clear she had been a well-disguised Sirusite woman all along.

"Project 616 and the vital Recorder unit represent Truth. *Total universal truth*," she said. "Thus I claim them on behalf of the Universal Church of Truth."

The skies above Alpha C exploded in quivering, volcanic flashes of warp-gate energy. The weather systems cauldroned into a huge, seething torus a hundred kilometers wide.

Forty immense Templeships of the Universal Church of Truth, massive space vehicles that looked like airborne cathedrals, entered reality with an abominable boom of displaced atmospherics. They hovered above the city, dwarfing *everything.*

At that point, most of the staff at Alpha C Orbital Traffic Control just gave up and went home.

The Universal Church of Truth did not wait for discussion or negotiation, or even surrender. The moment they appeared, the Templeships began teleporting hosts of Crusaders, led by Cardinals.

A ruthless, all-out assault of Timely Inc. Corporate Headquarters began.

CHAPTER FORTY-ONE

TRUTH OR DARE

ARNOK Gruntgrill lowers his tablet. His face is pale and agitated.

"All -tik!- kindsa flark has broken loose upstairs," he says to Xorb Xorbux. "I think...I think the -tik!- Badoon are here, too—and something *else*. The building's under attack. It sounds like chaos."

"I'd better get up there and—" Xorb begins.

"No!" says Gruntgrill. "The last thing I heard Hanxchamp scream was that we needed to complete the Datacore. We need to -tik!- integrate the Recorder. If we get the Core up to power, we can wield it, Xorb. We can...incapacitate the alien forces with a blink of an eye. We can banish them with a *thought*."

Xorb hesitates.

"You really don't understand the potential of the Datacore, do you?" Gruntgrill asks him. "Knowledge is power, and all knowledge is *all* power."

"I just thought Project 616 would enable us to control the market, be a jump or two ahead of our competitors," says Xorb. "You know...by knowing more than anyone else."

Gruntgrill shakes his head.

"It will make us gods, Xorb," he says. "It will make Timely Inc. into an omnipotent entity. By understanding reality down to its most minuscule detail, we will be able to control it, manipulate it. There will be no more disruptions to our market strategy. No more Kree-Skrull wars, no more Annihilation events, no more invasive threats like Galactus or Thanos. We will create total -tik!- galactic stability—and control all lives everywhere, forever. In the mega-corp future, even the DNA of individual beings will carry the Timely logo. It will be a Timely Universe, and we will be its masters."

"That sounds pretty flarking awful to me," grumbles Rocket. He and Groot are cuffed behind us, under the watch of the security guards. Gamora, also cuffed, is sprawled on the floor behind them.

"You shut your lip!" Xorb growls at Rocket.

He looks at Gruntgrill. "Get on with it, then. Hurry."

"You do not like this very much, do you?" I ask Gruntgrill.

"It -tik!- scares the willies out of me, frankly," Gruntgrill replies.

"Just get it done, Gruntgrill!" Xorb barks. "I like the sound of being a god."

Gruntgrill nods, and Roamer edges me toward the lip of the walkway. The Datacore blooms pink below us. I feel the crackle of the data inside me responding.

"I do not want to do this," I state.

"Quiet," Roamer tells me.

"I do not think you want to do this, either, Galadoran," I say, looking at him. He is unreadable.

"That interpolator device you use," I say, studying and recording the Timely unit bolted to his back. "It has taken you to me every time you used it. Because of its ability to place you in precisely the correct dramatic moment to affect destiny and universal continuity."

"That is its purpose."

"And each time, in effect, you saved me, or helped to bring me closer to my goal. Where *is* your place in the cosmic narrative, Spaceknight?"

"Shut up."

"I -tik!- said that to him," Gruntgrill calls out breezily. He makes a little false laugh. He is using a wall panel to operate a hoist that lowers an Adamantium cage from the ceiling. I know that I will be placed into that cage and then dipped into the Datacore, where my individual essence will be lost, and my stored data—which I now appreciate is vast beyond all measure—will be added to the map.

"I said that the flarking interpolator keeps reading him as a hero," Gruntgrill continues, working. "Even though he pretends to be a soulless -tik!- merc. Oh, well, he still got the job done in the end."

"*Are* you a hero?" I ask Roamer.

"Shut up."

"Are you a heartless being? Do you not care about the future that awaits us all?"

"Shut up."

"Time was, the Spaceknights of Galador would have fought to the last to *prevent* this from happening."

"Shut up *now*," Roamer snaps, the red light of his visor pulsing angrily.

"Very well. But do me one favor, if you will. Use the interpolator again. Right now. See where it takes you. See where the dramatic urges of creation believe you should be."

"I told you to be silent," says Roamer.

"Yeah, give it a shot," Rocket calls to him. "I'm a no-good ne'er-do-well, and even I found it in my hardened heart to give the doofus a helping hand."

"Be the flark quiet!" Xorb tells him, with an unnecessarily vicious gesture of his pistol.

The building shakes. Even down here, at sub eighty-six level, we feel it shudder. Almighty war is taking place above us. The cage swings, and Gruntgrill leans out over the guardrail to arrest it.

"Careful you don't fall in," laughs Xorb. "We don't wanna become morons instead of gods."

Gruntgrill shoots him a look.

"Flark off, Xorbux! You have no idea what's going on here! You -tik!- are only after the power!"

Xorb Xorbux aims his Subduematic at Gruntgrill. He clicks it to "kill."

"Get it done. Get it done now, you Kaliklaki waste of space," he says. "Or I waste *you.*"

"Would you -tik!- -tik!- step into the cage, Recorder?" Gruntgrill asks me.

Another blast shivers the building. The cage rocks again.

"I would rather not," I say.

"He's going to -tik!- kill me," Gruntgrill stammers.

"That would be preferable to what is about to happen," I reply.

"Please, get into the -tik!- cage!"

There is another shudder. The cage swings again.

"What the -tik!- flark is going on up there?" Gruntgrill asks.

CHAPTER FORTY-TWO

THIS IS WHAT THE -TIK!- FLARK IS GOING ON UP THERE

ROBED in red and maroon, the Crusaders of the Universal Church of Truth transmatted to the surface and charged into the Timely Corporate HQ wielding hatchets, swords, pikes, and blasters. The reception-desk staff stood little or no chance.

At the head of the invasion came the armored Faith Cardinals, towering cloaked figures of great power, who wore malevolent spiked-and-crested helms. They wielded ornate power blades and staves, which cut down or atomized anyone in their path.

"Matriarch!" said their leader, High Cardinal Navorth, as he used his ornate, triple-bladed power sword to rip aside a security shutter that was trying to close.

An image of the Universal Church's figurehead appeared before the High Cardinal in hololight form. The Matriarch was a supremely beautiful woman, the latest in a line of supremely beautiful women who had been elected to lead the zealots of the all-powerful Church. Dressed in a long, sumptuous gown and a veiled wimple, she sat beatifically on her throne in the command Templeship above.

"Speak, my Cardinal," she said.

"The outer areas have been secured, but there is blasphemous resistance," said Navorth. "Request permission to deploy the Black Knights."

"Request granted," said the Matriarch. "In the name of the one life, everlasting, nothing must stand in the way of our acquisition. The Church has waited too long for the appearance of a messiah who will conquer the Galaxy for us. Control of the Datacore will allow us to wield the Power Cosmic and rule the Universe for all time. Even the great Cosmic Abstracts will be obliged to bow to us in obeisance."

"I believe!" Navorth replied and sent a signal.

An instant later, the cohorts of Black Knights appeared in a series of transmat blinks. The Crusaders howled rallying cries of "I believe!"

Large, muscular, and powerful, the infamous Black Knights were drawn, like the Faith Crusaders, from many different races of the Cosmos. They were dressed in form-fitting black outfits and carried all manner of vicious close-combat weapons. They were the Universal Church's fanatical warrior elite—the most valiant Crusaders elevated to super-mortal power so that they could serve on the front lines and crush any and all unbelievers.

Bounding forward out of the swirling T-mat haze that had delivered them, the Black Knights cut into the ranks of the Timely security officers who blocked the entrances. The Black Knights soaked the walls with blood. They understood nothing about the concept of surrender.

Parts of the massive building exploded. The circle of Badoon megadestroyers had opened fire on the Templeships. The Templeships fired back. Two megadestroyers were hit. One sank limply, on fire, in a vast cloud of smoke. The other exploded and dropped onto downtown Alpha C, crushing buildings beneath it as it rolled and burned out.

The Templeships riddled Timely HQ with precision barrages. The *Pride of Pama* and the *Conscience of Sharra* fired at the Templeships, but they were pinned and took heavy return hits. The Nova heavy gauzed itself in an immaculate shield-robe of gravimetrics and its commander started to demand an immediate cease-fire.

Vicious fighting ripped through many floors of the immense Timely Inc. tower. Sub-Praetor Arach had called in reinforcements of Imperial Guardsmen and Metal Wing troopers from her ship. They arrived by transmat, as did elite Kree soldiers and Sentry units summoned by Sharnor. Nova Corps officers flew like rockets from the Xandarian heavy at Yaer's desperate command and swept down into the stricken building to engage all hostiles. The golden-helmed Corpsmen sent shock waves down corridors and hallways as they swept in, targeting anything and anyone with a weapon.

Ugly blisters of light formed and burst as Badoon teleport systems sent in fire-teams of War Brotherhood warriors. Intense shooting and power-blasts took out floors, blew down walls, and exploded vast windows, shattering picturesque, calming vista views.

On the Executive Boardroom floor, the fighting was especially intense. Sharnor the Accuser slugged it out in monumental hand-to-hand combat with three titanic Cardinals. Her Sentry units and troops fought back the waves of Faith Crusaders. Timely personnel fled in all directions.

"Find it, Una-Ren!" Sharnor yelled to her spy. The former Pama

Harnon had drawn a long-barreled laser disruptor and was shooting into the waves of attackers. "Find it and bring it to me!"

Una-Ren nodded and, catlike, slipped away.

"The Kree spy is taking off!" Centurion Clawdi yelled. She, Grekan Yaer, and Corpsmen Starkross and Valis were locked in a brutal fight with a host of Black Knights and a Sentry unit that had decided anything not Kree was fair game. The fight had taken them through several walls and into the main hallway outside the Executive Boardroom.

"She's onto something! Get her, Grekan!"

"But—" Yaer began.

"We can hold this off! Go!" yelled Clawdi.

Yaer dispensed gravimetric power through his gauntlets and put two Black Knights into a wall. Then he turned and blasted off after the Kree agent, moving like a heat-seeking missile along the hallway. He smashed several combatants out of his way.

The Shi'ar Guardsmen and their Metal Wing support were taking the brunt of both Badoon and Crusader assault in the annex to the Boardroom. Sub-Praetor Arach reared back and fired blue photon pulses from her spinnerets. Badoon War Brotherhood soldiers flew backward and fell hard. Warstar 34 was unleashing his full battery power at an oncoming, crimson-robed Cardinal who seemed to shrug off each blast with a twist of his energized staff. Dragoon and Ebon were battling face-to-face with marauding Crusaders and Black Knights. There was barely any space to use their powers.

"The leading Nova Centurion has just broken from combat!" Arach linked. "Ebon! You're the fastest! Find out where he's going!"

Ebon ducked a Black Knight's swinging dagger, punched him in the face, and looked helplessly at Dragoon.

"You heard her! *Move, girl!*" Dragoon told her, torching three Crusaders with a burst of pyrotech.

"On it, Sub-Praetor!" Ebon yelled, and lofted at once, knocking a Black Knight out of her way with a bolt of dark matter. She zoomed into a corridor that had been badly shot-up. A Badoon fire-team loomed in her path, firing their rifles at her. She shuddered and created a dark-matter shield that absorbed the lethal, dazzling shots, then sent the Badoon tumbling as she flew into them.

She tried to scan for traces of gravimetrics. Where was that Centurion? *Where?*

HANXCHAMP, Rarnak, and Wivvers had made it to the elevator banks.

"This *isn't* happening, this *isn't* happening," Hanxchamp kept saying to himself, trying to ignore the gunfire, explosions, and screams rattling through the building behind him. "In the name of Timely, someone *solutionize* this for me!"

"We have to get down to the Datacore, sir," said Blint Wivvers. The lift arrived with a ping.

"We can hide there," said Sledly Rarnak. "It's secure."

"And we can help Xorb and Gruntgrill finish the work," agreed Wivvers. "With the Datacore up to power, we can take out *all* of this craziness!"

"Good, yeah, good. Excellent," Hanxchamp nodded. They got into the elevator. Muzak was playing. Hanxchamp punched in his executive security codes.

"It *does* sound like a good idea," said Una-Ren, slipping into the car with them just before the doors closed. She aimed her elegant pistol at them. "Let's do that, shall we?" she smiled, cocking her head.

Blint Wivvers threw himself at her. Una-Ren fired twice, and the M'Ndavian head of Legal was hurled back into the corner. He slid slowly to the deck and expired.

"You *shot* him?" Hanxchamp gasped.

"A demonstration of what will happen to you if you don't cooperate from this point," she replied. "Take me to the Datacore, or I burn you both."

"Never trust a Kree," said the Skrull Rarnak acidly.

"Literally," Una-Ren agreed with a toxic grin.

The elevator began its rapid descent. As it traveled, muzak almost exactly like "The Girl From Ipanema" began to play.

GREKAN Yaer reached the elevator banks just as the doors closed. He had glimpsed Hanxchamp—and the Kree agent. *And* a gun. He ripped the outer doors open and prepared to dive into the shaft in pursuit of the descending express elevator. A disk of dark matter blocked him, and he rebounded back onto the carpet outside.

"You're in an awful hurry," Ebon said, landing beside him, her arms raised to unleash another dark-matter blast.

"You damned Shi'ar," Yaer said, getting up. "Hanxchamp's making a fast getaway. I think the Kree agent has him."

"Where are they going?" asked Ebon.

"Well, take the same wild guess that I did, Miss," said Yaer.

Shots hailed at them, peppering the front of the elevator bank, blowing chunks of wall and frame fascia out like confetti. They turned together, Centurion and Guardsman, and fired blasts that leveled the dozen War Brotherhood Devastation cadre warriors rushing at them.

Ebon looked at Yaer.

"I propose...how can I put it...cooperation?" she said.

"In the spirit of protecting the entire flarking Galaxy for our mutual good?" the Korbinite replied.

He held out his hand. They shook.

"Guardsman Ebon."

"Centurion Yaer."

"Let's go guard the Galaxy," she said.

"We'd better," he replied, "because no one else is doing the flarking job."

Side-by-side, they jumped into the yawning elevator shaft.

IN A side office, Mrs. Mantlestreek was crouching under a desk. It was comparatively safe down there. She had brought a tray of nibbles with her from the Executive Boardroom, just to keep her going.

"I'm sorry," she said politely into the handset she was holding, "Senior Vice Executive President (Special Projects) Odus Hanxchamp can't take your call right now. He's in a war zone."

CHAPTER FORTY-THREE

ONE WITH EVERYTHING

OF course, gentle reader, Centurion Grekan Yaer was wrong. Other individuals were *indeed* trying to guard the Galaxy. To the best of their handcuffed abilities.

"Get in the -tik!- cage," Gruntgrill says to me.

I sigh.

"Do it, robot-boy!" Xorb Xorbux cries, aiming his Subduematic.

I look back at Roamer one last time.

"Please," I say, "my final request. Try your interpolator."

His answer surprises me.

"I have," he says. "Three times. I have remained here."

"You see?" I ask, encouraged.

"I see nothing," replies the Spaceknight. "Get in the cage."

I step into the cage. I am shaking, gentle reader.

"Oi!" calls Rocket from behind us.

"What?" asks Xorb angrily.

"Steady with the gun, pal," Rocket says, raising his cuffed, disconcertingly human-like hands. "I just wanted to tell my pal there to stop singing."

"Ah yes," I reply. "Indeed. "Jump-ship Ju-ju" by the Lite Year Brothers. I just realized I was doing that. Sorry. Thanks for pointing it out. It wouldn't have been very dignified, going to my transcendental demise humming that."

"Just looking out for you, pal," says Rocket.

We share a last exchange of looks.

"You have been a good friend, Rocket Raccoon," I say. "A good and loyal friend, if an odd one."

"I am Groot."

"And you are, and always shall be, my Groot," I reply.

I suddenly realize something. Though our captors are humoring it because they take it to be a simple leave-taking, this last exchange has a deeper meaning. Rocket is talking about tenderly soaring and heartwarming soft rock, but his eyes are darting to the left, as if to indicate something.

I record. Unnoticed by the security guards surrounding Rocket and Groot, Gamora is no longer lying on the deck unconscious. There is no sign of her, except for a pair of open handcuffs on the deck.

Hope rises inside me. I play for time.

"Is this thing safe?" I say, shaking the cage around me so that it swings.

"Whoa! Don't -tik!- do that!" Gruntgrill cries.

"It doesn't feel safe," I say, doing it again. I keep waiting for Gamora to do whatever it is she's going to do.

Instead, Xorb Xorbux does whatever it is he's going to do. To wit, he punches me in the face with the butt of his pistol.

I fall back into the cage. He slams the door and presses the lever, and I start to descend toward the swirling Datacore.

I feel the heat of the Core. My entire casing starts to glow with painful energy. A nimbus of hot pink light surrounds me and grows more powerful.

I am about to become one with everything, my exploding data-load boosting the Timely Core to unprecedented levels.

"Look at this!" cries Gruntgrill, consulting a tablet. "It's already rising to ninety-one percent! It's incredible! -tik!- At this rate, we may even achieve the full one hundred percent!"

"Is that verified?" asks Odus Hanxchamp as he enters the chamber. Sledly Rarnak is by his side.

"Yes, sir, it's—" Gruntgrill begins. He stops. He sees the dark-eyed Kree agent he once knew as Pama Harnon. He sees the weapon she has aimed at the back of Hanxchamp's head.

"Is it confirmed, Arnok?" Una-Ren asks. "Make the answer accurate, or I will splatter Hanxchamp's brains—such as they are—across this entire chamber."

"-tik!- Yes."

"Lose the weapons, or Hanxchamp dies," says the Kree spy.

Xorb Xorbux curses, then drops his pistol. The security guards around Rocket and Groot slowly lower their pistols and Subdue-matic autoguns to the deck.

"You, too," says Una-Ren.

Roamer drops his blaster and sword.

"Excellent," smiles Una-Ren. "Now I think—"

She pauses. An odd look crosses her face. Then she falls forward.

The leering Black Knight behind her drags his blade out of her back as she topples. There are eight Black Knights in the shadows behind her, accompanying Cardinal Navorth and the Church's deep cover agent inside Timely: Allandra Meramati.

"The Datacore is ours, Cardinal," says Allandra. "And at an appropriately auspicious moment, too."

"I believe," he growls back. "Kill them all," he adds, as an afterthought.

"Now wait a moment!" Sledly Rarnak cries, leaping forward. The Cardinal's power sword takes the poor fellow's head clean off his shoulders. The Skrull in charge of Corporate Pamphlets lands on the deck in two pieces.

"I believe I issued a *command*," says Navorth.

Chaos ensues. Mayhem, indeed, although the word is now newly redefined to levels that might have previously been considered preposterous.

The Black Knights surge forward. Hanxchamp shrieks like a small child. Gruntgrill dives for cover. Xorb Xorbux and Roamer rush to retrieve their weapons. The security guards try to defend themselves against the onrushing Black Knights.

Rocket and Groot duck into the shadows.

Gamora appears like a ghost. There is a lot of blasting and screaming nearby. She slices the cuffs off Rocket and Groot with her swords.

"What's the plan?" she asks.

"We drag our pal out of that pit," says Rocket.

"What about all the rest of this?" Gamora asks.

"I am Groot," says Groot.

"Okay, fine," agrees Gamora. "You get the Recorder. I'll deal with everything else."

She leaps away. In a second, she is locked in feral combat with two Black Knights. Rocket and Groot rush for the main walkway.

Rocket pauses for a second to lift a pair of Subduematics from some of the slaughtered security guards. The Oh What the Flark Event Horizon is so far behind him now that it's just a dot to him. As he scampers, he double-fires the pistols and takes out a Black Knight. Roaring, Cardinal Navorth comes at him, his sword swinging, leaving trails of light in the air.

Roamer appears out of nowhere and smashes into Navorth. The two giants fall, grappling furiously.

"Wow," says Rocket. "Did the Spaceknight guy just switch sides?"

"I am Groot!"

"Yeah, he did seem to be wavering earlier, that's true. Trouble is, is he gonna turn back on *us* once he's finished with the right reverent poncy-cape there?"

"I am Groot."

"Fair point. The outcome of the scrap *is* in doubt."

Roamer and Navorth are engaged in a terrible struggle. They are both super-mortal, armored giants. Every blow they strike makes the air buckle. Dents and rips are appearing in Roamer's matte-black armor.

Rocket and Groot rush up to the edge of the walkway overlooking the Datacore. The cage is descending far below.

"You can't stop this! You won't!" Xorb Xorbux yells, leaping in front of them, his pistol aimed.

"Wanna bet?" snarls Rocket, and he shoots first.

Hit by a brace of Subduematic rounds, Xorb Xorbux topples backward off the walkway and falls into the Datacore pit. His plummeting body strikes the cage a glancing blow on the way down and makes it swing perilously. Xorbux disappears into the pink inferno.

"The percentile just dropped by one percent!" Gruntgrill cries from cover, studying his tablet.

"Flarking Z'Nox was as stupid as he was ugly," Rocket says to Groot. "Hey, Kaliklaki!"

Groot lifts the struggling Gruntgrill out from hiding and sets him on the deck.

"What's the score now, pal?"

"Uhm it's -tik!- ninety-five percent and rising fast! Ninety-six! Ninety-seven! -tik!- -tik!- -tik!- we're achieving *total datamap!*"

"Pull him back up!"

Gruntgrill shrugs. A stray shot has fused the lever of the hoist control.

"Flark!" says Rocket. "Groot, buddy! Haul him outta there!"

Groot reaches out and grabs the chain suspending the cage. He starts to pull with every fiber of power his massive body contains. The cage begins to inch back up.

With a fanatical scream, Allandra Meramati runs forward and plunges a power dagger into Groot's ribs. Groot screams with pain. The dagger stuck in his side seethes with lethal energy. Allandra Meramati grabs the protruding handle and begins to saw.

"You will not deny this!" she yells. "I believe!"

"I believe you have chugged the wrong Kool-Aid, lady," replies Rocket. He puts her down with shots from both pistols, straight-armed. *Boom! Boom! Boom! Boom!*

But Groot is badly hurt. He falls forward, the dagger crackling in his side. He topples into the Core. His grip on the chain gone, the cage drops again, violently.

Groot plunges into infinity.

I cannot save him. I cannot save myself. I am lit up with pink light. My mind screams.

This is the end. It is the beginning of a new era—but for me, it is the end.

CHAPTER FORTY-FOUR

WATCHED

THERE is peace down here. Absolute peace.

I float in a void. From far above, I hear shooting and yelling. I hear Rocket calling frantically for his friend Groot. I hear Roamer and Cardinal Navorth battling it out like utter furies. I hear the teleport bang as Sharnor the Accuser appears in the Datacore Chamber and starts throwing her weight around. I hear Gamora gleefully slashing Black Knights apart. I hear Ebon's dark-matter zap and Grekan Yaer's gravimetric slam as they sweep into the Datacore Chamber and try to contain the situation, without success. I hear Badoon War Brotherhood troopers storming the room, blasting at everything and everyone.

I hear Arnok Gruntgrill yelling, "Ninety-nine! *Ninety-nine -tik!- percent!*"

Ninety-nine percent. Almost there. The sounds recede. They fade.

I feel my mind draining.

I feel empty, yet full.

I am alone in a soft pink void. I feel and see and know *everything*. It is an extraordinary feeling, gentle reader—one that I will never be able to repeat. I am almost a *deity* in terms of my apprehension and ability.

I feel...

I feel as much in control of everything as...Ferris Bueller did in the movie of that name...

Uhm...the title of which is...well, it includes the words "Day Off" and an apostrophe "s." Just catering to your cultural...your...

What was I saying again, gentle reader?

I am getting very groggy.

I...

What?

Something. Did you just say something, kind reader?

Jump-ship ju-ju, I love your boog-a-loo, I love...

What was I saying?

Wait...

I am not alone in the void. Beside me hovers a giant robed figure with an even more disproportionately giant bald head.

"Who are *you*?" I ask.

"I am the Watcher," the figure says. "I am Uatu. I am of the oldest race of all. I watch and record to compile all aspects of knowledge of the Universe."

"Oh, a bit like me, then," I nod.

"No, no, I compile the *ultimate knowledge* of the Universe," he says.

"So do I."

"Yes, but not on *quite* the same scale."

"Okay."

There is a long pause. The Multiverse twinkles around us.

"So, uhm, you can hear me?" asks the Watcher.

"Yes."

"And see me?"

"Of course."

"Right," says the Watcher. "That's not supposed to happen at all."

"What can I tell you?" I ask him. "I can see *everything* right now. I am one with the Universe."

"I suppose that's to be expected, then," says the Watcher.

"Why are you here?" I ask.

"This is a moment of cosmic significance, Recorder 127. This is the moment when the very nature of Universe 616 changes forever."

"And you're down with that, are you, Mr. Uatu?"

"I am just a Watcher," he observes.

"But you could step in and act," I suggest. "You have the power."

"I do."

"But you won't."

"I'm still a little dismayed by the idea you can see me," admits the Watcher.

"What do I do?" I ask.

"In what sense?"

"I can't handle this. My databanks are exploding and melting. I am simply not capable of being the conduit of the Power Cosmic. The matter forges of Rigel made me well, but they did not build me for this."

"Then depose the power to someone who *can*," the Watcher says.

Then he fades away, big head and all.

"*One hundred percent!*" I hear Arnok Gruntgrill cry from far above.

I've just become a *god*, gentle reader.

Give me a sec, okay?

CHAPTER FORTY-FIVE

GREAT POWER, GREAT RESPONSIBILITY

I AM in the cage, swinging above the pink froth of the Datacore. I look up and see the sorely wounded Groot clinging perilously to the cage's chain above me.

I am one with everything. I do not want or need such power.

Depose, the Watcher said.

I know I have no other chance. Neither does the Multiverse.

I pulse the omnipotence out...and give it to Groot.

Why? I hear you ask, gentle reader.

Well, because I *trust* him.

Groot, hanging from the chain, lights up. The dagger impaling his ribs flies out of him and drops into the pink data-chaos below us. The wound it leaves closes and heals.

He coruscates with power.

"I am Groot," he says, surprised.

He's right. He *is* Groot. *Everything* is Groot.

"Send them away!" I cry. "Groot, I beg you! Send them away! You can do this. I have given you—*granted* you—the Power Cosmic."

Groot has become the most powerful entity in the Universe. He is omnipotent. He could, just now, do *anything*. Implode Galactus. Turn Thor inside out. Restart universal history.

But I *really*, really trust him.

"You're pretty much *glowing* down there, pal," Rocket calls from above.

"I AM GROOT!"

"Okay, that's fine, you're a *god*. That's great. Nifty. Now act godly-like toward your old pal. Sort this flark out!"

Groot does. Sharnor the Accuser vanishes. So do Grekan Yaer and Ebon. So do the Badoon and Roamer, and all of the fanatics of the Universal Church of Truth.

Groot grows more confident. He reaches out farther with his power. In the shattered building above us, hundreds of warriors disappear. The troubled skies above downtown Alpha C are suddenly empty of battlecruisers and Templeships.

I have underestimated Groot's nobility.

The power in Groot swells. It is blinding. Timely HQ is restored to its pristine condition. The swathes of downtown Alpha C crushed or flattened by the fighting are remade. The fallen and the wounded are made whole again. Even the dead are returned to life: alien warriors, Timely employees, innocent Alpha Centauran bystanders. As the dead Badoon, Kree, Xandarian, Shi'ar, and Universal Church faithful rise again, they vanish back to their places of origin.

"Amazing, pal!" Rocket calls down. "Just *amazing*! You put everything back the way it was! Good for you!"

"You have done the right thing, Groot," I say. "You have used the power responsibly."

"One last thing you gotta do, ol' buddy!" Rocket calls out. "One last thing to put right."

"I am Groot."

"Yes, you *do* know! You gotta get rid of the power...the power and the whole Datacore, so no one can ever use it again!"

"I am Groot."

"Yeah, yeah, I bet it's a temptation to keep it now you've got it," agrees Rocket from far above. "But you gotta do the right thing, pal. Come on, you're one of the *good* guys. You were raised in the royal houses of Planet X. You were brought up to understand the demands and responsibilities of power, and to rule wisely as a good ol' tree monarch if the time ever came! Come *on*, pal! Besides, I don't wanna hang out with a guy who's all *omnipotent* and stuff!"

Groot is tempted. I can feel he is very, very tempted to keep the power. But, of course, gentle reader, Groot does the right thing. The power bursts out of him as he casts it off. It radiates out across the infinite Multiverse, dissipating and fading into the cosmic background. The Datacore below us empties in a pink flash—its energies dispelled, its data scattered. The Datacore's systems fuse and burn out. Groot has made sure that it can never, ever be used again.

As his last act as a god, Groot creates a cosmic safeguard. If anyone, anywhere ever even *thinks* of trying to recreate the datamap in pursuit of such power, they will instantly forget *how* to do it.

The threat is gone. It can never return.

I am left in the cage, with Groot limply clinging to the chain above me. We swing gently in silence above a dark, burned-out, almost bottomless pit: the ruined chamber of the Datacore.

I hear Rocket whistle in relief.

"Hang on, pals!" he cries. "I'll fish you both out of there."

He turns to Gruntgrill and Hanxchamp. Nearby, Sledly Rarnak is sitting on the deck, feeling his neck, a puzzled expression on his face. Xorb Xorbux is leaning against a wall close by, in a state of shock.

"Don't just stand there!" Rocket demands. "Help me pull them up!"

"And *fast*!" Gamora exclaims, rushing to the guardrail. "We've got to get them up! The chain is damaged! It's going to give way!"

Her warning is already too late. Chain links fatigued by the immense cosmic energies creak. Stress fractures appear.

Links break and part.

Groot and I fall. We hurtle to our certain deaths.

There is a sudden smell of surprise twist, a waft of shock reveal, and a flash of light.

The Spaceknight appears above us. His flight systems screaming, he powerdives and grabs Groot with one hand and the cage with the other.

With immense effort, Roamer carries us back up and deposits us on the walkway.

"Buddy!" Rocket cries with delight, hugging Groot's leg.

"I am Groot!"

"Good to see you, too, Recorder-dude!" grins Rocket.

He looks at Roamer.

"Nice save," he says.

"I was cast far away by the Power Cosmic," replies Roamer. "I triggered the interpolator. This is, apparently, where the Universe needed me to be."

"I think the Universe is trying to tell you something," says Rocket.

"I think I will listen carefully to it and take its advice seriously," replies Roamer.

"Hang on! Hang on!" Hanxchamp cries. "These nutzookis just flarked up the biggest Timely project *ever*! They've cost us...more money than I can even *imagine*, and I can imagine quite a *bit* when it comes to money! They've *ruined* our corporate future! I want them *locked up*! They're going to *pay* for these crimes! Pay *big time*! Grab them, Spaceknight, and take them to—"

"I do not work for you, anymore," replies Roamer. He detaches the interpolator and hands it to Gruntgrill. "Thanks to this device, I realize I have not been working for you all along. It has shown me my error."

"Someone do something!" Hanxchamp squeals. None of his executives seem prepared to act.

"*Do something*!" Hanxchamp screams.

"We are," says Rocket Raccoon. "We're *leaving*."

CHAPTER FORTY-SIX

TAILS TO ASTONISH

LO, there must be an ending.

Oh, come *on*, gentle reader. If you're reading this, you must read comic books. I was culturally referencing for you again. Earth comic books do that sort of pronouncement *all* the time.

All the shooting and dying and exploding is done, and there will be no more screaming, panicking, or running away from jeopardy. My story is essentially over.

I just want to emphasize the gravity of what we have just been through. The Universe—the *Multiverse*—was just saved from a terrible fate.

Thanks, essentially, to a talking raccoon and a mobile tree. Yes, yes, other people *were* involved—but at the heart of it, it was down to them. Without them, you'd have "Timely Inc." stenciled on your cells. Without them, the future would be mindlessly endless and megacorporate.

They are Guardians of the Galaxy. Well, *Multiverse,* actually— but the title is not so zingy when it doesn't alliterate.

And so, I say goodbye to them.

"It's been an experience," I say as we approach the open landing ramp of the Nova Corps prowl cruiser on upper-landing-dock port 3447 of the Timely Inc. tower.

Gamora has already slipped away into the shadows, with a "See you later" to Rocket and a peck on the cheek to Groot. She has her own agendas to pursue until it is time for the Guardians to regroup and do their thing again.

Roamer has also departed, with a silent nod to us. I think he is heading back to Galador.

"Wanna come with us, bud?" asks Rocket.

"Where are you going?" I reply.

"Oh, thither and yon. Yon in particular."

"I must stay here," I answer. "I have summoned the Ark Fleets of Rigel. They are coming to collect and repair me, and to recover all of my dormant brethren in the Core below."

"Yeah?" says Rocket.

"I need to be downloaded and reformatted," I say. "I have been out in the Universe for too long."

"Okay, bud, good luck with that," says Rocket.

"Are you sad, Rocket Raccoon?" I ask.

"Nah, nah, just got some dust in my eye is all."

"I am Groot," says Groot, bending down and hugging me.

"Yes, you are," I say.

"If you're ever in need of an adventure," says Rocket, walking up the prowl cruiser's ramp, "you know, give us a call. Okay, Recorder-pal?"

"I am Groot," says Groot.

"I am Groot," I reply, with the warmest affection.

And then they are gone.

MANY of your years have passed since then, gentle reader. Though my databanks have been emptied by my Rigellian creators, I have deliberately chosen to retain the records of that high-spirited adventure, for personal reasons. I have also done my best to record the fortunes and destinies of the principal characters involved in the episode. I have absorbed and recorded them over the years through any data sources I can find.

I can share them with you, if you like.

Sharnor the Accuser returned to Hala as a "hero of the people." She announced to the Kree that she had single-handedly overturned Timely Inc.'s threat. She was feted and given decorations, and ultimately joined the staff of Ronan the Accuser, who celebrated her merits and presented her with an even bigger ceremonial hammer.

Una-Ren, aka "Pama Harnon," was equally feted as a hero, and continues to serve the Kree Stellar Empire as a top-class espionage agent. She was personally responsible for escalating three Kree-Skrull wars.

War Brotherhood Commander Droook spent seventeen years steering his megadestroyer fleet out of the distant fringe-world asteroid belt where Groot had, whimsically, deposited them. By the time he returned to the Badoon homeworld, there had been thirteen regime changes. Droook, as I understand it, still yearns for a Raccoonoid pelt to decorate the wall of his War Brotherhood wardroom.

Centurion Grekan Yaer returned to Xandar, and later married Centurion Clawdi. Between them, they produced six little prospective Corpsmen. Yaer served four more terms before he was promoted to Nova Prime, a post he held illustriously for nine Earth years. One of the reasons that the Worldmind chose Yaer for the prime position was the positive work he had done in forging closer ties with the Shi'ar.

Corpsmen Starkross and Valis both rose swiftly to the rank of Centurion.

Sub-Praetor Arach of the Shi'ar Imperial Guard served her empire devotedly until her death in combat, when she was unfortunate enough to find herself occupying the position of the hyphen in a Kree-Skrull war.

Guardsmen Warstar 34 and Dragoon continue to serve at the pleasure of the Shi'ar Imperator.

Guardsman Ebon achieved the high rank of Sub-Praetor toward the end of her career. This promotion was due in part to her strong collaborative work with the Xandarian Grekan Yaer. Affirmative exercises were established between the Guard and the Nova Corps, thanks to the friendship between Yaer and Ebon. Because of them, the Shi'ar Empire and the Xandarians moved forward in a new intent of mutual cooperation.

Pip the Troll still minds his bric-a-brac shop on Adjufar.

Sledly Rarnak quit his job with Timely Inc., claiming that he no longer had a "head for business." As all Skrulls do eventually, he felt it was time for a change, and he is now a modestly successful zunk farmer.

Using his legal nouse, Blint Wivvers took Timely Inc. to tribunal and won eighty-six trillion units in damages for "unexpected death in the workplace." He now runs his own burgeoning legal practice on Alpha C: Withers, Jimmini, Kerfarple & Associates.

Following said legal battle, Odus Hanxchamp became Junior Associate Under Supervisor in the 4006th-floor mail room.

Arnok Gruntgrill became Senior Vice -tik!- Executive President (Special Projects). He continues to annoy his secretary, Mrs. Mantlestreek.

Xorb Xorbux left Timely Inc. and went into private security work. His position as head of Corporate Security (Special Projects) was filled by an individual called Brango.

The Templeships of the Universal Church of Truth ended up (again, through Groot's omnipotent whimsy), perched on the event horizon of a black hole in Ultra Mega Sixty-Eight. It took them forty years to escape the gravity well. During that time, they went through eight matriarchs. One of them was Zania Orbal, aka "Allandra Meramati."

Cardinal Navorth, both before and after his escape from the Ultra Mega Sixty-Eight black hole, continues to be a total and utter bastard.

Roamer returned to Galador, renewed his vows, and now serves the Galaxy as a protector and avenger.

Gamora went on the run for six months, fleeing the vengeful agents of her disgruntled Negative Zone employer. Eventually, she decided to confront Annihilus to explain exactly why she had failed to deliver the Recorder to him and why he should get over it. This explanation involved her sinking both her swords down Annihilus's gullet. And thus she saved the Universe (again). But that is another record. Not this one. She continues to serve valiantly as Guardian of the Galaxy.

And you, gentle reader. You are part of this narrative, too. I have been checking in on you from time to time. Very glad work is going so well for you, and the new haircut really suits you. Let me tell you, I really laughed at that picture of a cat you posted on Facebook! How's your uncle? Is he doing okay now? Let's Snapchat!

Rocket and Groot? They're off the radar, under the wire. I look for them, but they're never there. True outlaws, I suppose. The only place I ever see them is on watch lists: Badoon, Shi'ar, Kree, Xandarian...

IN my mind, though, I can still picture them.

I remember our parting. Rocket reaches out a disconcertingly human-like hand. I shake it. I shudder, despite myself.

He doesn't seem to notice. He bounds up the landing ramp, and Groot follows him.

"Let's *go*, prowl cruiser!" I hear Rocket cry.

"Away from jeopardy again, pals?" the automatic voice replies.

"No, this time *toward beverages*. I need a non-scalding beverage like you wouldn't *believe*!"

"I am Groot!"

"Yeah, better still! Take us to the nearest *Timothy*!"

"Timothys locked on!" cries the automatic voice. "This vehicle says, let's make like an unfeasibly large gun and *shoot*!"

They depart in a gravimetric swirl.

The last thing I record is a disconcertingly human like-hand waving farewell to me from the prowl cruiser's cockpit window. Then the craft is airborne and gone.

It reassures me to know that they are out there somewhere. The Galaxy is a safer place while they are.

{end record}

Special Preview

SPIDER~MAN: KRAVEN'S LAST HUNT

BY NEIL KLEID

Adapted from the graphic novel
by J.M. DeMatteis and Mike Zeck

Coming October 2014

PROLOGUE

The hunter lifted his rifle from its case. He turned it in his hands and tested its weight. Running a palm along the stock and tightening the barrel in his grip, the hunter rested cool metal against his strong, calloused fingers, then lovingly placed the weapon on a nearby table with a reverence equivalent to mother and child. The rifle, a modified Remington, was one of a kind: handcrafted for the hunter alone, built atop the bones of a classic Model 700. Its case was a coffin, lined with velvet and burnished with copper. It lay open and resting in the heart of his lair.

Sergei padded from the room, which was situated at the center of his compound—a private sanctuary containing an accumulated lifetime of artifacts and memories. He walked deliberately, placing weight on his toes like a jungle cat, moving silently through his modest quarters and away from the casket and the waiting rifle. Waiting to be used, waiting for the inevitable end of the affair.

But not just yet.

Dressed in a cobalt robe barely cinched at the waist, Sergei moved to the rear of his townhouse, back where not even aides or servants dared tread. Here, in a secluded inner sanctum draped in exotic finery and littered with stuffed trophies—former adversaries dragged across land or sea in nets or cages, or draped over his shoulders, or ridden between his legs. Each had failed to best Sergei in his element, to defeat the hunter in his prime. He'd faced them all, from proud Lion to mighty Elephant; terrible Tiger to sleek Jaguar. They'd bared claw and tooth, roared and pounced, and Sergei took them one by one, claiming skin and bones for his own. Every animal. Every beast. The hunter had proved victorious against them all.

All but one.

Sergei drew the curtains, shutting out light, and shrugged aside his robe. Bare and alone, dressed only in hunter's skin, he circled the room and nodded to his enemies. His gaze landed on the midnight-blue of a fierce panther, jaws opened in a silent snarl. He padded past the looming figure of a mighty ape, arms raised as if to strike, but gave the imposing figure no notice. Arriving at a table in the back where waited an array of po-tions and candles hastily arranged on a small, silver tray, he moved through prepa-rations with little fanfare, distracted as he was by plans and mem-ories. Sergei lit incense, thin purple smoke rising from wicks to filter through the room, and swallowed several po-tions, the mixed herbs within serving to enhance his state of mind.

He turned back to the animals, stepped into the circle of beasts against which he'd proved his mettle and gained honor, and dropped to all fours. Sergei moved along the floor—the hunter no more, now adopting the ways and instincts of the Beast, using the limbs provided to propel himself along...to crawl. The herbs and drugs altered his per-ception, turned aside the hunter-as-man and allowed him to become the hunter-as-beast—though as he stalked imaginary prey, crawling beneath Elephant and Rhino, Sergei knew he was much more than that.

I am Kraven, he thought—the name echoing around his skull, across the room, off each trophy and every wall. I am Kraven, and

I am the Beast. He twisted it into a mantra, wore it for a crown as he pounced toward the panther, barely visible as the purple fog en-veloped its frame of blue and black. Sergei landed opposite the panther, opening his own mouth and growling in return. Then he cast his enemy aside, tossing the panther into a collection of or-nate shields and carefully stacked spears. The taxidermic prize and deadly weapons fell to the ground, scattering in a heap.

Sergei turned—no, crawled away and stalked another foe: an ape, tall and proud, rising up to cast a shadow across the hunter's naked form. Sergei rose to meet the furred behemoth, lifting his arms to match the simian's own, and drove his palm into the un-der-side of the ape's jaw, knocking head from body with a short, powerful blow and a primal, bloodcurdling scream of rage. The hunter reached out, grabbed the ape's body, and lifted it above his head, sinewy muscles flexed taut and firm from rage and exertion.

Sergei smiled, cold and dangerous through gritted teeth. My mind is rage and glo-ry, he thought. My heart: fire and pride. I am Kraven. My body is grace and power.

Bellowing like Elephant, rearing back with both arms, Sergei slammed the stuffed ape to the ground, shattering it and sending pieces out across the room, among the rest of the watching crea-tures. Breathing heavily, skin slick from sweat and smoke, he stumbled to the curtain and tore it aside, stopping only to retrieve his robe. The smoke filtered from the room, free to make its way into the rest of the lair, following the hunter as he strode down the hall toward the front of the compound.

Sergei paid the escaping smoke no mind, lost in thought and the mission at hand.

I am Kraven, the Beast, he lectured himself, but also Kravinoff, the man.

Securing the robe around his body, pulling arms back through the sleeves, Sergei cast the Beast aside—as he had the rifle—and walked on the flats of his feet, pushing through solid oaken doors to the thin warmth of the library. Surrounded by dog-eared books and faded maps, Sergei poured another drink—not a mind-altering potion this time, but a pleasant African red, aged to perfection in earthenware casks and laced with hints of poppy and lion's blood by master vintners. He decanted the wine into a heavy silver goblet, a remnant of a life he'd barely known, carried by his parents from Russia years before. He let the wine breathe, casting a gaze around the room at the goblet's cous-ins: items and heirlooms passed from Kravinoff to Kravinoff down through the years into his own undeserving, calloused hands.

"I am Kravinoff," he repeated aloud, to anyone who might be listening, man or beast. Kravinoff, Sergei knew, was a man—an old man, though few would believe it. Years had passed—long, hard, often fruitless years since he'd traveled overseas as a child, coming with his parents to this land of sheep and prey. He had been nothing more than a cub, a mewling pup riding the seas with his mother and wet nurse, traveling to the shores of a land without honor or dignity.

To look upon Sergei—his powerful form, his weathered face and jet-black hair—the average person might see a man of forty or younger. But the truth lay within the po-tions and herbs that Sergei imbibed. These herbs turned him from man to beast—from hunter to predator—but they also allowed him to retain youth, agility, stamina, and strength. In truth, Sergei Kravinoff had stalked the Earth for nearly a century.

And he had learned much, Sergei thought as he idly swirled the wine within his goblet. This land was not alone in its lack of honor. There had been no more room in Russia for such things: for aristocrats or culture. For honor or human dignity. Once the Cossacks came, once man became prey, hunted by other men who were nothing more than beasts in human skin...once they came for Sergei's family and fortune, it became necessary to seek new fortune in a new world that fattened, frightened men named Amer-ica.

But what the Kravinoffs lost, everything his parents had been forced to leave be-hind in their beautiful homeland—honor, dignity, pride—all of those things were bred in Sergei's bones long before the Trotskys and Lenins dragged Mother Russia into the pit. He carried them alone, inside his skin and within his cells, for the entire world seemed to have followed Russia's sad example. Where can one find dignity today? Sergei wondered. He stood at the desk in the center of his study, lapping at the wine and allowing the blood-red liquid to dribble down his chin and onto his wide, muscled chest. Honor, he asked himself, where is such a quality now?

He reached across the desk to a small intercom and jabbed a flat button with a thick, insistent finger. A bookshelf slid aside, its volumes no more than clever facsimiles, and a pair of nondescript doors parted to reveal a dimly lit chapel lined with rows of ceremonial candles. Sergei walked around the desk—placing weight back on his toes again, unconsciously returning to an animal's pace—and carried the goblet into the chapel. The doors slid closed behind.

I am Kravinoff, he thought once more, and were my father alive...were my mother alive...they would look upon this frightened, wounded animal called civilization without recognition, and with great fear. Sergei nodded to himself and drank deeply, wine splashing over his chin. He absentmindedly wiped it away on the back of his hand and moved farther into the soft glow of candlelight, shadows lengthening on the walls and windows to either side.

With great fear, Sergei thought. And great disgust.

He moved slowly to the center of the chapel, past rows of chairs and the dulled, prismatic colors of exquisitely designed stained-glass windows set into deeply niched walls. Finally, he returned to the coffin, waiting and resting on a platform before a larger window and a handful of silver candlesticks shaded to either side by lush, verdant floral arrangements imported from Madagascar, Moscow, and the Middle East. Sergei ascended the short staircase leading to the coffin and cast a brief glance at the modified Remington he'd laid on a nearby table. He set the goblet aside, resting it on the lip of the open coffin, and placed his hands to either side, staring up at the unlit candlesticks and impassive, decorative window beyond.

I am the man, he reflected. I am the Beast.

I am Kraven. The Hunter.

The hunter had found dignity in this world, but not in cities. No, the hunter had found it in jungles. He had seen honor not in the civilized, those who existed in a society that claimed to be honorable, but in the primal—in those who knew no law but that of tooth and fang, of kill or be killed. And as the hunter, he had found morality, found meaning—not in culture or arts, or in anything a supposedly civilized society created in an effort to prove itself better than animals. No, Kraven had found meaning in the hunt. And he had given his life to it.

But Time, like all good predators, had finally caught up with the hunter. And soon, there could be no escape from its cage of flesh. Herbs, roots, potions—they could keep him alive, yes, as they had long beyond Sergei's allotted time. But no potion could rejuvenate the hunter's dying spirit, and no herb would heal his heart, corrupted as it was by the weight of a corrupted age.

I was a child, Sergei thought, no more than a cub in his mother's jaws, carried along from one jungle to another. And in many ways, he believed, Sergei still was. But the meaning of the hunt had begun to fade, and the hunter's failures weighed upon his soul. His eyes ticked away from the window to the side table, where lay the rifle.

I will die soon, Sergei thought. I must die soon.

He turned back toward the open casket and carefully ran his hand inside, caress-ing the velvet and what lay within. Sergei's jaw set. He thought of Russia and his mother, of all the wrongs he had endured since coming to America. His fist clenched, grasping the object inside the coffin, and fingers entwined with the face of his enemy. With the skin of the Beast.

Slowly, Kraven lifted his hand and pulled a garment from the coffin—crimson and blue, emblazoned with the eight-legged sign of the Beast. He raised Spider-Man's costume to his face and traced the mask's wide, white eyes with a thick, coarse finger. Tears ran, unbidden, from the corners of Kraven's own eyes as he contemplated the task before him and studied his prey. He stared deep into the unseeing eyes of the Spider. He prepared for the hunt.

I will die soon, Kraven said to himself, using the mantra for focus like the steady beat of a jungle drum, echoing his earlier thoughts with fearful symmetry. I must die soon. He tightened his grip on the Spider's mask.

But not yet.

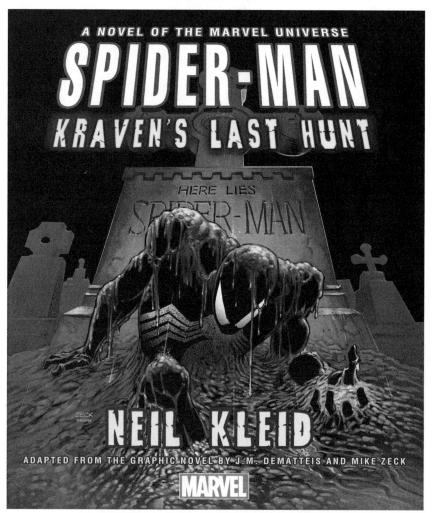

Spider-Man: Kraven's Last Hunt prose novel

Written by NEIL KLEID

Born to a rarified breed of Russian aristocracy, Kraven the Hunter had stalked and killed every animal known to man, and considered himself the world's best big-game hunter. It was this confidence that brought him to New York years ago, in an obsessive quest to hunt what he considered the city's greatest prey: Spider-Man. But his target eluded him time and again, mocking him at every turn. Now, after years of crushing defeats against the web-slinger, Kraven has hatched one last plan to best Spider-Man. In a stunning instant of shocking violence, Kraven stands finally triumphant over Peter Parker's seemingly dead body. And to prove that he is the hero's master…Kraven will pull on his costume and become him! Experience the classic, genre-defining Spider-Man shocker like never before in this new adaptation!

HC ISBN:978-0-7851-8970-1